RISKY FUTURES

Studies in the Circumpolar North

Series Editors: Olga Ulturgasheva and Alexander D. King

The Circumpolar North encapsulates all the major issues confronting the world today: enduring colonial legacies for indigenous people and the landscape, climate change and resource extraction industries, international diplomatic tensions, and lived realities of small communities in the interconnected modern world system. This book series provides a showcase for cutting-edge academic research on the lives of Arctic and Sub-arctic communities past and present. Understanding the contemporary Circumpolar North requires a multiplicity of perspectives and we welcome works from the social sciences, humanities and the arts.

Volume 6
Risky Futures: Climate, Geopolitics and Local Realities in the Uncertain Circumpolar North
Edited by Olga Ulturgasheva and Barbara Bodenhorn

Volume 5
Arctic Abstractive Industry: Assembling the Valuable and Vulnerable North
Edited by Arthur Mason

Volume 4
An Urban Future for Sápmi? Indigenous Urbanization in the Nordic States and Russia
Edited by Mikkel Berg-Nordlie, Astri Dankertsten and Marte Winsvold

Volume 3
Urban Sustainability in the Arctic: Measuring Progress in Circumpolar Cities
Edited by Robert W. Orttung

Volume 2
Sustaining Russia's Arctic Cities: Resource Politics, Migration, and Climate Change
Edited by Robert W. Orttung

Volume 1
Leaving Footprints in the Taiga: Luck, Spirits and Ambivalence among the Siberian Orochen Reindeer Herders and Hunters
Donatas Brandišauskas

Risky Futures

Climate, Geopolitics and Local Realities in the Uncertain Circumpolar North

Edited by
Olga Ulturgasheva and Barbara Bodenhorn

berghahn
NEW YORK • OXFORD
www.berghahnbooks.com

First published in 2022 by
Berghahn Books
www.berghahnbooks.com

© 2022, 2025 Olga Ulturgasheva and Barbara Bodenhorn
First paperback edition published in 2025

All rights reserved. Except for the quotation of short passages
for the purposes of criticism and review, no part of this book
may be reproduced in any form or by any means, electronic or
mechanical, including photocopying, recording, or any information
storage and retrieval system now known or to be invented,
without written permission of the publisher.

Library of Congress Cataloging-in-Publication Data
Names: Ulturgasheva, Olga, editor. | Bodenhorn, Barbara, 1946- editor.
Title: Risky futures : climate, geopolitics and local realities in the
  uncertain circumpolar North / edited by Olga Ulturgasheva and Barbara
  Bodenhorn.
Description: [New York] : Berghahn Books, 2022. | Series: Studies in the
  circumpolar North ; volume 6 | Includes bibliographical references and
  index.
Identifiers: LCCN 2022019195 (print) | LCCN 2022019196 (ebook) | ISBN
  9781800735934 (hardback) | ISBN 9781805390640 (open access ebook)
Subjects: LCSH: Climatic changes--Social aspects--Arctic regions. |
  Climatic changes--Political aspects--Arctic regions. | Arctic
  regions--Environmental conditions.
Classification: LCC GE160.A68 R57 2022 (print) | LCC GE160.A68 (ebook) |
  DDC 363.738/745613--dc23/eng20220722
LC record available at https://lccn.loc.gov/2022019195
LC ebook record available at https://lccn.loc.gov/2022019196

British Library Cataloguing in Publication Data
A catalogue record for this book is available from the British Library

ISBN 978-1-80073-593-4 hardback
ISBN 978-1-80539-743-4 paperback
ISBN 978-1-80073-594-1 epub
ISBN 978-1-80539-064-0 web pdf

https://doi.org/10.3167/9781800735934

An electronic version of this book is freely available thanks to the support of libraries working with Knowledge Unlatched. KU is a collaborative initiative designed to make high-quality books Open Access for the public good. More information about the initiative and links to the Open Access version can be found at knowledgeunlatched.org.

This work is published subject to a Creative Commons Attribution Noncommercial No Derivatives 4.0 License. The terms of the license can be found at http://creativecommons.org/licenses/by-nc-nd/4.0/. For uses beyond those covered in the license contact Berghahn Books.

Contents

List of Figures   vii

Foreword   viii
    Peter Schweitzer

Acknowledgements   xv

Introduction. On Constellations and Connected-Up Thinking in the Face of the Future   1
    Barbara Bodenhorn and Olga Ulturgasheva

Chapter 1. Activating Cosmo-Geo-Analytics: Anthropocene, Arctics and Cryocide   26
    Olga Ulturgasheva and Barbara Bodenhorn

Chapter 2. 'Tears of the Earth': Human–Permafrost Entanglements and Science–Indigenous Knowledge Encounters in Northeast Siberia   58
    Olga Ulturgasheva

Chapter 3. She'll Do What She Needs to Do   89
    Rachel Nutaaq Ayałhuq Naŋinaaq Edwardson

Chapter 4. Weathering the Storm: An Indigenous Knowledge Framework of Yup'ik Youth Well-Being and Resilience in Alaska   103
    Stacy M. Rasmus

Chapter 5. Journalism in Canada's Northern Territories:
Digital Media, Civic Spaces, Indigenous Publics   122
    Candis Callison

Chapter 6. People of the Cryosphere: A Cross-Regional,
Cross-Disciplinary Approach to Icescapes in a
Changing Climate   148
    Hildegard Diemberger and Astrid Hovden

Chapter 7. Risky Decisions, Precarious Moralities: The Case of
Autumn Whaling in Barrow, Alaska   176
    Barbara Bodenhorn

Afterword. Risk Constellations and the Politics of Polarity   206
    Michael Bravo

Index   213

Figures

2.1 Effects of permafrost thaw in the area of Sebyan.
© Olga Ulturgasheva   60

2.2 Deep hollow is about to trigger collapse of the mountain.
© Olga Ulturgasheva   70

4.1 A small herd of moose running on the beach near
Hooper Bay, Alaska. © Jan Olsen   110

6.1 Mount Kailash with prayer flags.
© Hildegard Diemberger   155

6.2 Oracle possessed by the Mountain Nyanchen Thanglha.
© Carlo Meazza   158

6.3 Glacial lake outburst flood in Limi. © Astrid Hovden   162

Foreword

Peter Schweitzer

Environmental and geopolitical discussions about the future of humanity have recently centred on the Arctic. This development can be seen as having been triggered by a bundle of complex interconnections, ranging from the rapidity of Arctic climate change to the multitude of untapped resources in the North to the technological advances enabling their extraction. These developments are being framed by political processes including signs of a new Cold War and uneven steps toward indigenous self-determination. While the Circumpolar North has emerged as a projection site for southern dreams of resource extraction, marine shipping, or – alternatively – wilderness protection, lived realities within the Arctic are far from homogeneous. It was only in the 1990s, after the dissolution of the Soviet Union, that the romantic notion of a Circumpolar North as a shared space, not only with similar environmental conditions but also with comparable social and cultural challenges, took a firm hold. Before that, the dichotomy between a Soviet Arctic and the rest prevented such shared points of view.

And yet those lived realities continue to reflect stark contrasts in social and political processes. It is not just the rising political tensions between the Russian Federation and the 'West' that threatens a unified Arctic perspective. Within the Circumpolar North, as the chapters in the present volume clearly illustrate, local and regional developments and living conditions seem not to be developing in parallel. Again, processes of political centralization and authoritarian leadership have limited the range of options for local and indigenous communities in the Russian Arctic severely. Even if only considering the non-Russian part of the North for a moment, it would be difficult to argue for its homogeneity. While decolonization and sovereignty have been important topics everywhere, the political realities are quite diverse. Greenland, a former colony of Denmark, is the only Arctic territory that will gain state sovereignty in the foreseeable future. The prototypical settler colonies of Canada and the United States, on the other hand, use post-coloniality quite regularly on the rhetorical and symbolic level without providing any prospect of political independence for its indigenous inhabitants. Again, there are important differences between home rule as practised in Nunavut, the northernmost territory that is demographically (and, thus, politically) dominated by Inuit, and Alaskan indigenous groups, whose aboriginal rights were 'bought off' by the Alaska Native Claims Settlement Act (ANCSA) and, thus, in the interpretation of some, extinguished. Still, even in Alaska certain forms of political self-determination can be found, such as in the North Slope Borough, the largest home rule Borough in the US.

The situation in northern Fennoscandia is complicated by a colonial history that is much older than Columbus' 1492 voyage and by a subsequent economic and political integration into southern Fennoscandia that makes any political partition unrealistic. Still, the fact that the Sami (or Saami) are the only indigenous inhabitants of the northern tip of Europe and have managed to create a powerful, transnational NGO that effectively represents and vocalizes its interests, the Saami Council, attests to the specific realities of Arctic mainland Europe. The only other Arctic indigenous NGO comparable in size, scope and strength of voice is the Inuit Circumpolar Council, which – similar to the Saami Council, which has member organizations in Finland, Norway, Sweden and Russia – unites Inuit living in Alaska, Canada, Greenland and Russia. In both cases, Russian participation in these organizations is qualitatively and quantitatively different from that of the other countries. Still, the symbolic gesture of acknowledging that the Russian Arctic is inhabited at its eastern and western borders by indigenous groups closely related by linguistic and kinship ties to groups primarily residing in the 'West' remains important. Finally, Iceland constitutes a unique northern assemblage: the only Arctic state that is located in its entirety north of 60 degrees northern latitude has no indigenous inhabitants, as the Viking settlers who arrived from the ninth century AD onwards only encountered some Irish and Scottish monks but no permanent population.

While the multitude of indigenous and non-indigenous lived realities in the Circumpolar North makes it reasonable to speak of 'Arctics' (see, particularly, the contributions by Callison, Ulturgasheva and Bodenhorn, this volume) instead of a supposedly homogeneous Arctic, climate change processes of recent decades have highlighted similarities again. What has sometimes been called the 'New Arctic', that is an Arctic environment threatened by enormous rates of change, might create a sort of community of common destiny in the face of profound changes in sea ice extent, snow cover, the state of permafrost, and other radical changes to the Arctic marine environment.

From the New Arctic to the People of the Cryosphere

Risky Futures, with its special focus on knowledge politics, voice, risk and non-human-centred cosmologies, does not limit itself to the Circumpolar North but extends its view to other world regions where low temperatures result in frozen water and frozen ground for large parts of the year. The cryosphere, as this part of the earth's surface is being called, is, apart from the Arctic, characteristic of high mountain areas. The Himalaya and neighbouring mountain ranges store more water in frozen form that any other part of the globe except for the North Pole and the South Pole, which justifies the label 'Third Pole' sometimes used in reference to the area. While other mountain ranges, such as the Andes or the European Alps, do not have the same extent as the Third Pole, they are nevertheless part of the cryosphere. And, in the same way as the New Arctic has been defined by melting snow and ice, as well as by thawing permafrost, these mountain regions have been among those most visibly affected by climate change. The similarities do not end with parallel environmental change processes. Like Arctic residents, mountain dwellers around the world have a long history of being marginalized by the state powers of the valleys. Similar to the Arctic, high mountain areas have been outside of (or, spatially speaking, above) lands suitable for most forms of agriculture, which has provided these relatively sparsely populated regions with the additional function of refuge from political and religious persecution. While 'people of the cryosphere' (Diemberger and Hovden, this volume) obviously lead extremely diverse lives under very different political, social and cultural circumstances, they share the fact that their homelands are located at the hot spots of climate change. The necessity to make a living in remote parts of the cryosphere has historically made mining and tourism dominant economic sectors in Arctic and mountainous regions. Today, ongoing environmental change not only enables resource extraction from previously untouched sites but also encourages new forms of tourism, such as 'last chance' tourism to the Arctic or to disappearing mountain glaciers. This points to a fundamental conundrum for the people of the cryosphere: industrial societies from (mostly) moderate climate zones have triggered climate change processes, which have affected the cryosphere earlier and more intensively than elsewhere. While there might be economic benefits for some in certain parts of the Arctic or in high mountain areas – through mining or tourism as mentioned above – there are negative (social, economic and cultural) impacts for most. Most importantly, however, climate change not only alters the natural environments for those who have contributed little to the accumulation of greenhouse gases in the atmosphere but it also changes the terms of engagements with these environments to dualistic notions of development vs. protection, conservation vs. growth. People of the cryosphere have neither destroyed nor protected the environments they depend on, for the simple reason that sustained livelihoods in fragile ecosystems require respect for and humility toward the more-than-human forces that govern these ecosystems (Ulturgasheva, this volume). In a way, global climate change has forced the dualistic rhetoric of industrial societies onto people of the cryosphere engaging with, adapting to and battling the impacts of lifestyles that contradict the values and codes of behaviour of their ancestors.

More-Than-Climate-Change

Despite the prominence of climate change in this volume and in the cryosphere, it is important not to fall into the trap of 'reducing the future to climate' (Hulme 2011), in the Arctic or elsewhere. Centuries of colonialism, discrimination or, at best, paternalism, have created social, economic and cultural problems that continue to haunt the Arctic and its inhabitants. This creates situations in which environmental change, no matter how dramatic it may be, is being reduced to an issue of secondary relevance. This is not due to ignorance or ecological illiteracy. On the contrary, the ability to live successfully in the Arctic for hundreds and thousands of years rests on careful observations and a deep understanding of the environment, which is not thought to be distinct from humans but a living system in which people are not the dominant actors.

The heterogeneity of the Arctic mentioned above is also reflected in how groups and settlements within the Arctic world relate to the issue of climate change. For one, different regions within the Circumpolar North are affected differently by climate change processes. For example, geology, building technology and other factors will determine to what degree houses and other structures of an Arctic settlement will be impacted by permafrost thaw. Likewise, coastal erosion depends on the physical make-up of a particular stretch of coastline in combination with what people do on that interface between land and sea. Finally, while many parts of the Arctic belong to regions where the notion of 'climate change' has been dominant in scientific and non-scientific discourses alike, other parts (such as the Russian Arctic) have not been part of regional or local conversations about global climate change until recently.

The issue cannot be reduced to the dichotomy of either acknowledging or denying climate change. It is about seeing this form of environmental change embedded within larger contexts of human-environmental relations. This includes, similar to the notion of the Anthropocene, a wider spectrum of ecological concerns rather than one limited to the climate. On the other hand, as the editors discuss in Chapter 1, it acknowledges that humans are part of the 'climate crisis' on every level, which involves politics, economics and cosmological understanding. Thus, 'more-than-climate-change' is about accepting the severity of climate change and the role of human choices in it, without assuming that people are almighty in their ability to combat or overcome it.

The Future of the Cryosphere and Its Peoples

The volume in front of you takes the reader from Alaska to Siberia, from Canada to the Himalaya and the European Alps. The stories along this journey speak as much of desperation and sorrow as they provide glimpses of hope and strong evidence of ingenuity and long-term resilience (Rasmus, this volume). So, what will the *Risky Futures* referenced in the title of this volume look like? One dramatic way of posing the question would be whether there will be an Arctic as we know it, that is an Arctic defined by snow and ice, the seasonal occurrence of which is an important enabler of Arctic livelihoods. In other words, is there a future for the cryosphere?

Of course, the answer rests with us humans, this strange species that managed to bring our planet to the brink of self-destruction. The good news is that an increasing number of people on earth are beginning to understand that we cannot afford to lose large parts of the cryosphere. While there was a time when people without winter sport ambitions and with homelands outside the cryosphere could shrug off the melting of snow and ice as if it wouldn't matter, today we understand that rising sea levels, reduced levels of reflection of solar radiation from the earth's surface, changes in ocean currents, etc., will affect everyone and not just people living in the Arctic. The 'right to be cold' (Watt-Cloutier 2015) is no longer just an issue for Inuit activists but should serve as a rallying cry for all of humanity.

It is clear that the entire cryosphere will not disappear in the foreseeable future. After all, high mountain areas will continue to receive precipitation in the form of snow for quite some time to come. Still, the climate change processes under way will significantly impact the lives of the peoples of the cryosphere. Thus, climate change will not just have direct impacts on the so-called natural environment of the Circumpolar North and beyond but also, at least indirectly, on its social environment and cultural activities. In short, it will become clear that – in our dependence on complex more-than-human environmental relations – we are all people of the cryosphere, who cannot afford to lose glaciers, ice or frozen ground, and need to insist on our 'right to be cold'.

Peter Schweitzer is currently Professor of Anthropology at the Department of Social and Cultural Anthropology of the University of Vienna. He is a founding member of the Austrian Polar Research Institute and served as its director from 2016 to 2020. He has been one of the two Austrian representatives to the Social and Human Working Group (SHWG) of the International Arctic Science Committee (IASC) and was the first chair of the SHWG, from 2011 to 2015. Schweitzer served as president of the International Arctic Social Science Association (IASSA) from 2001 to 2005 and is Professor Emeritus at the University of Alaska Fairbanks. His theoretical interests range from kinship and identity politics to human-environmental interactions, including the social lives of infrastructure and the community effects of global climate change; his regional focus areas include the Circumpolar North and the former Soviet Union. He has published widely on all of these issues.

References

Hulme, Mike. 2011. 'Reducing the Future to Climate: A Story of Climate Determinism and Reductionism', *Osiris* 26(1): 245–66.

Watt-Cloutier, Sheila. 2015. *The Right to Be Cold: One Woman's Story of Protecting Her Culture, the Arctic and the Whole Planet*. Toronto: Allen Lane.

Acknowledgements

The contributions to this volume were originally presented at a panel session 'Northern Futures? Climate, Geopolitics, and Local Realities' of the Royal Anthropological Institute/RAI meeting 'Anthropology, Weather and Climate Change' held at the British Museum, London in May 2016. We would like to thank warmly the Arctic Social Sciences programme of the US National Science Foundation, especially Anna Kerttula de Echave for generously supporting the Alaskan and Siberian participants' travel. We extend our special gratitude to the Royal Anthropological Institute for waiving the indigenous participants' membership and conference fees. We cordially thank Marion Berghahn and Anthony Mason at Berghahn Books for their patience and unquestionable belief in this book project. We would also like to acknowledge the significant contribution made by the two discussants on the panel, Michael Bravo and Peter Schweitzer. Finally, we are grateful to all of the panel participants for their part in the lively and productive discussion, and we wish, especially, to mention those who unfortunately were unable to contribute to the present volume: Niels Einarsson, Astrid Ogilvie, Glenn Juday and Marie-Jeanne Royer, whose presentations and interventions nevertheless formed a significant part of the dialogue that grew into this book.

Introduction

On Constellations and Connected-Up Thinking in the Face of the Future

Barbara Bodenhorn and Olga Ulturgasheva

> The processes of the Anthropocene have reversed the temporal order of modernity: those at the margins are now the first to experience the future that awaits all of us.
>
> —Amitav Ghosh, *The Great Derangement*, 2016

This is a book about the experiences, hopes, fears, responses and reactions of Circumpolar people who are engaging with rapidly shifting environmental circumstances. As reflected in our opening quotation, these changing conditions herald futures that may well be global, but that Arctic inhabitants are trying to imagine even as they develop strategies to cope with today's events – the future-made-present.[1] The volume reflects a day-long workshop held at the British Museum in May 2016. The discussion was well attended – packed out even – over the course of all three sessions – 'Because it was real', according to one attendee. We hope to retain that immediacy here, in a way that gives space to the many kinds of perspectives that contributed to our original discussions : local practitioners and observers (some of whom are one and the same); anthropologists, reindeer herders, ecologists, commercial fishermen, media specialists, whalers, geographers, trappers and others. Both the issues under consideration and the terms in which they are explored evade easy categorization. One of our discussants, Michael Bravo (who has written the afterword), summarized the entire workshop as an exposition of 'constellations of risks'. The editors have found the image compelling and encourage readers to see the whole as an exploration of the complexity of such constellations. We have divided our introductory remarks into two chapters: here we present the volume as a whole and explore a number of ideas which we feel have productively informed the anthropology of environmental processes in general. The first of these is an extended discussion about animacy, intimacy and vitalism, the combination which we suggest opens out an awareness of the multiple sensings of our surrounds; that awareness figures largely in the chapters to come. The second is a brief review of models of risk. Chapter 1 then sets out a series of concepts we feel are most pertinently relevant to imagining the possible futures that will envelop the lives of Arctic residents: the need to bring geo-politics and the cosmological into mutual view; the notion of the Anthropocene as a concept that is both powerful and another potential erasure of multiple voices; and, finally, the introduction of the notion of 'cryocide' to describe the risks faced by peoples across the globe who depend on ice-based landscapes for their existence. Although the contributions to come reflect a very wide range of issues and perspectives, they all reveal a commitment to examining abstractly understood climatological and geopolitical processes through the lens of local experiences and understandings.

On Decentring 'the Human' in Environmental Understanding

To capture some of the intellectual threads that might connect such a collection, in this introduction we propose a thought experiment: like so many, we start with Chakrabarty's (2009) assertion that a recognition of the Anthropocene as an idea that tells us something about human action as a determinant factor in geologic process invites – perhaps even requires – new ways of thinking. To approach this we want – as a beginning – to bring together three recent authors, all of whom are involved in what Ghosh (2016: 71) calls 'projects of imagination' that cross conventional disciplinary boundaries and, as such, may offer readers a way into the intellectual tenor of the volume overall: Amitav Ghosh's (2016) *The Great Derangement: Climate Change and the Unthinkable*; Elizabeth Povinelli's (2016) *Geonotologies: A Requiem to Late Liberalism*; and Kath Weston's (2017) reconsideration of 'the intimate' in her collection of essays, *Animate Planet: Making Visceral Sense of Living in a High-Tech Ecologically Damaged World*. In an important sense, all three might be considered post-humanist to the extent that none assumes that their focus can be restricted to human experience, human understanding, or human action – even though all of these are brought into their respective analyses. Thus, even through the conceptual lens of the Anthropocene, it is not the presence of 'the human' that is key here but rather the question of what happens to our thinking if we move away from humano-centric assumptions about past, present and future eventful processes. All three authors, then, recognize human activity as entangled in forceful ways in all sorts of non-human relations even as they propose ways of moving human actors from centre stage in their respective analytical frames. All three authors recognize that their shift in focus brings core contradictions into view. Weston (2017:10) frames her work as an attempt 'to describe a range of ecological intimacies through which people have co-constituted a world in which their finest technological achievements are implicated in habitat destruction'. Elizabeth Povinelli asserts, 'We must de-dramatize human life [even] as we squarely take responsibility for what we are doing. This ... may allow for opening new questions' (2016: 27). Such a statement is, of course, more easily asserted than realized. Ontological questions of conceptual framing, epistemological questions of evidence and knowledge, and ethical questions of the moral 'so what' in terms of responsible action are, we assume, in a constant state of mutual transformation. When we approach the subject of climate change from an actor's rather than a system's point of view, the analytical challenges multiply; not only is climate change, in Hulme's words, a 'wicked problem' (2009: 34), something he defines as 'essentially unique, with no definitive formulation, and [potentially...] symptomatic of yet other problems', but it is also (and most certainly in the Arctic) a 'threat multiplier' that has the potential to 'deepen already existing divisions and lead to the intensification of a range of conflicts' (Ghosh 2016: 143). Nowhere are these challenges more evident than in the Circumpolar North – where climatological processes take shape with ever increasing rapidity; geo-political desires bring nation states as well as local communities into intense confrontation; and struggles over whose voices count are the subject of constant negotiation. In our original call for papers, we explicitly invited our contributors to bring these factors into view. The results, we feel, meet Povinelli's exhortation to reframe our terms of reference as we open out new questions.

First, however, we would like to draw our readers' attention to the problem of time-as-signifier. As we shall see, one of Povinelli's quarrels with 'animism' as a concept is the degree to which its deployment effectively fossilizes not only indigenous knowledge, but relegates the people who inhabit animated worlds to some 'pre-modern' state of being and defines 'traditional knowledge' as a means to invoke that pre-modern past.[2] Despite Fabian's (1983) classic exhortations to anthropologists that they need to recognize their interlocutors as co-eval, the 'savage slot' continues to be invoked in many contexts. It should come as no surprise then to hear, even now, that Circumpolar peoples are often tagged as 'recently emerged from the stone age' (in Bodenhorn 1994: 7). At the same time, the Arctic is often characterized as the canary in the mine – the harbinger of the rest of the world's future. Whether as fossil or harbinger (or conceivably as a simultaneous both), the result of reaching for these sorts of images is – more often than not – to reduce the living inhabitants of these regions to signs: where 'we' (whoever that is) come from; where 'we' may end up. Thus we (the editors) want to establish two foundational points right at the start:

1. The accounts contained here reflect twenty-first-century struggles by people living in the Circumpolar North; they emerge from historical processes that are complexly contemporary (in the literal sense of sharing time with everyone else living in the twenty-first century). What Michael Bravo identified as 'constellations of risk' are being met with all the tools at our interlocutors' disposal: traditional, modern, scientific, practical, political and cultural. That conjunction of interests, knowledges and strategies is one of the core themes of the volume.

2. Nonetheless, what happens in the Arctic is also relevant for people not living in the Arctic – for thinking about resilience and creativity as well as for watching climatological processes as they unfold in real time.

For the rest of the introduction, we explore the provocations we feel Povinelli, Weston and Ghosh have to offer and then shift focus to consider the legacies of some classical models of risk. We conclude this part of our introductory remarks with an overview of the chapters themselves. In Chapter 1, we turn to the Arctic specifically and consider it as an eco-zone which acts as a planetary driver; we look at it as a politico/economic 'hot spot' that attracts multiples of competing interests and subsequently consider the implications of thinking about the Circumpolar North as a complex of cosmo-geo-politics. Finally, we introduce the notion of 'cryocide' to characterize the processes we feel have engulfed the worlds inhabited by ice-dependent peoples.

On Animism/Vitalism

> Our food consists entirely of souls.
>
> —Inuit shaman; in Barbara Bodenhorn, 'Whales, Souls, Children and Other Things that are Good to Share', 1988
>
> These things (baskets) is living. … now who can tell me what I mean, 'is living'?
>
> —Mabel McKay, in Greg Sarris, 'What I'm Talking about When I Talk about My Baskets', 1992
>
> This is not your great great grandmother's animism.
>
> —Kath Weston, *Animate Planet*, 2017

It is certainly possible to write powerfully about global climate change without recognizing that the globe's inhabitants have varying cosmological views about their surroundings and the processes which affect them.[3] Even Chakrabarty, with whom we began, assumes a unified 'anthro' in his vision of the anthropogenic climate change which drives the emergence of the Anthropocene as a geological era. But – as we shall explore in detail in Chapter 1 – one really cannot pay serious attention to the voices of Arctic peoples without acknowledging the importance of world views which are founded on ideas of human-non-human vital connectivity. Since recognizing the power of animated worlds continues to be controversial in much of academia, we want to begin our discussion by engaging with recent work that revisits the notion of animacy – and with it, its connection to intimacy.

Towards the end of her introduction to *Animate Planet*, Weston (2017: 26) muses that in current scholarship, 'everyone wants to rethink animacy but no one wants to be an animist'. She and Povinelli explore the debates around this conceptual complex in quite different ways. We feel the material in the present volume pushes both. While – as we shall explore below – we see how both authors rethink notions of animacy in creative and productive ways, we shall argue that it is quite important not to throw any vital babies out with the bathwater.

In *Geontologies*, Elizabeth Povinelli (2016) opens our frames of analysis by drawing a distinction between life/death and life(bio)/non-life (geo) as organizing principals. Western philosophy, she suggests, leans heavily towards the bio.[4] Geontopower, she argues, emerges from (and shapes) the ways in which this bio/geo nexus is organized conceptually to order human life politically and economically (and, by extension, the relations involving the rest of the planet). She proposes three figures – the Desert, Animism, the Virus – for understanding this dynamic. The desert (for which carbon is the major signifier) stands simultaneously for potential life – that vitality which can be created through the extraction of past lives contained in fossil fuels – life past and future, and an apocalyptic future when all life has become impossible.

Povinelli's attention to animism comes largely in the form of critique of the model (into which she slots, amongst others, the fossilized indigen, new vitalisms, and Gaia theorists) – which assumes that everything is life-filled. Such a starting point, she argues, closes down the possibilities offered by an awareness of non-life (2016: 18f). But her critique is actually considerably more nuanced than that.

To consider how Povinelli uses what she calls Karrabing analytics in order to push beyond conventional meanings of animism, it is worth exploring the figure of Tjipel – a presence/existent (Povinelli's term) on the Karrabing landscape where Povinelli has worked for decades.[5] At some point in her existence Tjipel was a young girl, murdered by an older man as she lay – face down – on the ground. Gradually her shape began to meld into the landscape, meandering, at times entwining with the vegetation on her edges, sometimes nibbling away at the random sand bank, at other times more rigidly confined by rock formations, occasionally disappearing altogether. At some points, her waters run clear and host many fish; at others, weighed down by tailings emptied into her waters by mining initiatives, she is sluggish and inhospitable. By listening to Karrabing talk about Tjipel, Povinelli suggests, an opening out process occurs. Karrabing, she asserts, are not interested in origin stories (Tjipel takes on this present form due to the murder, but she has other forms elsewhere); nor are they interested in the order in which things appear (who knows if rock fish precede or follow her appearance). Rather, they ask about directionality (where is she going?), orientation and relationality to other features in the landscape, including but not restricted to humans. A question of endless interest is why the creek offers fish to one person and not another. What is important for Povinelli is that Tjipel exists in multiple forms in multiple times – turning to and away from caring relations depending on circumstance. She is vital in her multiplicities but she is not an animated object/subject – not an entity with a soul. Her presence takes on many forms of being, blithely ignoring artificial boundaries between life/non-life and certainly not giving one precedence over another: vitality without singularity; existence without essence; existents which may turn toward each other in care – or may turn away (ibid.: 28). This recognition of relational energy that can be understood as story, event, co-constituting process and being without ever being fixed is, we feel, a productive move away from an understanding of 'anima' which fixes vitality to singular materialities.

Like Povinelli, Weston turns her attention to recent critiques of animism which – as a term – has been associated with the sort of evolutionist anthropology that assigns cosmological types to evolutionist hierarchies. To use the term is often to be tarred with a Tylorian brush (something both editors have experienced) (2017: 25ff). After noting what she considers the humanist character of the alternative model labelled 'perspectivalism', Weston turns her attention to forms of animation that she defines as co-constitutive rather than relational. Even as the term animism falls into disrepute, the sense that the world is replete with animating process comes to articulation across an increasingly broad intellectual landscape – but, in Weston's selection, not in ways that necessarily imply some form of social morality. Weston speaks of plants 'calling out' in warning to other plants, or in pleas for 'help' from insects – communications conducted via the release of pheromones; elsewhere Suzanne Simmard (2021) traces the ways in which 'mother trees' send nutrients to 'their' young via root systems.[6] Mochizuki (2011) speaks of 'a generation of Japanese people becoming nuclear fuel rods' in the wake of the Fukushima meltdown;[7] Weston herself (2017) explores the intimacies animated by the unwanted penetration of radioactivity in that same meltdown. This conjunction of what Weston calls 'animacies and intimacies' points away from assumptions about animation as in any way self-defined, or, indeed, necessarily social. In Weston's words: 'These twenty-first century eco-intimacies are not about separate-but-equal. Neither are they the products of relations between entities. ... Rather, these eco-intimacies are compositional; ... creatures co-constitute other creatures, infiltrating one's very substance' (ibid.: 33).

In some ways, Ghosh forms a bridge between Povinelli and Weston, focused squarely on questions of how humans engage with climate processes, by linking notions of coming-into-animation, intimacy, and the uncanny.

> The environmental uncanny is not the same as the uncanniness of the supernatural: it is different precisely because it pertains to nonhuman forces and beings ... Animals like the Sundarbans tiger and freakish weather events like the Delhi tornado, have no human referents at all.

> There is an additional element of the uncanny in events triggered by climate change, one that did not figure in my experience of the Delhi tornado. That is that the freakish weather events of today, despite their radically nonhuman nature, are nonetheless animated by cumulative human actions. In that sense, the events set in motion by global warming have a more intimate connection with humans than did the climatic phenomena of the past ... They are the mysterious work of our own hands returning to haunt us in unthinkable shapes and forms. ... [T]hey are instances ... of the uncanny intimacy of our relationship with the nonhuman. (2016: 32)

Note, his distinction is between human/non-human agencies, not life/non-life, or spirit/matter. Like Weston, his understanding of intimate and animating process is one of co-constitution and not necessarily of intersubjectivity. Like Povinelli, he provides a way of recognizing the impacts of human action without relying on a humano-centric world view. The recognition of 'the uncanny' as an important aspect of people's experiences resonates strongly with a number of our contributors, perhaps most dramatically in the accounts of Siberian reindeer herders for whom weather, topography and animals 'should' be known quantities but are today being experienced in unpredictable and unsettling ways.

So we come to the question of how to 'read' what is going on. In chapter three of *Geonotologies*, Povinelli notes that Karrabing aware that this vitality/energy/power does not just exist in the world, but becomes manifest in it. In a way that resonates with several of our authors, the key is that humans must learn to how recognize what is manifesting in any particular instance in order to decide what to do:

> The fundamental task of human thought – and thus the fundamental task of training humans how to think – was to learn how to discern a manifestation from an appearance; how to assess what these manifestations were indicating about the current arrangement of existence; and how to act properly given the sudden understanding that what is, is not what you thought it was. (Ghosh 2016: 58)

Mabel McKay (in Sarris 1989), a Kashaya Pomo basket maker and elder who has worked with Gregg Sarris for many years, has some provocative things to say that link the question of animacy with the question of learning. Sarris, himself brought up by Kashaya Pomo grandparents and currently in the Stanford English Department, had invited Mabel McKay to speak with his students about her skill as a basket maker. She said she would demonstrate rather than talk.[8] Luckily for us, she also spoke, showing herself to be a master teacher: 'it all starts from the beginning with roots. How the basket makes itself. Like two people meeting' (23); 'these things are living ... now who can tell me what I mean, is living?' (24). When asked, 'does it breathe?', she laughs. When asked, 'does it talk?' She responds, 'yeah, it talk all right. ... But how would YOU know? (ibid.)'. This is already pretty complicated stuff. On the surface it might seem like straightforward 'animism-as-social-relation' – basket and basket maker are both living; they can communicate; the basket maker at least is in some senses committed to acting properly towards the basket. But it all starts with the roots; and the basket tells Mabel how to make it. So whatever 'it' is, it exists before its material form. In Weston's sense, roots and basket maker are co-constituting the living that is the basket. In a Povinelli sense, the question of 'how would YOU know?' is entirely about manifestation. It's not just that roots and basket maker are in the same place, but that each is sensitive to the other. You have to learn how to recognize when you are being given instructions. And you need to know how to follow them. It seems that Mabel McKay is a bit more forthcoming about the learning process than Povinelli – although neither is providing a bullet point curriculum. 'What I'm talking about when I'm talking about my baskets', McKay says, 'is my life, the stories, the rules, how this thing is living, what they do to you' (25). It is not – as one member of the audience assumed – that McKay uses her baskets to tell the story of her life but rather that the stories, the rules and her life experiences provide her with a fund for understanding when, to echo Povinelli, roots are manifesting a basket with the vitality which affords them the agency to 'do something to you', or whether they are simply an appearance. In this volume, the problem comes when the frames of reference become unreliable: why in Siberia, for instance, bears 'go rogue' (Ulturgasheva, Chapter 2), what happens when open modes of thought become closed down (Edwardson, Chapter 3), or, if one assumes that 'the universe listens to everything', how to think about what it hears (see Rasmus, Chapter 4). In all of these instances, the felt urgency to respond to contemporary processes is made more complicated not only because of multiple sorts of overlapping risks but because it has become harder to figure out what is manifesting itself.

This brings us back to our concern with babies and bathwater. It is stimulating to think about animated intimacy which emerges from co-constitution which may have nothing at all to do with sociality or intentionality. It is helpful to think about multiplicities of Tjipel and the extent to which animacy can elude being fixed in a single thing or in a unique relationship. However, there are several 'yes, buts' here. Bodenhorn was introduced to the Iñupiaq concept of 'sila' (today translated as weather) in the 1980s. This, she was told, was an impersonal, implacable, unapproachable force. This was not an entity you could bribe with gifts, sacrifices or songs. You had to learn how to watch, be careful and stay alert.[9] But the world was also filled with 'iñua' – generally glossed by Iñupiat as soul or spirit, and literally translated as 'its person'. And when North Slopers have talked to Bodenhorn about whales and whaling over the years, it has been, more often than not, in terms of a moral, social, personal relationship. When Patrick Attungana (1988), a whaler and Episcopal Minister from Point Hope, addressed the Alaskan Eskimo Whaling Commission in the mid-1980s, he said a number of things: that whales see humans' actions and hear their interaction and decide 'to go camping' (i.e. to offer themselves up to a particular crew) based on whether or not they feel a welcoming campsite has been offered; if their bodies 'are treated tenderly', then the whale 'soul or spirit' will return to other whales to tell them that this was either a good place to go camping and that they will return the following year, or that a lack of generosity will drive them elsewhere. The whale gives itself to the entire community and expects to be shared by the entire community. This will continue 'if we hunt in harmony; this is what keeps us together'.[10] This is a powerful narrative that assumes intersubjectivity and moral sociality across (at least some) species boundaries. Although it of course cannot be taken as a mode of understanding that shapes all Iñupiaq behaviour, its footprint, so to speak, is present in contemporary discussions of how to proceed in social life. As Rachel Edwardson argues in this volume, this is a form of morality that continues intergenerationally through the circulation of whale and human DNA, mixed and melded with commensality. And it is a form of sentience explored by Rasmus at the level of the universe. Much as we welcome the conceptual openings out of our colleagues, we caution against a refusal to recognize the continuing strength of this form of animated relationality.

The notion of animism without its anthropological evolutionary baggage – without the question of whether or not ultimately this turns on the centrality of materiality – allows us to hear, see, feel, taste multiplicities of vital energies. That can include plants 'calling for help'; baskets that speak, but only if you know how to listen; creeks 'turning away'; and microbes upon microbes passing through and constituting the being-in-the-container they inhabit for moments, or for the entire span of their existence.[11] In virtually all of the chapters to come, it also helps us to understand moral relationality that extends beyond a humano-centric world and – crucially – reminds its practitioners that 'value' is not only that which can be calculated in market terms.

We give the final word in the section to Robin Wall Kimmerer. At the start of *Braiding Sweetgrass: Indigenous Wisdom, Scientific Knowledge and the Things Plants Have to Teach Us* (2013), Kimmerer, a Potawatomi elder and lecturer in Botany at SUNY, Buffalo, begins with an account of Skywoman's fall to earth; it is a journey she survives because geese gather to break her fall, and like any good guest she brings gifts: grasses, flowers and seeds which will become the basis of sustenance for humans and other living beings. 'Images of Skywoman', Kimmerer asserts, 'speak not just of where we came from, but how we might go forward' (2013: 5). On discovering that her ecology students framed human/nature relations only in negative terms (those of toxicity, pollution and over-exploitation), Kimmerer suggests that they had not grown up on the story of Skywoman (ibid.: 6). 'How can we begin to move toward cultural and ecological sustainability if we cannot imagine what the path feels like?' she asks, 'If we cannot imagine the generosity of geese?' (ibid.). Throughout her exploration of human-non-human interactions in northern New York, she repeatedly returns to her mantra: that we humans need to experience the world around us as something that requires our gratefulness. That contrast, between the need to be grateful and the assumed need to conquer, reflects one of the core tensions that trouble not only the contributors to the present volume, but many others who are also trying to reach a broader understanding of what we mean by 'climate change', its accompanying dangers, and our responsibilities to respond.

Recognizing 'Risk': On the Intersections of Hazards, Risks, Knowledge, Voice and Responsibilities

Since the mid-1990s when Iñupiat began to worry out loud about their ice, a steady stream of risk-related literature has appeared, much of it related to environmental unpredictability (see, for example, Gaul 2017; Richardson et al. 2011), threats to national security (e.g. Klare 2019), the perception of risk (Slovic 2010) and 'modes of uncertainty' (Samimian-Darash and Rabinow 2015). Of particular note is the work of Oreskes and Conway (2010) who set out in *Merchants of Doubt* a history of the concerted campaign to sow doubt in the reliability of scientific assessments concerning the risks presented by tobacco, acid rain and, most recently, climate change. Whereas, the authors argue, the campaign regarding tobacco was to challenge the interpretation of research results, the most recent interventions have been to demonize scientific expertise altogether. Thus, while we recognize ways in which scientific narratives can be used politically to diminish alternative forms of knowledge, we also see how scientific/indigenous collaborations can be the subject of a kind of double-barrelled dismissal. Our intention for the remainder of this section, however, is to pay close attention to some of the classical discussions that were developing at the same time as ice melt was starting to be of concern in the Circumpolar North. The literature we are considering thus reflects the ethnographic as well as the theoretical context of that time. Even more importantly, we feel that the ground they covered continues to provide fertile discussion in the present.

At the time that Bodenhorn was beginning to explore 'risky decisions' made by Iñupiaq whalers (see Chapter 7, this volume), the dominant model within government and scientific communities – what both Lupton (1999) and Fox (1999) called the 'techno-scientific/realist' approach to 'risk' – assumed that 'it' is out there. According to the British Medical Association (1987: 13), for instance, a hazard is something 'with the potential to cause harm'; the risk is the likelihood that it will do so. Thus the task of 'risk management' was to map causes in order to calculate, predict and limit effects; it was – and often continues to be – therefore presented as a technical procedure.[12] The British Medical Association (1987: vii) acknowledged that complete agreement in terms of what constitutes 'acceptable risk' was virtually impossible, and suggested that 'if people can agree upon the ways risks are measured and on the relevance of the levels of risk thus represented to the choices we must all make, then the scope for disagreement and dissent is thereby limited'. In the intervening decades, as we have noted, explosive global processes such as climate change, the increasing frequency of global pandemics, mass migration or the unintended consequences of technological developments have all generated a surge of risk analyses that these developments are thought to pose. The paradigm above, which posits the risk/hazard relation as one of cause and effect that is open to objective analysis, which in turn can produce effective management techniques, continues to exert a powerful presence on the landscape of environmental risk assessment (see both Gaul 2017, and Richardson et al. 2011, already mentioned).

With that context in mind, we turn to three bodies of social science work that gained attention in the 1980s and 1990s and strongly challenged the techno/science approach to risk which continues to hold sway in many quarters even in the twenty-first century. Although a great deal of thinking about risk has taken place since then, their footprints thus remain visible and their arguments provocative.

In *Risk and Culture*, Mary Douglas and Aaron Wildavsky (1982: 2) argue that 'fear of risk coupled with the confidence to face it has something to do with knowledge and something to do with the kind of people we are'. Different people worry about different things. '[T]o organise [in the face of perceived risk] means to organise some things in and other things out' (1982: 8). The nature of the perception of risk(s) and strategies for dealing with them, they argue, depend on organizational aspects of the social groups in question: whether groups are in core or peripheral positions and whether they are generally egalitarian or hierarchical in their social organization. Core groups tend to be present-oriented whereas peripheral ones tend to look to the future or to the past. These groups 'will never agree, because they are arguing from different premises' (1982: 175). The process – of identifying risk, assessing it and creating strategies with relation to its perceived implications – of considering 'goods' and 'bads' is thus moral and consequently always both cultural and political. Although Douglas and Wildavsky assert that the concern with 'risk' in the United States (their ethnographic field) has intensified radically since the 1960s, it is not 'about' modernity (1982: 14).[13]

Sociologists such as Ulrich Beck (1992, et al. 1994, 1996) and Anthony Giddens (1990, 1994) argue that this is not only about 'modernity', but about 'late modernity'. According to Beck (1996: 27), 'risk society' emerges as 'a phase of modernity in which the social, political, ecological and individual risks created by the momentum of innovation increasingly elude the control and protective institutions of industrial society'. Insurance companies, Beck argues, show us that the limits of this way of being have been reached. With new technological developments, the risk of a 'bad' outcome may be low, but the consequences of even a single failure may be limitless. As a result, insurance companies refuse coverage for most major research companies or limit it to almost meaningless amounts (1996: 33). In stage one, these consequences are systematically produced, but they are not subject to debate. In stage two, the hazards of industrial society dominate public and private debate. This debate he calls 'reflexive' (1996: 28ff), but clarifies that this is first in the sense of reflex and only subsequently in terms of critical reflection. Following on from

Simmel, Durkheim and Weber, Beck understands the process of modernization to be one of increasing individualization in which people are turned into the bearers of rights and duties, but only as individuals. His model, as well as Giddens', is very much one based on rational choice theory. What he calls (1996: 30) 'risky freedoms' are imposed on individuals without the latter being in a position – because of the great complexity of modern society – to make decisions in a knowledgeable and responsible way with regard to consequences.

Wynne (1996) challenges this position with a close and critical examination of the expert/lay knowledge model that assumes the former is objective and trusted by the latter. In part, his critique stems from the almost purely institutional emphasis in Beck's and Giddens' work. Drawing on case studies of sheep farmers in Cumbria and Andean potato growers, Wynne shows how scientists may often generate inaccurate predictions because they do not elicit local environmental knowledge (with serious consequences when those predictions form the basis of government or development policy). He shows how local knowledge may at times drive research, and become eclipsed when the researchers 'discover' what locals have been saying. And he emphasizes the extent to which silence should not be taken as evidence of 'trust' in expert opinion.

And there are those (e.g. Castel 1991; Lupton 1999; Fox 1999; Crook 1999) who tend to concentrate on Foucauldian governmentality: that 'complex form of power, which has … as its essential technical means apparatuses of security' (Foucault 1991: 102/3). The presentation of risk, Lupton (1999: 5) suggests, is a strategy of governmentality, one aspect of which is to suggest that it is ultimately controllable by following 'expert' opinion. Thus, Fox (1999: 19) explains, what for him was 'just a milk truck' was for his driving instructor a hazard – as was everything else on the road. Any analysis of the process of perceiving and acting on risk, then, must begin with a cultural analysis of why hazards are defined as hazards.

But we are also seeing some shifts in the conceptual make-up of this landscape. It remains commonplace in many settings that risk assessment is assumed to be a question of rational, objective judgement which is somehow disengaged from cultural factors. Because non-specialists are assumed to respond individually and subjectively to events around them, their opinions are generally considered to be 'biased' or 'anecdotal' in comparison to expert scientific assessment.[14] The tensions between natural and social scientists as holders of expert knowledge have often been played out on these grounds. Socio-cultural processes have historically not been considered, except insofar as these were considered with reference to the rational generation and implementation of management strategies by experts. Beck (1996) and Wynne (1996) noted, for instance, that major governmental institutions such as the National Science Foundation in the US and the European Union generally incorporated social scientists into their information gathering processes in the expectation that social scientists would be able to follow a 'hard science' paradigm in documenting, analysing and predicting outcomes of human responses to environmental policy shifts.[15] As we explore further in Chapter 1, the provocations of anthropocenic thinking have expanded both the scale and the boundaries of environmental modelling even though tensions behind the recognition of 'expertise' and 'evidence' remain subjects of lively debate when predicting the risk of undesirable environmental outcomes to human action (see, e.g., Sneath 2013). At the same time, however, in the demonizing of expertise that has characterized much public discourse in the US during the past decade, the deriding of expert knowledge as it pertains to risk, whether concerning climate change, gang violence or COVID, has frequently been heard in the Houses of Congress.

Still, perhaps one of the encouraging developments of the first decades of the twenty-first century has been a more genuine opening out – at least in some instances – of collaborative interactions between knowledge holders of different orders.[16] Several of the chapters in this volume reveal active sharing of knowledge between different sorts of experts: Eveny reindeer herders and permafrost scientists; public health experts and Yup'ik elders; and whale biologists and whalers.

Regardless of our recognition of collaboration, questions of voice remain. An awareness of the political consequences of eclipsing perspective, of refusing to listen to alternative voices is a theme that has fed through the present volume – from the elimination of the Arctic and its residents from news coverage of COP21 detailed by Callison, to the criminalization of any challengers to pipeline construction proposed by President Trump in 2019 and passed by the Senate in 2020.[17] This was aimed directly at Lakota defending their rights to clean water at Standing Rock. Lest we make too easy assumptions about these forms of silencing as either limited to the scientific/lay divide, or anti-colonial struggles between indigenous/modern knowledge holders, we need to recognize that the struggle over authoritative voice is one of power in the crudest sense. The demonization of science concerning environmentalism in general, climate change more specifically (including the US military's assessments of the risks to national security posed by it) and, more recently,

COVID, has been actively deployed in the service of industry and of politics for some time (see, for instance, Oreskes and Conway 2010; the subsequent *Merchants of Doubt* documentary, 2014; Klare 2019). Over the past several years, in the face of an active muzzling of the Federal agencies as a source of environmental and climate research results, perhaps ironically Native American news media such as *Indian Country Today* in the US or *The Narwhal* in Canada became important sources of cutting-edge reporting. Because so many Native American communities were – and continue to be – at the forefront of the toxic impacts of environmental degradation, it has been deemed crucial that they had access to all of the current information they could get.[18]

There is no need to reduce our anthropological understanding to a single line of analysis. This is not a contest for last theory standing. But in a world where – as Ghosh, Weston and Povinelli eloquently describe – having to bear the brunt of the consequences of human actions is unevenly distributed across humanity, as is the ability for voices to carry that are trying to make sense of those actions, and where – now more than ever – a dominant discourse of man (sic) over (sic) nature (sic) and the political economy it underpins continues in its ascendency even as it is contested on multiple fronts, we hope that the thoughtful discussions contained in this volume have the power to animate further explorations into the implications of risky Arctic Futures for Circumpolar residents as well as for others who take climate change seriously.

The Order of Chapters

As already mentioned, we have chosen to zoom in on specific issues that we feel inform the volume as a whole rather than undertaking a comprehensive literature overview. This has included a detailed discussion of animacy/intimacy as a key idea complex for taking indigenous voices into account; a conversation about the politics of environmental knowledge and voice; and finally, a discussion of risk as multi-faceted. These encompass two broad issues: a) the importance of recognizing the presence as well as the potential of non-humano-centric cosmological models; and b) how 'precarity' is experienced, communicated and acted upon. Both threads have been the subject of considerable discussion. We hope that the observations and insights in the chapters to come can open these discussions still further.

In Chapter 1, our attention is turned specifically to the Arctic, challenging the (still prevalent) fallacy that the Arctic – like the Antarctic – is barren, empty space and bringing our attention to the lived [lives= as= lived] of the peoples who have been occupying the Circumpolar region for millennia. In particular, we bring the geo-political and the cosmological into mutual view; we revisit the notion of the Anthropocene that has the capacity not only to revolutionize disciplinary boundary thinking, but also to homogenize 'anthro' to the detriment of non-mainstream peoples the world over. Finally, we suggest 'cryocide' as a term to describe the processes currently being experienced by peoples who inhabit ice-dependent landscapes.

Chapters 2, 3 and 4 provide ethnographic descriptions of those lived lives. In every account, unfolding events produce spiritual, cognitive and pragmatic disruptions. The sense of precarity that emerges from these multiple processes is equally complex and intertwined. By offering these narratives, we are not engaging in an exercise in homogenization. Eveny reindeer herders, Iñupiaq whalers and young Yupiit are not experiencing exactly the same unpredictability; nor are the resources and responsibilities which shape their responses the same. Nonetheless, we urge readers to recognize the importance of hearing non humano-centric world views across these chapters and to be aware that those senses of being in the world contribute to people's experiences of their homelands as zones of precarity that is as social and political as it is climatological.

In Chapter 2, Ulturgasheva provides a detailed account of recent Eveny reindeer herders' experiences with the violent and unpredictable ways in which extreme events are now a constant in their environment. The consequences of these include the appearance of 'rogue bears' fleeing forest fires from elsewhere who, it seems, do not understand the social contract between bears and humans; and it includes the unpredictable behaviour of the land/ice/riverscapes themselves. She explores some of the ways in which these reindeer herders understand such events and details the modes through which Eveny develop responsive strategies to them. This includes collaborative relations with Russian permafrost scientists who admitted to Ulturgasheva that they would have been unable to carry out their research without Eveny help. This first ethnographic chapter, then, reveals the importance of recognizing multiple modes of knowing that are neither centred on humans, nor pit 'science' and 'non-science' against each other. The politics of climate change in this instance emerge largely in the absence of a state that has retreated since the collapse of the Soviet Union, leaving Every for the most part on their own. Eveny do not assume that there is a single source of expertise and, in the face of precarious uncertainty, draw on all the sources at their disposal: their own observational skills, shamanic ritual practices, the mobilization of collective responsibility and a readiness to consult with scientists. The 'constellations of risk' put forward by Michael Bravo are met with constellations of responses. This is a story of adaptation and resilience, but it is not a story with a happy ending. None of the chapters in the volume are. The precarity is keenly felt; the uncertainty produces profound anxiety. But that leads neither to paralysis, dependency or inaction.

If Chapter 2 gives readers a view of collective action in the face of challenge, Chapter 3 brings internal political discord onto centre stage. Here Edwardson (an Inupiaq oral historian) explores in evocative detail how she has come to learn what it means to be in the world as an Inupiaq woman. In doing so, she provides a powerful, historicized account of tensions between what she identifies as the short-term and siloed thinking that Iñupiat have been subject to since the earliest arrival of commercial whalers and the more long-term, holistic world view that valorizes the moral imperative to protect the habitat of the whales on whom Iñupiaq communities depend. Like Eveny reindeer herders, Iñupiaq whalers are confronting uncertain and precarious changes in their marine environment which have profound implications for the moral, social relations Inupiat maintain with bowhead whales and other animals. At the same time, however, the North Slope of Alaska is oil rich and Iñupiat have struggled for decades to balance a determination to protect their habitat and to participate in the oil driven economy. In this instance, to echo Douglas and Wildavsky, what gets factored in and factored out is a matter of moral struggle by Iñupiat themselves. This has only been exacerbated by the increasingly intense complications that climate change introduces.

By the end of Chapter 3, then, we have already confronted a number of challenges to conventional depictions of Arctic socialities: that it is 'empty space'; that unbridgeable gulfs characterize 'traditional/scientific' divides; and that it is possible to talk about a unified indigenous view. The complexity of competing interests and the tensions it introduces into young people's lives – as well as the difficulties these youth find in bringing their experiences to articulation – is the subject of Stacy Rasmus's account in Chapter 4. Working in Yup'ik villages in southwestern Alaska, Rasmus has heard for years about the need to be able 'to weather the storms' – of unpredictable weather, intractable government authorities, and confusing social and economic messaging – particularly as these contribute to the risk of suicide amongst

Yup'ik young people. The Yup'ik universe, suggests Rasmus, is contracting and expanding at the same time. Here the gap is less about differences in opinion about future goals and more between generations who are hearing different things. In the face of less than effective One Health initiatives (which propose inclusion but are, in fact, imposed), one Elder told Rasmus, 'the weather is changing with the people'; the tides are no longer predictable and you need to be willing to wait them out – just as you need to wait out the emotional storms that have engulfed so many young people's minds – you need to wait until they are willing 'to open up their minds'. If one of our through lines has been about voice, this chapter importantly is about listening.

How people articulate what they know and how they negotiate discussions of response are issues that thread their way through these first chapters, but in Chapter 5 Candis Callison place 'voice' in the centre of the frame. In her chapter, Callison (a member of the Tāłtān people of British Columbia and media scholar) provides a forensic analysis of erasure as she offers a telling critique of media coverage of COP21. Here she details a growing absence of the Arctic as a space, or of Arctic residents who have expert knowledge of their places in the public media accounts covering the event. There were many indigenous participants at the Paris COP21 meetings (see, e.g., Fraser, forthcoming). Nevertheless, as Callison illustrates in great detail, the slight presence of 'the Arctic' and its residents that appeared at the outset of the conference simply slowly but steadily disappeared. It is not that Circumpolar peoples were prevented from attending the conference, but that their presence simply became a non-event. Their very considerable knowledge of a region that is one of the most rapidly changing in the world due to environmental shifts was not thought to be part of the overall conversation.

In Chapter 6, Hildegard Diemberger and Astrid Hovden return to the question of connections rather than the suppression or inclusion of voice. As with the first three ethnographic examples, the Tibetan nomads with whom Diemberger and Hovden work inhabit an animated landscape which residents engage with spiritually and practically. Like their Arctic counterparts they are ice-dependent – in this case on that of glaciers. As with Iñupiat and Eveny, they are keen observers of the world around them and interpret what they see according to a world view that does not place them at the centre of it. With these similarities in mind Diemberger and Hovden propose an inclusive view of new spaces and new connections. Here they champion the idea that reformulating our categories from 'the Arctic' to 'the cryosphere' allows us to think together the challenges faced by peoples living at high latitudes alongside those living in high altitudes. That, in fact, forms one basis to our question in Chapter 1 about whether we are now being confronted with what can only be termed 'cryocide'.

Finally, in Chapter 7, through her examination of strategic decisions made in the face of uncertain whaling conditions Bodenhorn returns to the idea that 'risk' in the Arctic is a highly complex set of phenomena which include physical, social, cosmological, political and economic elements. Thus, she brings the discussion back to Bravo's characterization of the volume as a depiction of constellations of risks.

Barbara Bodenhorn was Newton Trust Lecturer in Social Anthropology until 2013 and is currently Fellow Emerita of Pembroke College, Cambridge. Her most recent research interests focus on children's environmental knowledge as well as communally initiated responses to environmental change.

Olga Ulturgasheva is a Senior Lecturer/Associate Professor in Social Anthropology at the University of Manchester, UK. Over the last twenty years she has been engaged in a number of anthropological and cross-disciplinary studies exploring animism, human and non-human personhood, childhood and youth, climate change, resilience and adaptation patterns in Siberia, American Arctic and Amazonia. She is the author of *Narrating the Future in Siberia: Childhood, Adolescence and Autobiography among the Eveny* (Berghahn Books, 2012) and co-editor of *Animism in Rainforest and Tundra: Personhood, Animals, Plants and Things in Contemporary Amazonia and Siberia* (Berghahn Books, 2012). She serves as a Principal Investigator and co-Principal Investigator for two large international, collaborative research projects focusing on the dynamic of climate change in Alaska, Siberia and the Russian Far East funded by the US National Science Foundation and the European Research Council.

Notes

1. The title of the workshop was 'Northern Futures? Climate, Geopolitics and Local Realities'. We had originally proposed 'Arctic Futures?' as the title to the present volume and indeed it remains a central focus to the work as a whole. However, during the time it has taken to finalize this book, a number of other publications have appeared with almost identical titles, hence our shift to the notion of 'Risky Futures'.
2. Povinelli notes, for instance, that in Australia, 'traditional knowledge' can be put forward as evidence for continual historical presence in land claims

cases, but is not accepted in court as an explanation/analysis of current geopolitical/physical processes (2016: 103ff).
3. This list could be vast, but see, for instance, Jamail (2019); Klare (2019); or Rush's first-person accounts of environmentally extreme events that affect coastal erosion (2018).
4. Bodenhorn, however, is minded of conversations with Robert Suydam, an Arctic ecologist working in Utqiagvik who is explicit that it is the non-biological (soil, topography, weather, latitude) that determines what forms the biological can take (personal communication, July 2006).
5. This discussion is primarily a compression of chapter four, 'The Normativity of Creeks' (2016).
6. We recommend the PBS (2013) documentary, 'What Plants Talk About', for an exploration of communication in the absence of any sort of central organizing nervous system.
7. 24 October 2011, Mochizuki's blog Fukushima Diary, http://fukushima-diary.com. Accessed by Weston on 3 May 2016.
8. McKay was in fact recognized as an accomplished public speaker.
9. We are not staking claims to a unified cosmology here; Bodenhorn also read in Brower's late nineteenth century) diaries that he had paid shamans to arrange the right kind of weather for him to go out on the ocean.
10. See also Hess 1999.
11. This might seem self-evident to any biochemist aware of the constant swirling of microbes and other things that make up a human being, but it goes counter to basic anthropological assumptions of bodies as discrete entities. Helmreich (2009), Latour (1993) and Weston (2017), all from Science and Technology Studies, have (amongst others) explored such issues for some time.
12. See, e.g., Johnstone-Brydan 1995, Fox 1999, for analysis.
13. See also Douglas 1985, 1992.
14. The literature is substantial, but see, e.g., Hertz and Thomas 1983; Frankenfeld 1992; Johnstone-Brydan 1995; Wells 1996; see also Douglas 1985, which critically reviews some of the earlier scientific literature. See Wynne 1994, Wynne 1996: 77 and Gieryn 1999 for analyses of the 'expert'/'lay' divide.
15. Indeed, an NSF organized 'Human impact of global warming in the Arctic' conference held in Fairbanks in 1997 allowed a small number of social scientists to participate after considerable local academic protest that to hold such a conference without the inclusion of people who worked with people would be foolish. To be fair, the NSF has supported qualitative and descriptive anthropological research as well as quantitative and predictive work. As a first-time participant in what was predominantly a hard science conference, Bodenhorn was surprised by the degree to which the daily summing up sessions invariably presented the day's workshops in terms of agreed upon results. In classic Latourian fashion, dissent and uncertainty – much in evidence during the discussions – seemed to be almost entirely eclipsed.
16. Utqiagvingmiut (people of Utqiagvik, or Barrow) have a long history of working with scientists (see Brewster 2004); in 'Meeting Minds, Encountering Worlds (Bodenhorn 2013), I review three multi-year research projects in

Barrow, two of which had been initiated by Inupiat and a third which was actively supported by UIC, the village corporation. See also Konrad 2013, amongst others.
17. Senate bill 2299, passed 6 August 2020. https://www.congress.gov/bill/116th-congress/senate-bill/2299; see also Brown 2020 for a fuller discussion of the background of this bill.
18. This was the subject of considerable discussion at a conference on Indigenous environmental knowledge held in Princeton in December 2018, organized by Candis Callison.

References

Attungana, Patrick. 1988. 'Address to the Alaskan Eskimo Whaling Commission', *The Open Lead* (1)2: 16ff, trans. James Nageak.

Beck, Ulrich. 1992. *Risk Society*, London: Sage.

———. 1996. 'Risk Society and the Provident State', in S. Lash, B. Szerszynski and B. Wynne (eds), *Risk, Environment and Modernity: Towards a New Ecology*. London: Sage.

Beck, Ulrich, Anthony Giddens and Scott Lash (eds). 1994. *Reflexive Modernization*. Cambridge: Polity.

Bodenhorn, Barbara. 1988. 'Whales, Souls, Children and Other Things That Are Good to Share: Core Metaphors in a Contemporary Hunting Society', *Cambridge Anthropology* 13(1): 1–19.

———. 1994. 'Las ballenas y los Inuit', El Mar (volume theme). *SacBé* 1(1): 7–11.

———. 2003. 'Strategic Decision Making on the North Slope of Alaska', in A.P. McCartney (ed.), *Indigenous Ways to the Present: Native Whaling in the Western Arctic*. Edmonton: Canadian Circumpolar Institute Press; Salt Lake City: University of Utah.

———. 2013. 'Meeting Minds; Encountering Worlds: Science and Other Expertises on the North Slope of Alaska', in Monica Konrad (ed.), *Collaborators Collaborating*. Oxford: Berghahn.

Brewster, Karen. 2004. *The Whales, They Give Themselves: Conversations with Harry Brower, Sr.* Fairbanks: University of Alaska Press.

British Medical Association. 1987. *Living with Risk*. Chichester: John Wiley.

Brower, Charles, Sr. Diaries. multiyear diaries extended from the mid 1880s through to the early nineteenth century. Archived at the Rasmussen Library, University of Alaska, Fairbanks.

Brown, Alleen. 2020. 'Trump Administration Asks Congress to Make Disrupting Pipeline Construction a Crime Punishable by 20 Years in Prison', *The Intercept*. Retrieved April 2021 from https://theintercept.com/2019/06/05/pipeline-protests-proposed-legislation-phmsa-alec/.

Burchell, Graham, Colin Gordon and Peter Miller (eds). 1991. *The Foucault Effect: Studies in Governmentality*. Chicago: University of Chicago Press.

Castel, Robert. 1991. 'From Dangerous to Risk', in G. Burchell, C. Gordon and P. Miller (eds), *The Foucault Effect: Studies in Governmentality*. Chicago: University of Chicago Press, pp. 281–98.

Chakrabarty, Dipesh. 2009. 'The Climate of History: Four Theses', *Critical Inquiry* 35: 197–222.
Crook, Stephen. 1999. 'Ordering Risks', in D. Lupton (ed.), *Risk and Sociocultural Theory*, Cambridge: Cambridge University Press, pp. 160–85.
Douglas, Mary. 1985. *Risk Acceptability According to the Social Sciences*. New York: Russell Sage Foundation.
———. 1992. *Risk and Blame: Essays in Cultural Theory*. London: Routledge.
Douglas, Mary and Aaron Wildavsky. 1982. *Risk and Culture: An Essay on the Selection of Technological and Environmental Dangers*. Berkeley: University of California Press.
Fabian, Johannes. 1983. *Time and the Other: How Anthropology Makes its Object*. New York: Columbia University Press.
Foucault, Michel. 1991. 'Governmentality', in Graham Burchell, Collin Gordon and Peter Millers (eds), *The Foucault Effect: Studies in Governmentality with Two Lectures by and an Interview with Michel Foucault*. Chicago: University of Chicago Press.
Fox, Nick. 1999. 'Postmodern Reflections on "Risk", "Hazards" and Life Choices', in D. Lupton (ed.), *Risk and Sociocultural Theory*. Cambridge: Cambridge University Press, pp. 12–33.
Frankenfeld, Philip. 1992. 'Technological Citizenship: A Normative Framework for Risk Studies', *Science, Technology and Human Values* 17: 459–84.
Fraser, Richard. (forthcoming). 'After Paris: An Ethnographic Eye on COP21 and Beyond', in B. Bodenhorn (ed.), *In the Name of Climate Change: On the Politics and Pragmatics of Environmental Knowledge*. Oxford: Berghahn.
Gaul, Gilbert. 2017. *The Geography of Risk: Epic Storms, Rising Seas, and the Cost of America's Coasts*. New York: Macmillan.
Ghosh, Amitav. 2016. *The Great Derangement: Climate change and the Unthinkable*. Chicago: Chicago University Press.
Gieryan, Thomas. 1999. *Cultural Boundaries of Science: Credibility on the Line*. Chicago: University of Chicago Press.
Giddens, Anthony. 1990. *The Consequences of Modernity*. Cambridge: Polity Press.
———. 1994. 'Living in a Post-Traditional Society', in U. Beck, A. Giddens and S. Lash (eds), *Reflexive Modernization: Politics, Tradition and Aesthetics in the Modern Social Order*. Cambridge: Polity Press, pp. 56–109.
Helmreich, Stefan. 2009. *Alien Ocean: Anthropological Voyages in Microbial Seas*. Berkeley: University of California Press.
Hertz, David and Howard Thomas. 1983. *Risk Analysis and its Applications*. Chichester: Wiley.
Hess, Bill. 1999. *Gift of the Whale: The Inupiat Bowhead Hunt, a Sacred Tradition*. Seattle, Washington: Sasquatch Books.
Hulme, Mike. 2009. *Why We Disagree About Climate Change: Understanding Controversy, Inaction and Opportunity*. Cambridge: Cambridge University Press.
Jamail, Dahr. 2019. *End of Ice: Bearing Witness and Finding Meaning in the Path of Climate Disruption*. New York: The New Press.
Johnstone-Brydan, Ian. 1995. *Managing Risk*. Aldershot: Avebury.

Kimmerer, Robin Wall. 2013. *Braiding Sweetgrass: Indigenous Wisdom, Scientific Knowledge and the Things Plants Have to Teach Us*. Minneapolis: Milkweed Press.

Klare, Michael. 2019. *All Hell Breaking Loose: The Pentagon's Perspective on Climate Change*. New York: Metropolitan Books, Henry Holt and Company.

Lash, Scott, Bronislaw Szerszynski and Brian Wynne (eds). 1996. *Risk, Environment and Modernity: Towards a New Ecology*. London: Sage Publications.

Latour, Bruno. 1993. *We Have Never Been Modern*. Translated by C. Porter. Cambridge, MA: Harvard University Press.

Lupton, Deborah (ed.). 1999. *Risk and Sociocultural Theory: New Directions and Perspectives*. Cambridge: Cambridge University Press.

Merchants of Doubt. 2014. A documentary directed by Robert Kenner and produced by Participant. Release date 14 December 2014.

Mochizuki, Iori. 2011. Blog. Fukushima diary, http://fukushima-diary.com. Accessed by Weston 3 May 2016.

Oreskes, Naomi and Erik Conway. 2010. *Merchants of Doubt: How a Handful of Scientists Obscured the Truth from Tobacco Smoke to Global Warming*. London: Bloomsbury Press.

Povinelli, Elizabeth. 2016. *Geontologies: A Requiem to Late Liberalism*. Durham and London: Duke University Press.

Richardson, Katherine, Will Steffen and Diana Liverman. 2011. *Climate Change: Global Risks, Challenges and Decisions*. Cambridge: Cambridge University Press.

Rush, Elizabeth. 2018. *Rising: Dispatches from the New American Shore*. Minneapolis: Milkweed Editions.

Samimian-Darash, Limor and Paul Rabinow. 2015. *Modes of Uncertainty: Anthropological Cases*. Chicago: University of Chicago Press.

Sarris, Greg. 1992. '"What I'm Talking about When I Talk about My Baskets": A Conversation with Mabel Mckay', in S. Smith and J. Watson (eds), *De/colonizing the Subject: The Power of Gender in Women's Autobiography*. Minneapolis: University of Minnesota Press, pp. 20–33.

Simmard, Suzanne. 2021. *Finding the Mother Tree: Discovering the Wisdom of the Forest*. New York: Penguin/Random House.

Slovic, Paul (ed.). 2010. *The Feeling of Risk: New Perspectives on Risk Perception*. New York: Earthscan Books.

Sneath, David (ed.). 2013. 'Seeing Environmental Process in Time: Questions of Evidence and Agency', *Cambridge Anthropology*, Special Issue, 31(1).

Trahant, Mark. 2021. *Indian Country Today*. Retrieved April 2021 from Digital Native American news journal, https://indiancountrytoday.com/

Valkenburg, Govert. 2012. 'Sustainable Technological Citizenship', *European Journal of Social Theory* 15(4): 471–87.

Wells, Geoff. 1996. *Hazard Identification and Risk Assessment*. Rugby: Institute of Chemical Engineers.

Weston, Kath. 2017. *Animate Planet: Making Visceral Sense of Living in a High-Tech Ecologically Damaged World*. Durham and London: Duke University Press.

Wynne, Brian 1992 Misunderstood Misunderstnading.Social Identities and Public Uptake of Science. In. Public Understanding of Science 1 (3) https://doi.org/10.1088/0963-6625/1/3/004.
———. 1996. 'May the Sheep Safely Graze? A Reflexive View of the Expert-Lay Knowledge Divide', in S. Lash, B. Szerszynski and B. Wynne (eds), *Risk, Environment and Modernity: Towards a New Ecology*. London: Sage Publications, pp. 44–83.

CHAPTER 1

Activating Cosmo-Geo-Analytics
Anthropocene, Arctics and Cryocide

Olga Ulturgasheva and Barbara Bodenhorn

In our introduction we laid out several concepts we feel are pertinent to understanding environmental processes in general: the need to recognize multiple worlds and the positions humans actors occupy within them; the urgency of acknowledging that expert knowledge emerges in many forms and that this knowledge may be communicated in many ways; and, finally, how peoples across the globe are experiencing and responding to uncertainty, unpredictability and precarity invites a continuing consideration of 'risk' as an analytic.

The present chapter draws upon those ideas but turns readers' attention more specifically to issues that influence our contributors' analysis of Arctic conditions. In this we consider the Arctic as a specific ecozone which has generated a significant body of environment-related research, much of it subject to the questions of voice we introduced in the Introduction. We also examine the Circumpolar North as a particular cosmo-political zone which continues to register the nineteenth-century colonial footprints of Russia, the US, Canada and Denmark; these in turn have generated innovative and persistent pushback on the part of local residents across the region. We then explore briefly the extent to which it remains a global hotspot – politically, economically, and ecologically – with tensions between those who want to exploit its non-renewable resources and those who focus more on the protection of its renewable resources which carry moral and spiritual weight in terms of interspecies sociality. The Anthropocene as a concept mobilizes so many of these issues simultaneously that we have reserved a separate section to discuss this. We pay particular attention to indigenous critiques of the idea, which leads us to consider the Anthropocene with relation to the cosmological as reflected in origin stories. This leads to a section that explores the ways in which people use stories to think through the present. Finally, we suggest the notion of 'cryocide' to describe all of the processes described above. Scientists such as Wadhams (2017) and Jamail (2019), mentioned in the Introduction, have paid serious attention to the implications of the disappearance of ice cover in the Arctic. By cryocide, however, we are not only referring to the disappearance of the physical substance, but also to the human and other bio systems that depend on it for their continuity. In this, we strongly agree with Diemberger (Chapter 6) that it is productive to consider 'people of the cryosphere' as linked and facing similar challenges. In the contributions that follow, then, readers are invited to consider the implications of world views in which humans are not at the centre; they are urged to listen to voices that reveal new kinds of knowledge and imagine new sorts of connections; and they are confronted with the complex geo-political realities that play major roles in the challenges Circumpolar peoples face on a daily basis.

The Arctic as a Shifting Zone

The news that the Arctic is the fastest-warming region on the planet has not been on the radar of public attention until recently. In public discourse, the Arctic has often been associated with a cold, empty, pristine, ambiguous, even liminal land (see Bravo 2017; Tasch and Tasch 2017)[1] even as it was associated with utterly imaginable riches: gold, baleen, timber, furs, oil. In recent years, reports on global warming and rapidly changing climate have started to transform mainstream perceptions of the Arctic from a remote, uninhabited area into a territory of crucial environmental and geopolitical importance (Pfeffer 2009; Klare 2019).[2] The Arctic as an ecozone, rather than as an econo-military space, has suddenly become visible as tangible and very fragile. This transformation of the public perception of the region, albeit slow, indicates that it is no longer easy to ignore the fact that the Arctic is changing at an accelerated rate, and global feedbacks to its transformations are emerging through a cluster of environmental disasters simultaneously happening across all continents. Although climate modelling foresaw such phenomena as 'Arctic amplification' a decade ago (see Holland and Bitz 2003;

Cohen et al. 2014), polar climate models have consistently underestimated the speed with which the warming has intensified since then (Barnosky and Hadly 2016; Jamail 2019; O'Reilly 2016).

On Knowledge, Collaboration, Voice

Reports from Arctic indigenous communities about the disturbing dynamic with which the weather patterns, lands and animal behaviour were changing have been emerging for several decades. In *The Earth is Faster Now*, Krupnik and Jolly (2002) were among the first social scientists in Alaska to work with local experts to highlight Yup'ik views of how they perceived environmental changes. Conrad Oozeva, from Saint Lawrence Island, teamed up with Krupnik in 2004 to publish *Watching Ice and Weather our Way* (Oozeva et al. 2004). Genuine collaborations which reflect indigenous voices and concerns about the environment rather than simply co-opting them are well established in the North; the extent to which such collaborations include indigenous initiatives should not be ignored (see, e.g., Berkes, Huebert and Fast 2005; Berkes 2012; Bodenhorn 2001, 2013a, 2013b; Brewster 1997, 2005; Cruikshank 2004; Fenge 2001; Fienup-Riordan and Rearden 2012; Ford 2001; Hastrup 2013b; Bodenhorn and Ulturgasheva 2017, 2018; Ulturgasheva 2014; Ulturgasheva et al. 2015; Williamson 2011). The Inuit Circumpolar Conference, the Alaska Eskimo Whaling Commission and the Nunavut government, amongst others, have likewise been key indigenous-led institutions in supporting the gathering together and dissemination of detailed regional evidence of environmental changes. Independent indigenous voices have also made themselves heard in the North: Yup'ik scholar Oscar Kawagley (2006) makes a powerful argument for recognizing the importance of non humano-centric world views; Greenlander Karla Williamson (2011) explores the bases of resilience in 'An Ecology of Stories'; Zach Kunuk (a co-founder of Isuma, a First Nations' owned production company) produced the world's first Inuktituk film on the subject in his 2010 documentary *Inuit Knowledge and Climate Change*.

Despite this wealth of information, these reports have been, for the most part, either dismissed or utilized only in scientific reports intended for use by managerial elites (see Bravo 2009). Looking critically at such selectiveness by the media, in her contribution to this volume Candis Callison highlights that mainstream narratives about climate change tend to obscure the importance of knowledge of and expertise about the climate change dynamics in the Arctic. Instead, they use the Arctic as a proxy for other issues, such as the expansion of extractive territories by prominent economic stakeholders, a 'new Cold War' between the US and Russia, or conflicts between the oil industry and environmental groups. While media reports on the Arctic are abundant in concerns over polar bears, indigenous voices, whether alone or in collaboration with scientists such as the ones noted above, are rarely heard in national and global media; newsmakers habitually reduce the experts from indigenous communities down to subjects for coverage or research instead of holders and producers of active knowledge. Callison writes that 'the meaning is prescribed by scientists and political or industry figures – rarely by Indigenous and/or Arctic-based experts' (Callison, this volume). Scientific reports, she continues, which tend to view indigenous expertise as 'a potential global and scientific resource', are more often than not entangled with political obstructions and agendas of socio-political institutions that serve as constraints rather than opportunities for indigenous communities' empowerment and participation in decision-making. Hence, 'experiments in democratizing science have ironically served to reinstate the authority of science by subtle means involving erasure of the very public being invited to participate' (Ellis, Waterton and Wynne 2010, cited in Callison, this volume). Such practices persist, pointing to current structures of exclusion which are continuously reproducing a highly territorial 'silo effect' that prevents much-needed voices from participating at the centre of knowledge production.

TEK: A Road Paved with Good Intentions?

We would be remiss to ignore the promise and the pitfalls of an institutional effort to 'bring indigenous voices in'. In *Traditional Ecological Knowledge: Concepts and Cases*, Julian Inglis (1993) provides historical context for the idea, pointing to the importance of Agenda 21 of the Earth Summit in Rio de Janeiro in June 1992 which recognized the contributions of indigenous knowledge holders to environmental understanding. An initial meeting which was attended by indigenous peoples and other experts was held as part of a Common Property Conference and proposed two goals: to facilitate the gathering of knowledge useful at the community level and, more broadly, to promote the incorporation of traditional ecological knowledge (TEK) into policy. A number of local governance entities saw the initiative as promising, and participated in documentation efforts (see Fenge 2001 on emerging collaborations across a number of Canadian First Nations communities; Ford 2001, whose focus was entirely on Inuit communities; Royer et al. 2013; and Royer 2016, working with Cree communities). But criticisms also emerged from several directions. Cruikshank (2004) argued forcefully against the fragmentary nature of TEK, which flies in the face of the holistic and context-dependent knowledge practices of most Canadian First Nations people. In Cruikshank's view, TEK constitutes 'modernist recasting' of indigenous onto-epistemologies that 'continues to present local knowledge as an object of science rather than as intelligence that could inform science' (Cruikshank 2005: 257). When codified as TEK and incorporated into the frameworks of North American management science, such interactive, lively, experiential knowledge as Athapaskan knowledge about glaciers is recast and labelled into categories within the Western managerial paradigm. Thus, sentient and social spaces in which knowledge is produced and circulated are turned into 'measurable commodities called "lands" and "resources"'. In this regard, Cruikshank has been insistently highlighting that 'indigenous peoples face double exclusion, initially by colonial processes that expropriate land, and ultimately by neo-colonial discourses that appropriate and reformulate their ideas' (2005: 259). And 'double exclusion' has the potential to lead and, historically, has led to complete erasure and denial of the indigenous expertise.

Relatedly, Wenzel (2004) noted that many management and conservation policies being developed for northern Canada made 'selective use' of TEK. These were notable for their omission of any recognition of the spiritual nature of environmental understanding on the part of northern hunters. As an alternative, Wenzel offers *Inuit Qaujimajatuqangit,* the guiding principle of the Nunavut Government which takes the social/moral basis of animal human interactions as a starting point. From Hawaii comes the critique of Wehi et al. (2018) who note that Native Hawaiian teaching is based on story, allegory, and imagery rather than 'facts'.

The increasing intensity of extreme environmental pressures in the region is making visible how important it is to challenge the reproduction of what are in effect colonial practices and to highlight the need to destabilize this hegemonic state of affairs. The original workshop – as well as the present volume – emphasizes the importance of listening to Arctic residents for their local expertise. It is not accidental that the list of contributors to this volume includes Arctic residents and indigenous scholars, namely, Rachel Edwardson, an Iñupiaq from Barrow (Alaska), Candis Callison, a member of the Tāłtān Nation from British Columbia (Canada), Stacy Rasmus, a Lummi-Athabaskan scholar based in Alaska, and Olga Ulturgasheva, an Eveny from northeast Siberia. But, we hasten to add, the volume neither siloes nor exoticizes 'indigenous knowledge' as something apart; instead, it offers a complex account of thinking about the Arctic that includes multiple perspectives, with local voices at the core and not at the periphery of the discussion. The latter also resonates with the urgent need for collaborative, cross-sector, cross-border efforts in looking for insights to inform Arctic-led pathways towards resilience and adaptability; these insights include a recognition of the limitations of a science-alone approach to environmental understanding. While questioning the hegemony of a positivist approach, Wilkinson and colleagues relevantly state:

> All knowledge is incomplete and tentative. This is why focusing 'just on the facts' as a positivist [scientist] might see them is too narrow a foundation for real-world problem-solving. The key to successful joint problem-solving is to recognize the strengths and limitations of the focus each may have and to create a process wherein many voices and multiple methods and streams of understanding are valued and used. (Wilkinson, Clark and Burch 2007: 23)

It is increasingly recognized that 'neither Western science nor traditional knowledge is sufficient in isolation to address all complexities of climate change' (Jolly et al. 2002). Collaborative, cross-sectoral partnership, by enhancing the capacities of the experts and other knowledge holders to comprehend the phenomena of changes in their complexity, has created a stronger potential to provide insights and tools for addressing those changes. Hence, the volume calls for the opening of spaces for collaboration as well as the inclusion of unheard and/or silenced heterogenous voices; we thus urge readers to recognize that 'the Arctic' is not a monolith – ecologically, socially or politically. Nor, by the same token, is it as exceptional as it is often portrayed. Although some extreme conditions are unique to the Arctic, the need for rapid, inventive and effective responses to unpredictable events is one facing many peoples across the world. The latter is intrinsically related to the human capacity for adaptability and adjustment to different scales of exposure to the technogenic catastrophes and dramatic environmental transformations associated with climate change (see Petryna 2003; Scheper-Hughes 2005; Ghosh 2016; Weston 2017).

Introducing Feedback Loops as an Analytic

In her discussion of the consequences of the Chernobyl nuclear plant explosion, Adriana Petryna rightly asserts that 'to enhance our capacities to deal with surprise, we need new models of science and politics that take the word "adaptation" – in all its divergent meanings and human practices – seriously' (2003: xxvi). In this regard, Veena Das's discussion of the need for new models in the face of what she calls 'critical events' becomes even more pertinent, especially when she exhorts that 'radical unfamiliarity requires novel forms of thinking – thinking that is often not forthcoming because of the human propensity for reaching for the tried and true' (Das 1995, cited in Bodenhorn and Ulturgasheva 2018: 109).

Correspondingly, Petryna's discussion of the atrocious consequences of the nuclear plant explosion calls for new developments in climate-science modelling and practice informed by a 'user-inspired science', a strategy that embraces rather than denies the limitations of any scientific account of potential or calamitous environmental disruptions' (2003: xxvi). Given that worldwide unpredictability is becoming more of a norm rather than an exception, the challenge is to craft a tentative strategy that includes a detailed and balanced consideration of the limitations and productive potential of each account, whether scientific or public. It is the accounts of survival and lived experiences by those who have gone through environmental calamities that become vital for ascertaining human capacities to adapt and negotiate safety. Hence, the contributors to this volume ask what the implications of the Arctic experiences might be for our understanding of human responses to global processes more broadly:

- Can humans adequately respond to multiple threats induced by climate change?
- What types of knowledge and tactics are required to reduce the uncertainty of increasingly erratic climate events and to shape new patterns of adaptability reflexive of and responsive to local particularities?
- How do affected communities make sense of critical events like storms, landslides, wildfires or flash floods?
- Are humans able to mitigate risk situations and calamities when available strategies and resources are getting increasingly unreliable and stretched too thin?
- What preparation and risk mitigation techniques are emerging and being articulated by affected communities? Are humans capable of

predicting potential ecological disasters while experiencing profound uncertainty? Is the latest dynamic adjustable at all, and are human populations likely to be able to adapt? If so, what are the limitations of existing adaptation models and potential occlusions to adaptability and resilience?

Alongside this set of questions, the unsettling and complex dynamic of fluctuations make previous cause-and-effect connections less convincing and unclear. It also interrogates the reliability of the calculations regarding the rate and dynamic of climate change provided by positivistic science (Krebs and Berteaux 2006; Keith et al. 2008; Coreau et al. 2010). For example, if a decade ago any connection between dramatically disappearing ice in the Arctic and the scale of Californian wildfires could be seen as ungrounded by sceptics of climate change, now this previously unlikely connection is increasingly becoming accepted. Two seemingly unconnected disasters have recently pointed environmental scientists to dramatically changing patterns of wind distribution, contributing to the slow distribution of streams of cold air that result in abnormally hot weather for mild climates (Box 2012). It should be noted that a glaciologist and Greenlandic Ice Sheet specialist, Jason Box, has been connecting the circulation of forest fire ash in the jet stream to accelerating ice melt in Greenland since at least 2012. Through his *Dark Snow* project, he has been discussing the impacts of forest fires, focusing on the jet stream carrying ash from Siberia to Greenland and the implications of this dynamic on ice melt for a decade or more. According to his observations and assessments, deceleration of the wind speed and lack of cold air have recently resulted in severe weather fluctuations globally, increasing the likelihood for freezing weather in warm climates and heatwaves in northern areas, extreme rainfall or droughts in the regions closer to the equator, and severe floods or enormous wildfires across the Arctic and Subarctic regions (Barnosky and Hadly 2016; Overland et al. 2019). Changing environmental patterns seem to link apparently unconnectable dots and, by doing so, have the potential to underscore the continuities of seemingly disparate events. Since the linear cause-and-effect connections in understanding the character of change do not suffice anymore, new ways of conceptualizing the connection are required for understanding the implications for dealing with the issues of risks, human security and environmental sustainability. Figuratively speaking, the connection with a new texture, nature and direction is calling for new conceptual models of perceiving it.

What is also becoming increasingly obvious in the light of violent fluctuations induced by warming air temperatures is that the ice-free Arctic is no longer located in the distant future but is lurking just around the corner; indeed, it is here in some parts of the Arctic at certain times of year (see Wadhams 2017). These emerging non-linear and self-modifying cascades of linkages generate new cross-system feedback loops within the Arctic ecosystems. If we look at the 2020 summer reports on Alaskan and Siberian wildfires, the systemic impact of permafrost melt, and the effects of the COVID-19 pandemic on top of all these, we can speak of the severe propagation of risks and uncertainties across the region, making an already fragile cryosphere even more fragile while turning the region into a hot spot for emergencies (Kormann 2020). The regime of 'run-off' pressure producing cascades of linkages is indicative of the co-occurrence of poly-systemic feedbacks, i.e. responses to multidirectional and simultaneous effects of the permafrost melt across human and non-human realms (AMAP 2017). This, in turn, will consequently generate all sorts of hindrances for the governance of disaster preparedness, lowering and significantly reducing human capacity for survival and resilience.

This dynamic has been associated with the Anthropocene, i.e. an era of severe environmental destruction continuously induced by a corporate system's voracious appetite for endless expansion and accumulation of wealth at the expense of natural resources and fragile ecosystems (Eriksen 2016). However, the notion of the Anthropocene and its timescale may not sound sufficiently alarming in indicating the extreme urgency and high 'run-off' pressure that will push all sectors of societies, especially military and medical services, to get involved with more and more rescue and relief operations, stretching budgets and interfering with their emergency capabilities.[3]

The Anthropocene as an Analytic Incorporating Cosmopolitics

As we mentioned in our Introduction, the Anthropocene – like animism – is another term of great controversy as well as great potential for the editors' understanding of Arctic environmental processes. Crutzen and Stoermer (2000) argued that recent human participation in global environmental processes has been so profound at the geological level that scientists need to conceptualize the earth as moving from the Holocene to the Anthropocene. We humans have to be recognized not only as a factor in the geological process but as the dominant factor in its current shifting manifestation.[4] For historian Dipesh Chakrabarty, this argument opened conceptual doors that challenged silo thinking – collapsing social and natural sciences as modes of knowing (2009). More recently, Hastrup and Hastrup (2015: 1) have called for 'creative undisciplining' in order to engage anthropologically with rapidly shifting global processes.

But the notion that 'we humans' have propelled the planet into the Anthropocene has created quite a bit of pushback. James Moore, for instance, proffers the term Capitalocene (2014) as an alternative to highlight the fact that the impacts are generated not by all human action, but rather by actions that both constitute and are constituted by a capitalist enterprise. And scholars such as Candis Callison (2018), Amitav Gosh (2016) and Zoe Todd (2015), amongst others, robustly point out that the people who are often least involved in capitalist industry are the first to suffer its effects in terms of environmental degradation. The ideology of colonialism needs to be added to that of capitalism. They are linked, but not the same. The Arctic as a geo-political zone dramatically plays out these tensions.

While we agree with the above, we suggest a further reading that recognizes the Arctic not just as a complex of geo-political issues but as a swirling nexus of multiple cosmo-political zones. Before we consider technologies of resource extraction or the political organization of access to those resources, we should consider foundational ideas about human being-in-the-world. From the fifteenth century, the dominant ideology behind 'Westward expansion' reflected forms of Christianity, which not only justified conquest in terms of conversion but also assumed that the earth had been created by God to give to humans for their use.[5] Many traditions of The Book are not only humano-centric but humano-privileged. The model that humans are not only separate from the rest of the world but somehow above 'it' thus has long pre-capitalist roots. By the nineteenth century this cosmological model had become overlaid with further ideas of evolution – read as 'progress' – as well as of assumptions about the inevitable scarcity of resources. This, in turn, underpinned the valorization of private property as a way of saying what is 'mine' is not 'yours',[6] and what I have is never enough.[7]

Although the authors of these arguments assume that they reflect universal truths about human nature, we also need to consider the presence of alternative cosmological models that are contemporary rather than prior to these ideas. Most Iñupiat today, for instance, are devout Christians who nonetheless conceive of their position in the world as one of mutuality and reciprocity with other animals.⁸ So we turn to William Oquilluk and Lauren Bland's accounts of Iñupiaq history in *The People of Kawerak* (1973). According to Iñupiaq oral narratives of northwestern Alaska, the history of the world is the history of nine disasters. It is a story of change, but not progress. And it is a story of human adaptive agency. In an early disaster, the sun goes behind the moon for four days, the earth freezes, and most living creatures die. Only four families survive this disaster, and when they emerge with the return of the sun, everything has changed, and they realize 'they had to think with their minds in order to survive'. They do this, through observation, experimentation and communication. One man watches a spider spin her web and imitates her to invent fishnets; another notices a leaf floating down the river and thinks about how to incorporate that in the form of a boat. A child inadvertently catches a fish when he goes to the river for water in mid-winter, tosses it to one side, and later realizes that the flash-frozen result is edible. The world has changed. People need to change with it; anyone – even a child – may come up with solutions. But you have to share what you are learning with others. That profoundly non-capitalist concept continues to hold sway for many Arctic inhabitants. In Raymond Neakok Sr's words, 'you have to tell what you know – that's one of the rules' (Bodenhorn 1997: 123).

And it offers a model of animal-human morality. In the story of the Eagle-Wolf Messenger Feast, Oquilluk tells how the development of human sociality emerged from the morality of animal–human relations. In this account a single hunter behaves disrespectfully by not returning the heart of a slain eagle to its Mother. The animal spirits do not punish this behaviour but rather teach the hunter how to act properly in a world that includes others. They teach him how to thank the Mother Eagle by singing, dancing and preparing a great feast, and exhort him to share what he had learned with his kin. The first great feast, however, is not exclusive to the group but incorporates others – animal spirits who have taken on human form in order to appear as guests.⁹ In this single collection of stories, then, readers are offered the possibility of thinking about change that is distinct from progress; about recognizing the threats of human action to the well-being of non-humans which can be met by changing human behaviour rather than punishment; about responses to risky conditions which are collective and inclusive rather than assigning blame in order to decide who pays.

We have already talked about 'voice' as a question of politics, pointing in particular to Callison's contribution to this volume. What we wish to emphasize here is that this is not simply a question of ignoring what people are saying today, but that these models depend on spatial and temporal 'tricks' which have the effect of diminishing-whilst-encapsulating peoples and their multiple forms of knowledge. Non-capitalist becomes pre-capitalist and therefore not relevant to contemporary realities. As with our discussion of TEK, forms of knowledge that have developed over generations based on observation and practice become reduced to 'tradition' which is often dismissed as exotic and 'out of date' rather than being recognized as twenty-first-century observations of twenty-first-century conditions.

It makes a difference for imagining future actions if you begin from a position of humano-privilege or humano-responsibility, if you begin from an assumption of scarcity which drives competition, or plenty which thrives on cooperation, if the earth is conceived of as a resource for human use, or if humans are assumed to be part of a web a sociality that depends on reciprocity for its continuation. It makes a lot of difference if 'change' is not always calibrated in terms of 'progress'. That is what we mean by cosmo-geo-politics. However, whereas cultural theorists such as Douglas and Wildavsky (1982) set out such differences in order to assign characteristics to groups of people, what we emphasize here is the counter productivity of such a move. In the Arctic – as in many other places – these very powerful cosmo-political ideas move, shift and mix up. You can believe in the Bible and in the moral sentience of whales; you can celebrate the whale at Nalukataq (the communal feast to mark a successful whaling season, which is centred on giving thanks to the whale) and disagree with your neighbour about whether or not to work with oil companies. The ideas are cultural in that they are deeply felt, but they do not map easily onto 'sides'. That is why cosmo-geo-politics renders discussions of the Anthropocene so difficult.

Stories as Scaffolding for 'Weathering the Storm'

The stories we have been listening to reveal fundamental information about the cosmo-political: how people imagine their place in the world. But, as Julie Cruikshank (1998) noted in The *Social Life of Stories*, narratives may also serve as a sort of scaffolding that frames human responses to events in the present.

In the chapter by Ulturgasheva readers will learn how Eveny reindeer herders draw on their stories, on their spiritual relations with the animals, on their practical knowledge and on their flexibility in order to respond to extreme and unpredictable environmental events (see also Ulturgasheva and Bodenhorn 2016). It is clear to them they must 'think in their minds in order to survive'. But the reindeer herders came to London not only to talk about the extremes of mudslides and flooding rivers; they also wanted to talk to others about geopolitics – about the growing interest of extractive companies in their territory. The risky future is not just about 'climate' but about 'environment' more comprehensively. Rachel Edwardson, born and bred in Barrow, Alaska, and a member of a whaling family, reveals starkly what that future might bring. Barrow families remain committed to whaling as a foundational act that, in Patrick Attungana's words, 'holds our families together'. At the same time, however, they rely on the resources of the Iñupiaq Arctic Slope Regional Corporation, whose profits are drawn largely from the oil industry. As Edwardson seeks a way through the dilemmas posed by these competing interests, one hears strong echoes of Iñupiaq stories that tell of whales coming back to people who 'treat their bodies tenderly' and with respect. She re-creates the acts of her grandfather in order to imagine what future her son might be able to expect.

The powerful insights offered by Iñupiaq stories resonate as well with the discussion by Stacy Rasmus in this volume, who looks at Alaskan Yup'ik teachings (*qanruyutet*) and ways of living (*yuu'yaraq*) to argue that it is the continuity of Yup'ik relational connections to the land, animals and waterways that helps Yupiit to 'weather the storms' and sustain the community's well-being.[10] Drawing from the Yup'ik notion of 'weathering the storm', her discussion illustrates that, having moved to the domain of the socio-economic, occupational and political pressures in recent decades, the terms for survival and adaptation have dramatically changed. Young Yupiit need to learn to weather new type of storms. According to Yup'ik elders these storms 'may not necessarily be the ones causing waves and whiteouts outside on the water and land; instead, it may be the swirling swells of emotion or freezing pangs of lonesomeness one feels on the inside that needs instruction and tools for coping and finding safe harbour'. Rasmus's account suggests that as long as the human–animal connection upon which Yup'ik teachings are based is sustained and the Yup'ik seasonal harvest continues, resilience and the capacity of the Yup'ik communities to weather the storms will be maintained.

What the Yup'ik account has shown is that continued and systemic insistence on and institutional imposition of cultural homogeneity and humano-centric ideologies are always intended to reduce human and non-human resilience, i.e. the capacity to live, adjust to and develop with change and uncertainty (Ulturgasheva et al. 2014; Escobar 2018). As Rachel Edwardson's account in Chapter 3 also suggests, the costs – especially for young people – may be tragic, but the roots of resilience are deep, and strategies to foster it continue to emerge. The institutional, systemic and cross-sectoral acceptance of diversity and the existence of distinct worlds where humans and their non-human companions, including cosmologically important non-human actors, would prevent neo-colonial, humano-centric obstructions.

Cryocide

As we stated above, the thrust of technocratic and modernizing economic forms has been driving global environmental changes, which have lately led to threats of the complete loss and disappearance of the cryosphere around the world. These processes are not unique to the Arctic. Chapter 6 by Hildegard Diemberger and Astrid Hovden shows that a similar dynamic is observed in the regions characterized by the largest accumulation of ice outside of the two poles, i.e. the Himalayas and the Alps. Diemberger and Hovden relevantly emphasize that the high-altitude cryosphere of the Himalayas, the Alps and the Arctic can be seen as linked by comparable experiences of human responses to vanishing ice, i.e. the process we shall call 'cryocide'. The process of the cryocide could be compared with a 'ticking timebomb', the effects of which will not stay solely in three high-altitude regions. The effects will accelerate the emergence of the new risks, all of which have the potential of going, literally, viral. And, as the latest pandemic of COVID-19 has shown, the scale for the 'new viral' may exceed human cognitive and infrastructural capacities to contain the onset of new risks. Furthermore, the new risks will turn out to be an old type of risk or a dormant one. What is clear is that carbon dioxide is not the only risk stored in the layers of permafrost. Permafrost has always been an ancient refrigerator for the remains of life that once thrived in the Arctic, including microbes, pathogens, viruses, ancient plankton, insects and amphibia. After being frozen, these ancient species have never completely disappeared, and it is likely that continuous permafrost thaw will soon offer them a chance for a second life. The prospects for various frozen creatures that hibernated in permafrost to re-enter this world are getting higher, and this includes the possibility for 'zombie' viruses now hidden in the sub-surface ground to re-emerge (see Omazic et al. 2019; Evengård and Thierfelder 2021).

In anthropological studies, the focus on interactions between humans and the cryosphere has been peripheral to the anthropological studies of the Circumpolar North and anthropology in general. Although the premise that nature and society cannot be viewed separately and should be understood as mutually implicated has been crucial for Arctic ethnographies since the last century, ice as a methodological and analytical focus through which climate history can be revealed emerged as critical through the works of Canadian anthropologist Julie Cruikshank. Cruikshank's (2005) monograph *Do Glaciers Listen?* has shown the generative potential of an ethnographic and historical focus on such non-human agents as glaciers. The book's focus is on the glacial landscape of the Saint Elias Mountains, an area on the border between Canada and the United States, which is homeland for both Tlingit and Tutchone people. Her account offers a penetrating examination of the complex encounters between European colonizers and Athapaskan-speaking groups. The main question posed in the book title reveals how an Athapaskan onto-epistemology of human–glacier relations provides sophisticated guidance and an 'imaginative grist for comprehending and interpreting *shifting* social circumstances' (2005: 8). This includes the physical and socio-economic impact of Euro-American settler colonialism's expansion on glaciological ecology, leading ultimately to the disappearance of glaciers. In our view, Cruikshank's monograph not only signalled the emergence of an anthropology of the Anthropocene but also foresaw recent methodological developments such as cosmopolitics and multi-species ethnography in which plants, mountains, features of the landscape and cosmologically important animals are indispensable for highlighting central political and epistemological stakes in the field of environmental security and sustainability (see de la Cadena 2010, 2015; Kimmerer 2013).

One of the revelations pertinent to our discussion lies in the details of Cruikshank's take on the production of knowledge about glaciers by Athapaskan elders and Euro-American scientists. According to Cruikshank, if geophysical science objectifies glaciers as inanimate storages of data about melting, trace metals and biological organisms, Athapaskan narratives about glaciers include them in human–non-human sociality as agents affecting people's destinies and human history. By examining Athapaskan recollections about the history of human relations with glaciers, Cruikshank elegantly challenges the concept of the environment as a data depository that can be extracted and operationalized to meet utilitarian demands. While 'shrinking glaciers' are now characterized, by scientific journals and international media, as the 'categorical evidence of climate change' (Roe, Baker and Herla 2016), Cruikshank's account has shown that Athapaskan oral traditions have long rendered these 'advancing and waning' glaciers as capable of responding to human action. Inspired by Cruikshank's approach, the contributions by Diemberger, Hovden and Ulturgasheva in this volume also illustrate how distinct and powerful bodies of knowledge about human–glacier or human–permafrost relations need to be appreciated in their totality, rather than fragmented into data.

Another author whose work we feel merits discussion in the framing of this volume is Kirsten Hastrup. She has also focused on the agency of ice while examining the history of climate change but has examined specifically the experiences of a rapidly changing icescape by Greenlandic hunters from a productive angle of the cryolens. Her discussion examines the ways in which various actors, including scientists, early explorers and indigenous hunters, have interacted with Greenlandic icebergs and glaciers. As Hastrup puts it succinctly, 'it is the ice which holds together the environment, or – indeed – splits it up, and which provides the leitmotif of poetry, story and science' (2013b: 64). In other words, ice is a powerful force with its own aesthetic, episteme, narrative and social agency. Ice can stand for itself in any argument, so she asserts: 'ice is its own argument; it is not for us to argue its case' (51). She looks at scientific perceptions of environmental change from the perspective of the nineteenth-century Arctic explorers who, so to speak, engaged in a complex argument with the powerful non-human agent that is ice. Hastrup's discussion eloquently shows the difficulties the nineteenth-century explorers encountered while trying to capture the High Arctic topographically. The nature and dynamism of the Greenlandic ice have long resisted explorers' cartographic attempts, as it actively obscures the process of mapping the icy lands that can appear or disappear as a result of either melting or freezing. Ice defeated explorers' attempts to signify the icescape, as their representations failed to capture the enormity, energy and power of the ice, intrinsically dynamic, unobjectifiable and unmappable. The ice remains at the heart of Hastrup's account, exuding presence and continuously deriding early Arctic explorers' constructions of the region.

Non-scalability of the Arctic Cryosphere and Limits of Human Adaptability

Hastrup's historical perspective provides a critical take on the non-scalability of the entire world of the Arctic cryosphere with its human and non-human inhabitants, as it has already reached a point of no return (Hastrup 2013c, 2020). The continuous activity of extractive industries has not ceased from destroying the Arctic environment, for decades steadily driving environmental disasters and ruining regional landscapes and ecologies. Billions of tons of carbon dioxide coming from fossil fuels that continue to enter the atmosphere annually are amplifying the dynamic of ecological ruination (Le Quéré, Peters and Andres 2014). The regional histories of industrial development, whether it is Alaska, Siberia, Greenland, Canada or Fennoscandia, have often illustrated that after decades of intensive mining and extraction permafrost-bound lands tend to transform irreversibly into environmental ruins. Neither monetary compensation nor new technologies of regeneration, habitat restoration, re-creation or recultivation will be sufficiently effective in returning these landscapes to ecological health, much less to an earlier state.

In our view, this particularly applies to a revivalist project called Pleistocene Park undertaken by Russian scientists (Popov 2020). This dystopian park was established 7 kilometres (4 miles) away from the town of Chersky in northeast Siberia in 2018. The project implementers believe that by populating a stretch of 160 square km (62 square miles) with genetically engineered beasts that are a cross between elephants and woolly mammoths, as well as yaks, horses, sheep and oxen, they will revive the grasslands spread as it was during the Pleistocene epoch, i.e. the glacial geological period that began 2.6 million years ago and ended 12,000 years ago. Reversing that process and reviving the grasslands, they argue, could be the key to preserving permafrost. The plan to reintroduce large mammals that could tamp down moss, knock down trees and churn up the soil is meant to allow the grass to flourish again. In this romanticized view of the Pleistocene era, the grass had the capacity to reflect sunlight and capture more carbon in its roots than today's flora. By reintroducing and reoccupying the area with long-gone mammals, the project – which requires roughly 3,000 animals and $114 million of investment – hopes to slow down the degradation of permafrost and keep the Siberian tundra frozen (*The Economist* 2020). The project may be a provocative and costly thought experiment, but just like any technological fix, this looks too simple for a wickedly complex problem.

In these regards, the discussion by anthropologist Kath Weston, of techno-revivalists who aim to resuscitate ecologies across continents and regions, presents quite an important and pertinent take on de-extinction projects of this kind, which more often than not perpetuate the colonialist's gaze (see Weston, in press). According to Weston, what these revivalist projects share is a conviction that older ways of doing things, including the re-creation of the Pleistocene grasslands in the Arctic tundra, might make a difference when it comes to climate change. Often, the desire to tame climate change propagated by such revivalist projects as the Pleistocene Park is woven into the fabric of quest narratives that turn, as Weston puts it cogently, 'the one-way story of technological progress on its head by arguing that sometimes the only way to go forward (so to speak) is to go back'. We concur with Weston that environmental transformations on a geological-epoch scale can never be confined to one isolated activity, such as the grazing habits of large mammals with hooves. One must recognize that myriad other factors influenced and intervened in the course of environmental change, factors that include such disruptions as the multiple forms of development that changed the chemical and organic composition of the soil, flora and fauna irreversibly.

What is missing in the revivalist hype surrounding Pleistocene Park is the voice of Siberian indigenous populations who have been living in this area for eons and who have never been consulted on how this type of ambitious dystopian endeavour unfolding in front of their eyes could impact their livelihoods and sense of security. Nor were they asked how those newly introduced animals might affect either the population of their herds of domesticated reindeer or the hunted animals upon which their entire lives depend. Would those genetically revived animals compete for the areas of habitation and overgraze the reindeer pastures vital for the indigenous communities' well-being and continuance? Would all these regenerational activities take place at the expense of their own lives and the lives of their future generations? As the Arctic indigenous accounts have shown before, there is a world of difference between approaching the permafrost-bound land as a resource to be preserved and approaching the permafrost as a sentient being who weeps with 'firing tears' when it is destroyed, as Ulturgasheva details for the Eveny case in this volume, or who speaks when it breaks, warning Tlingit, who know how to listen, of a flood unleashed in retaliation for insulting treatment (Cruikshank 2005).[11]

The disappearing cryosphere, as well as dramatic permafrost thaw induced by anthropogenic factors, foreshadows new types of hazards and disasters which will subsume human and non-human, society and environment together. The non-scalability of the Arctic environment prompts us to raise urgent questions regarding how we understand human and non-human capacities to avert risks and hazards; how we take into account the increasing vulnerability of communities; and how we comprehend the relationship of multi-species feedbacks to new and emerging forms of 'normal'. We need to take on board the availability and accessibility of resources, knowledge and strategies that people utilize to deal with the latest challenges associated with climate change, and we need to undertake a careful consideration of the environmental futures that require 'a big enough and right-minded vision' (Jamail 2019: 221).

The narratives of the dramatic change offered by the indigenous inhabitants of the Arctic and international climate scientists (see Krupnik and Jolly 2002; Marino 2015; Crate and Nuttall 2016; Nakashima, Rubis and Krupnik 2018) are ceaselessly pointing to a profound sense of unpredictability and uncertainty generated by the change. These are the reports of the unprecedented extinction rate of animals, birds, insects and plants whose livelihoods have relied on the fragile ecology of the cryosphere. A melting cryosphere accelerates the likelihood for thousands of towns and villages located along the Arctic coastline to be threatened by thawing permafrost, storms, rising sea levels and loss of the sea ice (see Bodenhorn, this volume; Jamail 2019; Ulturgasheva, this volume). All of the above will only intensify in the course of the next couple of decades, with methane released by rapidly thawing permafrost.

Geopolitically, with the dramatic disappearance of the cryo-world, the region is likely to turn into a major point of volatility in the territorial disputes and resource conflicts between nation-states and corporations (see also Klare 2019). One cannot escape foreseeing the glimpses of a militarized future in the Arctic. As the ice is melting away, drilling for gas and oil is intensifying, and new shipping routes are opening, along with the recognition that protection of national and corporate interests will be hard to maintain, as they are neither adequately equipped nor properly aware of the nature of risks in a new and unfamiliar Arctic (Nuttall 1998; Goodell 2017). Although ice melt and the rising waters emerged as major risks several decades ago, there is still no comprehensive plan of what to do about it infrastructurally, politically, economically and ideologically. So far, there is an assumption on all levels (governmental, municipal, international, local and individual) that when the situation is critical and urgent, somebody else (perhaps scientists) will invent something that will save them from a calamity. But nobody will come up with any solutions unless there is a substantial effort to develop far-reaching plans which include a detailed consideration of potential and most probable risks as well as long-term strategic visions.

The understanding of complex networks of risks and the strategies undertaken to ameliorate them will depend on how they are interpreted and articulated, and by whom. In the time of neoliberal calculations, when risk has quickly become a measure for financial stability or instability serving as a tool for financial technologies through which capital moves, risk comes to be institutionalized, elaborated and analysed in terms of the care of the self. But, as Geeta Patel has earnestly shown, linearity of speculations and calculations from within neoliberal subjectivity, with its obsession with privatized efficiency and commodification of risk, is susceptible to producing and reproducing human and non-human vulnerabilities (Patel 2016: 284–91). An eloquent discussion of the flaws of the monetary disaster response and environmental risk (mis)management has been provided by Elizabeth Marino (2015; see also Marino and Faas 2020) through her work with the Iñupiaq community on the island of Shishmaref, Alaska. She shows how the governmental disaster response protocol applied in calculations of the imminent threat of disastrous flood to the village due to sea-level rise and coastal erosion was antithetical to climate change adaptation and preparation. In the government officials' view, the only sensible response to the imminent threat posed by radical erosion of the island could have been an organized relocation, something the villagers themselves voted for in 2014. However, the estimated costs for relocating the village of Shishmaref to the site preferred by the community amounted to 180 million US dollars (Marino 2015: 45–58), an amount that was deemed unfeasible.

Moreover, there were bureaucratic obstacles to the implementation of this plan, specifically the view of the government that, since the disaster had not happened yet, there was no way emergency funds should be spent on organizing relocation. There was (and still is) no corresponding agency for pre-emptive disaster planning or risk reduction in this type of case where erosion increases exposure to flooding hazards. There is no clear course of action in response to the threat of potentially catastrophic flooding today. But one of the possibilities, or as they call it possible disaster responses, was to rebuild the village 'without improvement'. That is to say, to rebuild with minimal costs. This increases the local population's distrust in the ability of the government to deal with the environmental degradation and intensifies an ongoing process of marginalization of such communities as Shishmaref. Indeed, as of 2019, four years after the publication of Marino's work, next to nothing had actually taken place to rectify an ever-worsening situation.[12] What we observe in all these cases is the contradiction and even the clash of modernities: on the one hand, there is a constant need for certainty (there is a need to shape a particular policy on the basis of certainty rather than probability as well as a need on the basis for risk assessment); on the other hand, the acceptance of uncertainty becomes more evident (2015: 93–97).

While problematizing the neoliberal model of risk as a matter of calculating costs and benefits, Barbara Bodenhorn examines how risk is perceived and interpreted by Iñupiaq whalers of Barrow, Alaska, and explores the basis for the actions they take when they are involved in complex and uncertain situations that require immediate decisions (see also Bodenhorn 1997, 2013a). In her discussion in this volume she offers a critical review of how social scientists have been looking at the models and processes of identifying risk, assessing it, and creating strategies with relation to its perceived implications. The account shows that risk assessments and considerations of potential hazards are always positioned at the intersections of ethical, cultural, social and political assumptions, all of which affect how the decisions that humans take are modelled and how knowledge is manifested in those decisions. Her account thus illustrates that their decisions involve a multilayered understanding of risk, which they talk about in ways that 'express an acute understanding of connections across a number of systems'. These include but are not limited to the languages of complex calculations, an explicitly moral language of risky relationships between humans and whales, languages of responsibility, timing, shortage and vulnerability.

Cosmo-Geo-Analytics

Risks associated with a melting cryosphere and rapidly disappearing ocean and land ice have important implications for the methodological approach of our volume; the process of melt provides us with a conceptual grid for capturing the dynamic of the latest environmental changes in the Arctic. Such cryo-formations as glaciers, permafrost, icebergs and snowdrifts, which are rapidly disappearing, highlight the crucial roles they have been playing in contributing to the continuance of diversity and multiplicity of lives and worlds, including that of humans. Conceptually, the changes that are associated with a transition from one form to another, when a solid, well-shaped substance such as ice is transforming into formless and fluid water, create the effects of dissolution, dissipation and substantive changes that may re-emerge in the patterns of resilience and adaptation. These effects are considered in the contributions to this volume. They attend to the impacts of and feedbacks to the melting cryosphere that we have chosen to call cryocide. These include the issues of environmental uncertainty, complexity and risk (Bodenhorn, Diemberger and Hovden); communication, voice and politics of knowledge (Callison, Edwardson); collaboration, adaptation and resilience (Ulturgasheva, Rasmus). The contributions to this volume illustrate how Arctic populations understand and respond to the changes from within distinct horizons of knowledge and modes of sociality; they point to productive moments of collaboration with scientists and other stakeholders. The accounts exemplify the extent to which cosmological, geological and social processes are entangled. They point to the need for shifts in the geopolitical map of knowledge production that view cosmo-geo-social processes as mutually implicated and inter-constituting.

It is the rapidity and scale of destruction wrought by extractivist alliances between states and corporations that make Anthropocenic processes so dramatically visible in the Arctic. The region has been imagined by capitalist investors and other types of predatory extractors as an up-for-grabs economic frontier, and this has proved to be an ecologically damaging conceptualization (Brightman, Grotti and Ulturgasheva 2006/7). We hold that what is currently being damaged are the diverse worlds of other-than-human persons upon which indigenous communities depend. The contributions to the volume show how indigenous concerns about ecological catastrophe are often articulated with cosmologically important animals in mind. As Rachel Edwardson's account has shown, the concerns articulated by Alaskan Iñupiaq hunters in their political negotiations with the oil company over the ocean resource use included whales, whose presence was not recognized by the oil company representatives during the meeting. Edwardson's account involved the whale as a cosmologically central other-than-human, Iñupiaq progenitor and master spirit, and an important political actor. By involving whales, Iñupiat did not mean to prove the reality of whales; what they meant was to show how whales are central to Iñupiaq continuation and survival. Central to Edwardson's argument – and very pertinent to our examination of social risk – is her discussion of 'silo thinking', which characterizes disagreement in her community. Even though most Barrow families are connected to whaling in one way or another, some are more 'pro development' than others. 'If you are not at the table, you're lunch' and 'the ice is going to melt anyway, we need to think about an ice-free future' are statements Edwardson has heard from whalers who favour oil development over whale protection. For Edwardson, one of the greatest risks facing her children's future – a future connected to a moral sociality with whales and a strong positive sense of what it means to be Iñupiaq – is the inability within the community to break free of people's individual silos to think creatively about what is to come.

In a similar vein, the Siberian account of human adaptive agency illustrates the cosmological centrality of reindeer and points to an assemblage of cosmo-geo-ecological sensitivity that has been informing human–permafrost engagement and adaptation strategies for Eveny reindeer herders. The contribution to the volume by Ulturgasheva provides an account of the kinds of expertise, mindset and sensitivity that are required for responding adaptively and dealing with the environmental unpredictability that characterizes living on and from the permafrost-bound land (see also Ulturgasheva 2012, 2016). Eveny reindeer herders' expertise, which relies on their patterns of mobility, tactics of flexibility and divination rituals, revolves around the complex understanding of the interdependence of human and non-human elements, such as permafrost, lichen, reindeer and humans. The interdependence has been central to reindeer herders' ability to negotiate their communal safety and well-being.

This expertise has never been static and it evolved in response to all sorts of environmental shifts and perturbations. The need to stay attuned to the rhythms of all interrelated human and non-human elements, as well as the recognition of relational symmetry and interdependence, has been central to the human capacity to survive and quickly adapt to any changes. The ability to survive and thrive has required (and continues to require) not only a knowledge of animals' predispositions and proclivities, but also a mastery of orientation and movement across the landscape. Crucially, it also requires the capacity to stay attuned to all elements of what Ulturgasheva's interlocutors called a web of mercifulness: humans have always remained at the mercy of wild and semi-domesticated reindeer; reindeer have been at the mercy of lichen, which in turn has been at the mercy of permafrost which has stayed solid owing to the mercifulness of lichen. Since all elements in this human–non-human community have been bound by inter-reliance, their safety and continuance have been determined by an asymmetric assortment of cosmo-geo-ecological dependences.

Iñupiaq and Eveny accounts of how human lives and social relations depend significantly on whales and reindeer are ultimately linked to their understanding of cosmology and resource politics. They manifest *sila*-thinking (see Edwardson, this volume) that stands in contrast to the silo-thinking we problematized above. In this regard, we agree with Marisol de la Cadena that indigenous politics often transcend or exceed the boundaries of mainstream politics as an exclusively human domain from which non-human forces are banned (2010: 335). De la Cadena's notion of cosmo-politics (or universal politics), which calls for the inclusion of non-humans (or as she calls them 'earth beings') into political negotiations in the capacity of political subjects, reshuffles the humano-centrism of hegemonic antagonisms pertaining to the domain of the political. Our volume expands this inquiry further into the field of the geo by demarcating a set of much-needed de-hierarchizing, de-silo-ing paradigms of knowledge production. As we shall see throughout this volume, the cosmo-geo-analytics that takes cosmo-knowledge seriously and respect the existence and subjectivities of non-humans is required to activate a more inclusive take on geopolitical processes themselves, as such cosmo-geo-politics could enable political forces to challenge hegemonic biopower thinking that is currently driving official (non)-responses to the irreversible forces of Anthropocene. This volume constitutes an attempt to recalibrate an understanding of the knowledge production process that responds to new horizons of knowledge that are not siloed within agendas of dominant enclaves of scientific knowledge owners. The contributions are instances of how diverse constellations of risks and sudden shocks (e.g. pandemics, extreme climate events such as hurricanes or tsunamis, presidential elections and economic crisis) prompt activation of the cosmo-geo-analytics facilitating the development of novel forms of engagement with complex impacts of climate change. Hence, we propose a cosmo-geo-analytics capable of articulating epistemological configurations that can include non-human beings such as whales, wolves and bears, but also powerful geomorphological entities – hyper-animistic forces such as permafrost or a hyper-object of wildfire – that constitute the cryo-ecologies of the Circumpolar lands. This, we suggest, both engages with and goes beyond some of the current re-examinations of animist thinking that we have already discussed, and offers an analytical perspective that is applicable on multiple scales from the intimate to the planetary. At a moment when the Arctic and its peoples are at the centre of rapid climate change, we further suggest that it is crucial that we do so when thinking about Arctic futures.

Olga Ulturgasheva is a Senior Lecturer/Associate Professor in Social Anthropology at the University of Manchester, UK. Over the last twenty years she has been engaged in a number of anthropological and cross-disciplinary studies exploring animism, human and non-human personhood, childhood and youth, climate change, resilience and adaptation patterns in Siberia, American Arctic and Amazonia. She is the author of *Narrating the Future in Siberia: Childhood, Adolescence and Autobiography among the Eveny* (Berghahn Books, 2012) and co-editor of *Animism in Rainforest and Tundra: Personhood, Animals, Plants and Things in Contemporary Amazonia and Siberia* (Berghahn Books, 2012). She serves as a Principal Investigator and co-Principal Investigator for two large international, collaborative research projects focusing on the dynamic of climate change in Alaska, Siberia and the Russian Far East funded by the US National Science Foundation and the European Research Council.

Barbara Bodenhorn was Newton Trust Lecturer in Social Anthropology until 2013 and is currently Fellow Emerita of Pembroke College, Cambridge. Her most recent research interests focus on children's environmental knowledge as well as communally initiated responses to environmental change.

Notes

1. See Hastrup 2013b and Callison 2014 for a critical consideration of these constructions.
2. During the Cold War, both the USSR and the US used their Arctic territory as a strategic buffer. George Edwardson recounted to Bodenhorn in 1985 how, when fishing on an inland river, he would watch MIGS fly low and fast along the waterway, testing to see how far inland they could get before being picked up by US military jets. 'I'm sure we were doing the same thing on the other side', he surmised. When oil was discovered, and statehood was established in the 1950s, Alaska became a territory to fight over, not just fly over. The Circumpolar nations have recognized the Arctic for its strategic military importance and for its economic potential for many decades. Even though the USSR, the US, Canada and Denmark/Greenland have separately recognized the presence of 'their' indigenous populations since the mid-1970s, indigenous presences have largely been seen as a hinderance to 'progress'; their views and knowledge have not been solicited. And the

claims they make to their land and resources must be continually defended. Our point here is that the ecology of the Arctic as a minimalist, and therefore vulnerable, ecosystem has only relatively recently become part of the public discourse concerning the region.
3. The US military has been the most consistent arm of the Federal Government to keep track of the consequences of climate change as a matter of national security. See Klare 2019 for an extended discussion of 'the view from the Pentagon'.
4. See Ehlers and Krafft 2005 for an excellent collection of essays reviewing early twenty-first-century treatments of this concept. In their introduction, the editors trace an awareness of the impacts of human activity on geologic processes from the mid-nineteenth century. They identify Turner and colleagues' work, *The Earth as Transformed by Human Action* (1990), as pivotal in their bringing together 'nature' and 'society' as co-drivers of environmental and climatological processes. The concept remains somewhat controversial even in geological circles.
5. This was by no means a monolithic process: Russian Orthodoxy reigned in Siberia, and on Kodiak Island in Alaska; Sheldon Jackson divided rural Alaska up like a missionary pie in order to avoid proselytizing competition; Moravians, Catholics, Presbyterians and others each received 'their' territory. Anglo- and Francophone Canada generally followed Protestant/Catholic denominations. Greenland's colonizers were largely Protestant.
6. See Robert Wright's (2004) historically informed critique of the trope of 'progress' – according to him, one of the most pernicious ideas to inform 'Western thought'. The book combines well with Fabian's long-standing exhortation to anthropologists to recognize others as co-eval, and not The Other (1988).
7. The intellectual history behind this is too long to go into here, but Hobbs, Locke, Marx and Weber all develop their arguments from a standpoint that assumes individual human desire is infinite, thus creating inevitable scarcity and competition.
8. See Bodenhorn 2000 for an extended examination of Iñupiaq discussions of this.
9. In a similar way, Robin Kimmerer (2013: 9ff) relates a Potawatomi origin story in which Skywoman falls to earth, is first supported by the wings of geese, then is let down on a turtle shell, and is finally able to settle on Turtle Island due to the generosity of a muskrat, who brings her a fistful of muddy soil from the bottom of the sea.
10. The distinction between Yup'ik/Yupiit follows the same general rule as that for Iñupiaq/Iñupiat: the former is singular and adjectival (Yup'ik skills; Iñupiaq stories) whereas the latter refer to a collective of people (young Yupiit find it challenging to deal with governmental agencies).
11. In *Salvaging Nature*, research sponsored by the UN, Marcus Colchester (1994) details the long – and widespread – history of tensions between conservationists who 'want to preserve' lands and indigenous peoples who have, in fact, been preserving them while they have lived there. They are then displaced – generally without consultation – because preserved spaces

are meant to be 'wild' and 'pristine' places that can be enjoyed by tourists rather than inhabitants.
12. As of 2019, no major steps had yet been undertaken to address either environmental threats on the island or the complex needs required for relocation (Hofstaedter 2019).

References

AMAP. 2017. *Snow, Water, Ice and Permafrost in the Arctic (SWIPA)*. Oslo: Arctic Monitoring and Assessment Programme (AMAP).

Barnosky, Anthony David and Elizabeth Hadly. 2016. *Tipping Point for Planet Earth: How Close Are We to the Edge?* London: William Collins.

Berkes, Fikret. 2012. *Sacred Ecology: Traditional Ecological Knowledge and Resource Management* (third edition). New York: Routledge.

Berkes, F., et al. 2005. *Breaking Ice: Renewable Resource and Ocean Management in the Canadian North*. Calgary: University of Calgary Press.

Bodenhorn, Barbara. 1997. 'People Who Are Like Our Books: Reading and Teaching on the North Slope of Alaska', *Arctic Anthropology* 34(1): 117–34.

———. 2000. 'It's Traditional to Change: A Case Study of Strategic Decision-Making', *Cambridge Anthropology* 22(1): 24–51.

———. 2013a. 'Meeting Minds; Encountering Worlds: Science and Other Expertises on Alaska's North Slope', in M. Konrad (ed.), *Collaborators Collaborating*. Oxford: Berghahn Books, pp. 225–44.

———. 2013b. Book Review of *Inherit My Heaven: Kalaallit Gender Relations*. *Arctic* 66(4): 500–501.

Bodenhorn, Barbara and Olga Ulturgasheva. 2017. 'Climate Strategies: Thinking through Arctic Examples', *Philosophical Transactions of the Royal Society A* 375(2095): 20160363.

———. 2018. 'Envisioning Arctic Futures: Digital and Otherwise', *Museum Anthropology Review* 12(2): 100–19.

Box, Jason. 2012. Interview in *Chasing Ice*. National Geographic documentary with James Blog. Produced by Jeff Orlowski et al. Released November 2012.

Bravo, Michel. 2009. 'Voices from the Sea Ice: The Reception of Climate Impact Narratives', *Journal of Historical Geography* 35(2): 256–78.

———. 2017. 'A Crypolitics to Reclaim Our Frozen Material States', in E. Kowal and J. Radin (eds), *Cryopolitics: Frozen Life in a Melting World*. Cambridge, MA: The MIT Press, pp. 27–57.

Brewster, Karen. 1997. 'Native Contributions to Arctic Science at Barrow, Alaska', *Arctic* 50(3): 277–88.

———. 2005. *The Whales, They Give Themselves: Conversations with Harry Brower, Sr.* Fairbanks, AK: University of Alaska Press.

Brightman, Marc, Vanessa Grotti and Olga Ulturgasheva. 2006/7. 'Introduction: Rethinking the "Frontier" in Amazonia and Siberia: Extractive Economies, Indigenous Politics and Social Transformations', Special edition of *Cambridge Anthropology* 26(2): 1–12.

Callison, Candis. 2014. *How Climate Change Comes to Matter*. Durham, NC: Duke University Press.

——. 2018. Keynote speech. International Symposium convened by Dr Candis Callison (University of British Columbia, Canada) and Prof Simon Morrison (Princeton University, USA) on 'Indigenous Communities and Climate Change in North America and Russia'.

Chakrabarty, Dipesh. 2009. 'The Climate of History: Four Theses', *Critical Enquiry* 35: 197–222.

Colchester, Marcus. 1994. *Salvaging Nature: Indigenous Peoples, Protected Areas and Biodiversity Conservation*. Geneva: UNSAID.

Cohen, J. et al. 2014. 'Recent Arctic Amplification and Extreme Mid-Latitude Weather', *Nature Geoscience* 7(9): 627–37.

Coreau, A. et al. 2010. 'Exploring the Difficulties of Studying Futures in Ecology: What Do Ecological Scientists Think?', *Oikos* 119: 1364–76.

Crate, Susan and Mark Nuttall. 2016. *Anthropology and Climate Change: From Encounters to Action* (second edition). Walnut Creek, CA: Leftcoast Press.

Cruikshank, Julie. 1998. *The Social Life of Stories: Narrative and Knowledge in Yukon Territory*. Lincoln, NE: University of Nebraska Press.

——. 2004. 'Uses and Abuses of "Traditional Knowledge"; Perspectives from the Yukon Territories', in D.G. Anderson and M. Nuttall (eds), *Cultivating Arctic Landscapes: Knowing and Managing Animals in the Circumpolar North*. Oxford: Berghahn.

——. 2005. *Do Glaciers Listen? Local Knowledge, Colonial Encounters, and Social Imagination*. Seattle: University of Washington Press.

Crutzen, Paul and Eugene Stoermer. 2000. 'The "Anthropocene"', *Global Change Newsletter* 41: 17–18.

Das, Veena. 1995. *Critical Events: An Anthropological Perspective on Contemporary India*. Delhi: Oxford University Press.

de la Cadena, Marisol. 2010. 'Indigenous Cosmopolitics in the Andes: Conceptual Reflections beyond "Politics"', *Cultural Anthropology* 25(2): 334–70.

——. 2015. *Earth Beings: Ecologies of Practice across Andean Worlds*. Durham, NC: Duke University Press.

Douglas, Mary and Aaron Wildavsky. 1982. *Risk and Culture: An Essay on the Selection of Technological and Environmental Dangers*. Berkeley: University of California Press.

The Economist. 2020. 'One Russian Scientist Hopes to Slow the Thawing of the Arctic', 16 December 2020. Retrieved 8 March 2021 from www.economist.com/christmas-specials/2020/12/19/one-russian-scientist-hopes-to-slow-the-thawing-of-the-arctic.

Ehlers, Eckart and Thomas Krafft (eds). 2005. *Earth System Science in the Anthropocene: Emerging Issues and Problems*. New York: Springer.

Ellis, Rebecca, Claire Waterton and Brian Wynne. 2010. 'Taxonomy, Biodiversity and Their Publics in Twenty-First-Century DNA Barcoding', *Public Understanding of Science* 19(4): 497–512.

Eriksen, Thomas Hylland. 2016. *Overheating: An Anthropology of Accelerated Change*. London: Pluto Press.
Escobar, Arthuro. 2018. *Designs for the Pluriverse: Radical Interdependence, Autonomy, and the Making of Worlds*. Durham, NC: Duke University Press.
Evengård, Brigitta and Tomas Thierfelder. 2021. 'CLINF: Climate-Change Effects on the Epidemiology of Infectious Diseases, and the Associated Impacts on Northern Societies', in D. Nord (ed.), *Nordic Perspectives on the Responsible Development of the Arctic: Pathways to Action*. New York: Springer, pp. 49–70.
Fabian, Johannes. 1988. *Time and the Other: How Anthropology Makes its Object*. New York: Columbia University Press.
Fenge, Terry. 2001. 'The Inuit and Climate Change', *Isuma* Winter: 79–85.
Fienup-Riordan, Ann. 2020. *Nunakun-gguq Ciutengqertut/They Say They have Ears through the Ground: Animal Essays from Southwest Alaska*. Fairbanks, AK: University of Alaska Press.
Fienup-Riordan, Ann and Alice Rearden. 2012. *Ellavut: Our Yupik World and Weather: Continuity and Change on the Bering Coast*. Seattle: University of Washington Press.
Ford, Violet. 2001. 'From Consultation to Partnership: Engaging Inuit on Climate Change', *Silarjualiriniq* 7: 2–4.
Ghosh, Amitav. 2016. *The Great Derangement: Climate Change and the Unthinkable*. Chicago: University of Chicago Press.
Goodell, John. 2017. *The Water Will Come: Rising Seas, Sinking Cities, and the Remaking of the Civilized World*. New York: Back Bay Books.
Hastrup, Kirsten. 2013a. 'Anticipation in Thin Ice. Diagrammatic Reasoning among Arctic Hunters', in K. Hastrup and M. Skrydstrup (eds.), *Anticipating Nature: The Social Life of Climate Models*. London: Routledge, pp. 77–99.
———. 2013b. 'The Ice as Argument: Topographical Mementos in the High Arctic', *Cambridge Anthropology* 31(1): 52–68.
———. 2013c. 'Scales of Attention in Fieldwork: Global Connections and Local Concerns in the Arctic', *Ethnography* 14(2): 145–64.
———. 2020. 'Emerging Landscapes: Geosocial Relations in Thule'. Paper presented for Arctic Cultures Workshop, Cambridge, UK, 8–9 January 2020 (unpublished).
Hastrup, Kirsten and Frida Hastrup. 2015. *Waterworlds: Anthropology in Fluid Environments*. Oxford: Berghahn Books.
Hofstaedter, Emily. 2019. 'Amid an Erosion Crisis, Shishmareff Takes Small Steps toward Expansion'. Retrieved 25 March 2021 from www.knom.org/wp/blog/2019/06/28/amid-an-erosion-crisis-shishmaref-takes-small-steps-toward-expansion/#:~:text=Shishmaref%20is%20a%20san.
Holland, Marika and Cecilia Bitz. 2003. 'Polar Amplification of Climate Change in Coupled Models', *Climate Dynamics* 21(3–4): 221–32.
Inglis, Julian. 1993. *Traditional Ecological Knowledge: Concepts and Cases*. Ottawa, Ontario: Canadian Museum of Nature/International Development Research Centre.
Jamail, Dahr. 2019. *The End of Ice: Bearing Witness and Finding Meaning in the Path of Climate Disruption*. London: The New Press.

Jolly, D. et al. 2002. 'We Can't Predict the Weather like We Used To: Inuvialuit Observations of Climate Change, Sachs Harbour, Western Canadian Arctic', in I. Krupnik and D. Jolly (eds), *The Earth Is Faster Now: Indigenous Observations of Arctic Environmental Change*. Fairbanks, AK: Arctic Research Consortium of the United States, pp. 9–125.
Kawagley, Oscar Angayuqaq. 2006. *A Yupiaq Worldview: A Pathway to Ecology a nd Spirit*, 2nd ed. Long Grove, IL: Waveland Press.
Keith, D. et al. 2008. 'Predicting Extinction Risks under Climate Change: Coupling Stochastic Population Models with Dynamic Habitat Models', *Biology Letters* 4: 560–63.
Kimmerer, Robin Wall. 2013. *Braiding Sweetgrass: Indigenous Wisdom, Scientific Knowledge, and the Teachings of Plants*. Minneapolis, MN: Milkweed Editions.
Klare, Michael. 2019. *All Hell Breaking Loose: The Pentagon's Perspective on Climate Change*. New York: Macmillan.
Kormann, Carolyn. 2020. 'A Disastrous Summer in the Arctic', *The New Yorker*, 27 June.
Krebs, Charles and David Berteaux. 2006. 'The Problems and Pitfalls in Relating Climate Variability to Population Dynamics', *Climate Research* 32: 143–49.
Krupnik, Igor and Dyanna Jolly. 2002. *The Earth Is Faster Now: Indigenous Observations of Arctic Environmental Change*. Fairbanks, AK: Arctic Research Consortium of the United States.
Kunuk, Zacharias, Ian Mauro and Norman Cohn. 2010. *Inuit Knowledge and Climate Change* (in Inuktituk with English subtitles). Iglulik Isuma Productions.
Le Quéré, C. et al. 2014. 'Global Carbon Budget 2013', *Earth System Scientific Data* 6: 235–63.
Marino, Elizabeth. 2015. *Fierce Climate, Sacred Ground: An Ethnography of Climate Change in Shishmaref, Alaska*. Fairbanks, AK: University of Alaska Fairbanks.
Marino, Elizabeth and A. Faas. 2020. 'Is Vulnerability an Outdated Concept? After Subjects and Spaces', *Annals of Anthropological Practice* 44: 33–46.
Mitchell, Timothy. 2009. *Carbon Democracy: Political Power in the Age of Oil*. London: Verso.
Moore Jason. 2014. The Capitalocene, Part I: on the nature and origins of our ecological crisis. Retrieved 20 January 2017 from http://www.jasonwmoore.com/upload/The_Capitalocene_Part_i_ June-2014.pdf.
Morrow, Phyllis and Chase Hensel. 1992. 'Hidden Dissension: Minority–Majority Relationships and the Use of Contested Terminology', *Arctic Anthropology* 29(1): 38–53.
Nakashima, Douglas, Jennifer Rubis and Igor Krupnik. 2018. 'Indigenous Knowledge for Climate Change Assessment and Adaptation: Introduction', in D. Nakashima, I. Krupnik and J. Rubis (eds), *Indigenous Knowledge for Climate Change Assessment and Adaptation*. Cambridge: Cambridge University Press, pp. 1–22.
Nuttall, Mark. 1998. *Protecting the Arctic: Indigenous Peoples and Cultural Survival*. London: Routledge.

Omazic, A. et al. 2019. 'Discrepancies in Data Reporting of Zoonotic Infectious Diseases across the Nordic Countries – a Call for Action in the Era of Climate Change', *International Journal of Circumpolar Health* 78(1): 1601991.

Oozeva, C. et al. 2004. *Watching Ice and Weather Our Way*. Washington DC: Arctic Studies Center, Smithsonian Institution.

O'Reilly, Jessica. 2016. 'Sensing the Ice: Field Science, Models, and Expert Intimacy with Knowledge', *Journal of the Royal Anthropological Institute* 22(S1): 27–45.

Oquilluk, William and Laurel Bland. 1973. *The People of Kawerak: Legends of the Northern Eskimo*. Anchorage: Alaska Pacific University Press.

Overland, J. et al. 2019. 'The Urgency of Arctic Change', *Polar Science* 21: 6–13.

Patel, Geeta. 2016. *Risky Bodies & Techno-Intimacy: Reflections on Sexuality, Media, Science, Finance*. Seattle: University of Washington Press.

Petryna, Adriana. 2003. *Life Exposed: Biological Citizens after Chernobyl*. Princeton, NJ: Princeton University Press.

Pfeffer, William Tad. 2009. 'People and Place in the Far North: A Vision of Life, Community and Change', in S. Jakobsson (ed.), *Images of the North: Histories, Identities, Ideas*. Amsterdam: Rodopi, pp. 81–90.

Popov, Igor. 2020. 'The Current State of Pleistocene Park, Russia (An Experiment in the Restoration of Megafauna in a Boreal Environment)', *The Holocene* 30(10): 1471–73.

Roe, Gerard, Marcia Baker and Florian Herla. 2016. 'Centennial Glacier Retreat as Categorical Evidence of Regional Climate Change', *Nature Geoscience* 10(2): 95–99.

Royer, Marie-Jeanne. 2016. *Climate, Environment and Cree Observations: James Bay Territory*. Cham, Switzerland: Springer.

Royer, M.-J. et al. 2013. 'Linking Cree Hunters' and Scientific Observations of Changing Inland Ice and Meteorological Conditions in the Subarctic Eastern James Bay Region, Canada', *Climatic Change* 119: 719–32.

Scheper-Hughes, Nancy. 2005. 'The Disaster and Its Doubles', *Anthropology Today* 21(6): 2–4.

Tasch, Jeremy and Weiwei Tasch. 2017. 'Ambiguity in an Ambiguous Region: Risk Conundrums in the Arctic', in R. Kaspersob (ed.), *Risk Conundrums: Solving Unsolvable Problems*. London: Routledge, pp. 147–62.

Thompson, Andrea. 2012. 'Arctic Wildfire Soot Darkening Greenlandic Ice Sheet', *Scientific American*, 7 December 2012. Retrieved 26 March 2021 from www.scientificamerican.com/article/arctic-wildfire-soot-dark/.

Todd, Zoe. 2015. 'Indigenizing the Anthropocene', in H. Davis and E. Turpin (eds), *Art in the Anthropocene: Aesthetics, Politics, Environments and Epistemologies*. London: Open Humanities Press, pp. 241–54.

Turner, B. et al. 1990. *The Earth as Transformed by Human Action: Global Change and Regional Changes in the Biosphere over the Past 300 Years*. Cambridge: Cambridge University Press.

Ulturgasheva, Olga. 2012. *Narrating the Future in Siberia: Childhood, Adolescence and Autobiography among the Eveny*. Oxford: Berghahn Books.

———. 2014. 'Attaining Khinem: Challenges, Coping Strategies and Resilience among Eveny Adolescents', *Transcultural Psychiatry* 51: 632–50.

———. 2016. 'Spirit of the Future: Movement, Kinetic Distribution and Personhood among Siberian Eveny', *Social Analysis* 60(1): 56–73.
Ulturgasheva, Olga and Barbara Bodenhorn. 2016. 'Arctic Futures? Climate, Geopolitics and Local Realities', *Witness the Arctic: Chronicles of the NSF Arctic Science Section* 20(3): 23–30.
Ulturgasheva, O. et al. 2014. 'Arctic Indigenous Youth Resilience and Vulnerability: Comparative Analysis of Adolescent Experiences across Five Circumpolar Communities', *Transcultural Psychiatry* 51(5): 735–56.
Ulturgasheva, Olga, Stacy Rasmus and Phyllis Morrow. 2015. 'Collapsing the Distance: Indigenous Youth Engagement in a Circumpolar Study of Youth Resilience', *Arctic Anthropology* 52(1): 50–60.
Vitebsky, Piers. 2005. *The Reindeer People: Living with Animals and Spirits in Siberia*. Boston: Houghton Mifflin; London: HarperCollins.
Wadhams, Peter. 2017. *Farewell to Ice*. London: Allen Lane.
Wehi, P.M., M.P. Cox, T. Roa and H. Whaanga. 2018. 'Human Perceptions of Megafaunal Extinction Events Revealed by Linguistic Analysis of Indigenous Oral Traditions', *Human Ecology* 46: 461–70.
Wenzel, George. 2004. 'From TEK to IQ: Inuit Qaujimajatuqangit and Inuit Cultural Ecology', *Arctic Anthropology* 41(2): 238–50.
Weston, Kath. 2017. *Animate Planet: Making Visceral Sense of Living in a High-Tech Ecologically Damaged World*. Durham, NC: Duke University Press.
———. In press. 'Techno-Revivalism: Mobilizing "Tradition" to Address Climate Change', in B. Bodenhorn (ed.), *In the Name of Climate Change: The Politics and Pragmatics of Shifting Environmental Conditions*. Oxford: Berghahn Books.
Wilkinson, Kim, Susan Clark and William Burch. 2007. *Other Voices, Other Ways, Better Practice: Bridging Local and Professional Environmental Knowledge*. Yale: Yale School of Forestry & Environmental Studies 14.
Williamson, Karla. 2011. *Inherit My Heaven: Kalaallit Gender Relations*. Nuuk: Department of Culture and Education, Government of Greenland.
Wright, Ronald. 2004. *A Short History of Progress*. Toronto: Anansi Press.

Chapter 2

'Tears of the Earth'
Human–Permafrost Entanglements and Science–Indigenous Knowledge Encounters in Northeast Siberia

Olga Ulturgasheva

In May 2016 the Royal Anthropological Institute hosted an international conference 'Anthropology, Weather and Climate Change' held at the British Museum in London during which the co-editors of this volume convened a day-long panel session titled 'Northern Futures? Climate, Geopolitics and Local Realities'. One of the highlights of the panel session was a presentation by Eveny reindeer herders, who travelled from northeast Siberia to speak at the conference. While expressing their concerns about climate change, the Eveny spoke about the increased likelihood of risk situations in the areas of their subsistence and travel, including floods, wildfires, unprecedented loss of the domesticated reindeer, and overwhelming changes in flora and fauna.[1] The reindeer herders spoke about the plans of the Russian and international extractive companies to start mining gold and silver on the territory of reindeer pastures, which will inevitably lead to an ecological catastrophe, contamination of rivers that supply vital fresh water, and the transformation of boreal forests and meadows where reindeer graze into ecological ruins. Their emphasis on how human and animal safety is severely undermined by the long-lasting effects of forest fires, accelerating permafrost thaw, prompted the panel to discuss and consider the effects of wildfires across the Arctic. The reindeer herders supported their discussion by video- and photo-evidence of several environmental calamities they have experienced over the previous two years, including a dramatic landslide.

Using a mobile phone camera, one of the reindeer herders managed to video-record how a geyser of muddy water flashed out of the dry ground. It looked as if a subterranean river came out suddenly after being pushed up by thawing permafrost. The scary footage of the environmental calamity took the audience members' breath away as they were silently watching a startling dynamic of the floods erupting from below and engulfing the reindeer herders' campsite in minutes. The video captured how people were trying to flee the flooded area to safety, hurriedly yet calmly. People were moving fast but nobody panicked and screamed out in fear. The visual testimony of the intensification of ecological fragility and rapidity of environmental degradation in the Siberian Arctic provided by the reindeer herders raised serious questions about the scale of the environmental risks and the human capacity to avert ecological disasters.

To a large extent, the Eveny presentation of the effects of permafrost thaw back in 2016 served as an eloquent articulation of the environmental crisis and visual evidence of cryocidal processes discussed in Chapter 1. It also portended the current regime of high run-off pressure that generates multidirectional and simultaneous responses to permafrost thaw across human and non-human domains. The report offered by the reindeer herders continues to reverberate, with the grimness of current news about deforestation rate as a result of intensive logging, droughts, flash floods and wildfires (Jamail 2019: 133–55). Every year Siberia loses several kilometres of land as it erodes, either slowly turning into post-cryogenic, unliveable ecological ruins disappearing under the muddy waters of melted permafrost or disappearing entirely under encroaching ocean waters in coastal areas of the Siberian Arctic. The dramatic changes in the cryosphere are attributed to a number of anthropogenic activities associated with oil and gas extractive industries, military initiatives and hydrocarbon developments, all of which have been continuously generating chemical and radioactive contamination, significantly contributing to the rapid degradation of permafrost.

Four years after that conference panel, in July 2020, a spell of abnormally hot weather across large territories of Siberia saw nearly 300 wildfires blazing at once, causing record high carbon emissions. The gigantic wildfires are accelerating the pace of permafrost thaw while amplifying the pace of ecological degradation. In March 2021, meteorologists already predicted that in the forthcoming summer

Siberia would face a similar type of extreme weather which will inevitably cause more wildfires (Physorg 2021).

The startling dynamic of cryogenic changes and predictions articulated by the reindeer herders serve as an invitation to discuss the human capacity to adapt, predict, avert risk situations and negotiate safety in the face of profound unpredictability. They also invite us to consider available models for ascertaining the collective and individual ability to mitigate current and future environmental calamities. Recent revelations about the speed and intensity of the permafrost thaw and the amplified rate of ecological degradation have pointed to limitations and underestimation of the scientific models (see Shakhova et al. 2010; DeConto et al. 2012; Lovejoy 2013). Numerous reports have confirmed that the accelerated speed of degradation is currently on track to far exceed projections. This stresses the necessity to activate and shape those forms of collaboration that could open up new channels for addressing climate change and transgressing mainstream knowledge (Allen, Breshears and McDowell 2015;

Figure 2.1. *Effects of permafrost thaw in the area of Sebyan.*
© *Olga Ulturgasheva*

O'Reilly 2016). The latter requires consideration and recognition of plural worlds as well as thinking at more-than-human scales.

The debates surrounding the concept of an Anthropocene have recently facilitated a critical view of European anthropocentrism and rampant capitalism as conceptual sources of the planetary condition of endlessly worsening environmental degradation and loss of biodiversity (Moore 2015; see Introduction, this volume). With regard to this, the process of the Anthropocene associated with the colonial destruction of diverse and plural worlds is rightfully viewed as a product of 'colonialist one-worldism' (Escobar 2020) and 'a scenario of the end of the world' (de la Cadena and Blaser 2018). Building on the latest calls to challenge the dominant man-centred paradigm, my ethnographic consideration of human–permafrost entanglements will echo the arguments developed by Marisol de la Cadena (2015), who advocated inclusion of heterogeneously entangled worlds in political disputes over land use and human–non-human security. It will also resonate with Arturo Escobar's critique of the developmentalist-liberal world vision embedded within the modernist ontology of separation. Escobar pertinently stresses that knowledge hierarchies with the divisive pattern of scientists/experts developing, changing and modifying 'ignorant'/'primitive' indigenous groups have long prevented a true dialogue between different conceptions of the worlds or 'cosmovisions' (Escobar 2018, 2020).

I also agree with Escobar that any attempt to arrange such a dialogue will face institutional and systemic obstinacy, resisting the possibility of putting the complexity of indigenous pluriversal cosmovisions into a symmetrical interchange with the dominant anthropocentric (man-centred) ontology of natural scientists who tend to prioritize objective factors and straightforward cause-and-effect links in their understanding of the scenarios of change. To enable such dialogue, it would make sense to critically evaluate the lessons from the past, from which there is currently a refusal to learn or which are intentionally silenced and erased. Therefore, this chapter aims to identify the prerequisites for arranging such a dialogue by considering rare examples where the dialogue and partnership were possible, even temporarily.

Based on ethnographic research in two reindeer herding communities in northeast Siberia in 2014–2020, my discussion will look at how the latest environmental changes associated with permafrost thaw are navigated and articulated by Siberian Eveny reindeer herders. First, to foreground my discussion of the Eveny cosmovision of environmental change, I critically evaluate the latest theoretical takes on human–non-human relations with a special focus on the post-humanism versus animism debate. Then, I shall look at how the latest dynamic of permafrost thaw in Siberia is being understood through both the scientific and the indigenous lens. This will include an overview of recent cryogenic and anthropogenic transformations which affect the local ecosystem, hydrology and more-than-human worlds. Finally, I examine the instances when reindeer herders' knowledge was pivotal for scientific research in northeast Siberia. However, the scientists' inability to recognize and properly document their joint effort was due to a mindset which was locked in a 'one-world' vision. The discussion will provide an account of what types of expertise and sensitivity are required for collaborative dealing with environmental unpredictability and the latest dynamic of climate change.

On the Reindeer-Morphic Model of the World

Before I move to the discussion of the reindeer herders' responses to the latest dynamic of environmental degradation and permafrost thaw, I would like to introduce the Eveny legend about the creation of the Earth.[2] The legend goes as follows:

> People did not live on the Earth before, they used to live in the sky. They lived very well there. Once a woman got expelled from her native sky because she rejected a marriage offer from a man she did not love. Having been rejected by people, she left the sky riding an eight-legged reindeer. Reindeer and woman were riding for a long time until the reindeer got very tired and suddenly fell out of the sky. When they both landed on water, the eight-legged reindeer advised the woman to pick hair from its fur and throw it in the water. In water, the reindeer hair transformed into wooden logs out of which the woman made a raft. Then, the reindeer advised the woman that she had to kill him and butcher his body. She followed the advice, and as soon as she butchered the reindeer carcass, the reindeer hide turned into the earth, then skull and bones transformed into mountains, hair turned into a forest, hair lice turned into wild reindeer. When she was breaking bones, the sound of breaking bones turned into thunder and the last reindeer breath turned into wind. Then his heart turned into a hero, lungs turned into a boy and a girl. This is how the Earth was created. (Dutkin and Robbek 1978: 156)

This aetiological myth about how a reindeer became an originator of the Earth with the help of a woman carries a very important point for my discussion. The story highlights that Earth and its features, including humans, have been engendered as a result of actions taken by a woman, and all features of the Earth are continuous with the non-human – reindeer – pointing to a zoomorphic or reindeer-morphic model of the world. It is a model of the world that posits the Earth as being in a post-reindeer condition and highlights that all features of the world are mutually constitutive and closely interconnected through their genesis. Here, humanity is conceived in its existential interconnectedness with non-human elements of the world, i.e. all features of the world are interwoven in the earth–reindeer–human assemblage. Given the dramatic speed with which the Siberian environment is transforming in response to climate change and environmental degradation, the myth, with its strong emphasis on the interdependence and interconnectedness of human and non-human, becomes especially pertinent.

Such emphasis on interconnectivity has a special resonance with the recent sociological and philosophical strand that prioritizes non-human over human while focusing on post-human, extra-human or non-human sensibilities. Post-humanism, conceived as a response to ongoing environmental catastrophe and as an explicit critique of imperial capitalism, posits a new type of relationality which is more generally receptive to worldly alterity and epistemic multiplicity (Haraway 2008; Kirksey and Helmreich 2010; Wolfe 2010; Hodder 2014). The post-humanistic trend in social theory is an important contribution to ecological thinking in resistance to the dangers posed to life in the age of the Anthropocene (Braidotti 2009; MacCormack 2012); however, knowledge accumulated by indigenous groups (referred to as either indigenous knowledge, traditional environmental or ecological knowledge, or ethno- or native science) often continues to be ignored by post-humanism, which, like other 'postmodern' philosophies including poststructuralism and postcolonialism, typically does not reference the scope of indigenous knowledge in the recent spate of publications outlining its parameters (see Bignall, Hemming and Rigney 2016). There is a tendency in the post-humanist field to distance oneself from and ignore any ideas related to indigenous knowledge and indigeneity, diminishing these to a romantic expression of otherness or an essentialist, defensive response to the domination of Western colonialism, simultaneously prioritizing Eurocentric theoretical perspectives even as they critique Enlightenment ideas (see particularly Raffles 1999, 2002, 2011; Tsing 1999, 2005, 2011). In other words, although they aspire to decentre man, they remain ethnocentric, 'leaving "the anthropological machine" of Western humanism essentially untouched' (DiNovelli-Lang 2013: 140).

While simultaneously giving a cold shoulder to anything indigenous and striving to erase the boundary between multiple species, many post-humanists erect new divisions, once again reinstating hierarchical distinctions between an Enlightened First World and a colonized Indigenous Fourth World. This is the kind of divisiveness that stems from a dominant one-worldism, i.e. the modern cosmovision based on an ontology of separation. Such ontologies divide 'the human from non-human (culture from nature) and distinguish the "civilized" (European, moderns, rational people) from the "non-civilized" (primitives, barbarians, underdeveloped people, nonmoderns, terrorists)' (Escobar 2020: 123). Following this modernist, bio-colonial vision, the 'non-civilized', non-Western subjects could only be contingent assemblages and products of systemic/colonial forces, and their struggle for recognition and autonomy is rendered futile because the perspectives, experiences and positions they hold and defend are destined to dissolve in the networks of externally imposed, colonial, structural and institutional forces.

Furthermore, elision or omission of indigenous knowledge has also to do with the latest critique of animism. The term 'animism' is rejected by opponents who tend to reduce the notion, linking it to a desire to remain either mired in the past, i.e. evolutionism, or trapped in a set of worries about proving the reality of a non-human other, i.e. radical alterity or perspectivism.[3] By reducing indigenous knowledge down to a 'noble savage' trope, the critique of animism dismisses the extent to which the twenty-first-century Siberian hunters and reindeer herders continue to understand more-than-humans to be enlivened by animist relationality. This is the kind of relationality and expertise that has been relying on a symmetrical fusion of human and non-human that recognizes sentient qualities of the earth, the earth that is defined by actions of humans and non-humans.

As an epistemological and ontological stance, animism has been questioning human exceptionalism for more than a century. Yet post-humanists often criticize animism for its anthropomorphism besides its relationality and attribution of personhood to non-humans, i.e. a view of every object as a potential human-like subject. But, as Signe Howell has eloquently shown, post-humanists' desire to 'think beyond the human' is confronted by a similar predicament of being stuck within the same 'reality' question to which they found no satisfactory solutions (Howell 2016: 59). By ditching animism, 'post-humanism obstructs appreciation of indigenous ontologies because the post-humanists too easily seek to conflate them with the Western one' (58).

Despite the ongoing critique of animism by post-humanists, the scholarly inquiry into animacy and animation continues to spark interest from a wide range of analytical angles. If the early anthropologists like Tylor and Frazer used the term animism to classify peoples according to social evolutionist hierarchy, the subsequent generations of anthropologists who have conducted ethnographic research with shamanic and animist societies worldwide have heavily problematized the evolutionary classifications of their predecessors and criticized their Eurocentric assumptions about the superiority of humans over non-human beings. The old evolutionist theory of animism was updated by several generations of scholars, including Signe Howell (1984), Nurit Bird-David (1999, 2006) and Barbara Bodenhorn (2000, 2004) among many others.

The new take on animism posits that the boundary between humans and non-humans is permeable and that personhood extends beyond the confines of the human body. Due to the latter developments in the theory of personhood, unbounded potential for identification and continuity between humans and non-humans continues to be identified as a prominent feature of animist thinking (Howell 1984, 2016; Pedersen 2001; Willerslev 2007; Brightman, Grotti and Ulturgasheva 2012; Rival 2012, 2016; Willerslev and Ulturgasheva 2012; Ulturgasheva 2017 and many others). Lately, several productive attempts to rethink animism have extended the inquiry on animism beyond the notion of 'soul'. Nowadays, the concept of animism is undergoing continuous reinvention and is even being applied in the highly technological and experimental setting of robotics laboratories, illustrating the power of 'technological animism' even in the absence of souls and soul theory (Richardson 2016).

As the Introduction to this volume highlighted, new animacies emerge from ecological ruins generated by capitalist expansion and environmental destruction (Povinelli 2016; Weston 2017; see also Murphy 2008; Fortun 2014; Shapiro and Kirksey 2017). Within new animacies lies the principle of unbounded co-constitution that weaves human and non-human intimacies, whether microbial, viral or chemical, spreading through the entire fabric of bio-, techno-, eco- and socio-existences, i.e. 'life that becomes not-life, an other-than-life, a becoming-nonliving' (Thacker 2005).

Since creatures alongside chemical and toxic 'other-than-life forms' co-constitute, intrude upon and invade other forms of human and non-human existencies in and through their substances, they generate intimacies that enliven new animacies. However, the kind of humanism or anthropocentrism this analytical angle challenges largely comes out of Western, industrial and post-industrial humanity, charged with the neo-liberal fetishization of an individual. The latter implies that the post-humanist/STS focus on animacies and intimacies selectively prioritizes a post-industrial/industrial context to highlight the irrelevance (or 'humano-centrism') of those forms of animism that such an approach associates with the anthropological past-perfect. The latter begs the following questions.

Do new animacies truly and holistically encompass our understanding of human and non-human existences across and beyond life and non-life forms? Are they also running the risk of lumping diverse takes on animist human–non-human entanglements into one box labelled humano-centrism? How really humano-centric are animist ways of being and knowing? If we prioritize microbial and viral animacies and discard forms of animism that continue to be practised, for example, by our Siberian interlocutors, would it only confirm the primacy of the natural sciences and dualistic humanism once again? If animist relationality is really and fully anthropocentric, what kind of 'anthropo- or humano-centrism' does it stand for and is it guilty of?

In response to this set of questions my further discussion will show that Eveny reindeer herders' ways of dealing with the latest environmental upheavals and their attempts to reduce environmental uncertainty through divination rituals continue to emphasize the persistence of animist relationality that encompasses both humans and other-than-human beings. This is the kind of relationality that reflects 'human proclivity to anthropomorphize' (see Howell 2016: 44); however, it is far from positing either radical otherness or human exceptionalism.

The Siberian Eveny legend about a reindeer as a creator of the earth is particularly eloquent in these regards, as alongside the relation it equally reproduces co-constitution, i.e. if the reindeer constitutes the earth and earth constitutes the reindeer, then humans are constituted of reindeer and reindeer are constituted of humans. If we use the language of post-humanists, the story about the reindeer would be essentially a story of rapid evolution of microbes constituting reindeer or it would be an account of a reindeer microbiome transmitted and expanded across species including humans. Both versions of the story, i.e. animist and post-humanist, are quite different but they do not seem incompatible from a broad perspective. If we accept the anti-dualist symmetry of two conceptual schemes, we shall see two different angles of the same animate matrix where the animist angle emphasizes relation and the post-humanist one highlights co-constitution.

It is also important to acknowledge that animist cosmologies and shamanic ways of thinking and perceiving the world continue to be crucial for human adaptation in Siberia and the entire Arctic region in general. So nowadays the question of adaptability and human capacity to survive and cope with the latest environmental challenges requires attention to nuances of people's lived experiences, including their relations with animist/spiritual forces of the land.

Hyper-animism of Permafrost

Permafrost is an important climatological feature of the entire area of northeast Siberia (and all of the Circumpolar region), so any changes within its characteristics generate a number of simultaneously occurring risk situations, subjecting local communities to potential and ongoing infrastructural and ecological disasters. The history of regional development has shown that the dynamic and unpredictable nature of permafrost obstructed the development and management of any construction and engineering projects in the region. Permafrost always resisted and defied human control.

Given that the notion of permafrost has been shaped by the modernist ontology of separation and emerged as a scientific object from within the positivist, Enlightenment-driven epistemology, the existing discourses on permafrost are mainly associated with the technogenic, man-privileging perspective (see, for example, Streletskiy and Shiklomanov 2016; Chu 2020; Streletskiy 2021). Within the development-centred, modern cosmovision, permafrost is mainly conceptualized as an archive of the geological, genetic, palaeontological or mineralogical data and a technogenic obstacle that continues to impact industrial and development projects in the Russian Arctic. There is no space in the modernist ontology for a body of knowledge that takes into account the frozen ground as the entanglement of cosmological, geological and ecological processes, i.e. the onto-epistemology that includes the earth-ice formations constituting permafrost as agents affecting people's destinies and human history.

The need to stay attuned to the rhythms of all interrelated human and non-human elements, together with the recognition of relational symmetry and interdependence, has been central to the human capacity to survive and adapt to the permafrost-bound land. Such perception of the land also enabled an understanding of it as an elusive, viscous and unpredictable force. The Eveny engage with permafrost as a container of shamanic or animistic spirit forces, nurturing provider and contributor to human and more-than-human livelihoods and security. This vision of the land is filtered through the animist matrix in which the land emerges as a power saturated with the potential for animacy and transformation. In this sense, permafrost could be characterized as, borrowing from Timothy Morton (2013), a hyper-object. As an animist hyper-object, permafrost engenders and animates social dramas, sustains wildlife and holds imminent and anticipated futures.

The term 'permafrost', literally the combination of two words, 'permanent' and 'frost', evokes a sense of permanence along with an association with immovable, monolithic, eternally frozen ground. However, contrary to what the term evokes, its morphological and cryogenic characteristics often point to its plasticity, impermanence and sensitivity (see also Cruikshank 2005 and Hastrup 2013). This supposedly eternally frozen ground has the propensity to transform its shape in response to any slight internal movements. Permafrost consists of several horizontal layers composed of a mixture of alluvia, sediment, frozen rocks and large ice deposits that intermittently alternate between fluid and solid states (Alekseiev 2016: 41–110). These layers are dynamically interacting with each other, turning one into another while co-constituting and reconstituting their states and textures. The upper layer (about 10–20 metres thick) is a stratum which is sensitive to any drastic fluctuations in seasonal weather conditions, while freezing to the bottom in winter and melting in summer. It is the frozen field located below the surface layer that is defined by scientists as permafrost. The estimated thickness of the layer is in the 20–1,500 metres range.

The temperature of internal ice layers is never permanent and stable, as it is characterized by intermittent changes in temperature, either reaching up to 0 or 1 degree Celsius or falling drastically to −21 degrees Celsius. Because of the fluctuations in temperature, subterranean layers of the ice ground are mutually able to deform, reform and reproduce by expanding in all directions, either amplifying or decreasing responses across layers. Such a state of permafrost points to highly energetic geological masses. The state of aggregations depends on the scale and pace of interaction between internal subsurface temperatures and external air, in addition to the interactive dynamic between internal water channels and seasonal weather fluctuations. Subterranean ice formations are mobile and highly sensitive to changes in an internal temperature regime often affected by external factors such as prolonged rains or intensive floods (Nekrasov and Deviatkin 1974).

Permafrost is an important factor in the process of surface and subsurface water exchange, regulating subterranean and surface water flows into the network of rivers. When the exchange becomes unbalanced, it leads to an intensified interaction between permafrost and fresh water that contributes to an increased transience of bodies of water such as lakes and lakelets. When internal ice layers melt, the unfrozen open ground turns into lakes filled with ground water rich in minerals. Moved by strong winds, such lakes can migrate at a rate of 5–10 metres per year across the territory. While remaining still, the lakes generated by melting permafrost burn the ground, producing an effect that Eveny refer to as a *khokki necherek* or, translated from the Eveny language, the 'hot teapot' effect. If a hot teapot is put on ice, the teapot will melt it, producing a shallow hole. The mobile lakes are producing similar shallow holes just like hot teapots.

Strong winds play a crucial regulatory role, since, moved by the winds, lakes are prevented from burning or heating the ground further. By changing location, such lakes provide the space for the permafrost to reconstitute its layers. Hence, the permafrost manifests an amazing plasticity or capacity to retain equilibrium between receiving and giving the ice form. In that sense, Arctic winds and transient lakes act like a natural sculpting mechanism that first deforms and then reforms the ice grounds. Wind acts as a powerful agent, making the lake follow the direction the wind blows. The interactive dynamic between wind and a migrating lake challenges the fixity of the landscape by exercising their own constitutive and reconstitutive power.

According to Eveny, migrating lakes are both a good and a bad sign: on the one hand, a transient lake is an indicator that permafrost is melting, but on the other hand, owing to their capacity for transience, it allows the ground to reproduce or reconstitute the ice formations that it loses while melting. Such natural ice reconstitution may happen over one winter; however, if temperatures are not cold enough it often leads to a number of cryogenic catastrophes. All of the above only intensifies the instability of an already shaky and movable surface consisting of marshy hollows, ravines and gullies. When all the natural protective layers needed for containing movements within subsurface grounds are destroyed or get out of balance, the internal grounds become unstable and erupt as a landslide.

Here we are dealing with quite a sensitive landscape characterized by a high likelihood of transience, eruption, movability and flammability. Moving across such a sensitive landscape always promises a

Figure 2.2. *Deep hollow is about to trigger collapse of the mountain. © Olga Ulturgasheva*

variety of risks throughout all seasons. In the perception of Eveny reindeer herders, permafrost has always been an enormous animating force and animist shape-shifter, involved in an ever-changing, uneasy relationship with its surface layer, the land. It is also a powerful imaginative and transformative force that animates and changes the shape of the earth, just like the reindeer from the aetiological myth. As a non-human powerful person, subterranean ice grounds can be generous and nurturing as they replenish mountain streams and local rivers along which Eveny move. Or they can change their mood, erupting suddenly and causing huge obstacles for human movement along rivers and streams. Such land is saturated with its capacity for transience and mobility, making lakes move and mountains disappear.

Migrating lakes and collapsing mountains point to the profoundly deterritorializing effect of melting permafrost. These manifestations of transience, plasticity and changeability serve as signifiers of the modes of co-constitution and connectivity that enliven and animate life forms. This transformable, highly animate nature of permafrost has always been part and parcel of a responsive social world, as the shape-shifting cryogenic landscape has necessitated a high scale of human–animal mobility and sociality extending beyond humans. Hence, permafrost serves as a matrix for hyper-animation where an interactive, transformative dynamic is activated by the movements and plasticity of life forms that are continuously erupting, co-constituting, reconstituting, submerging or emerging again. The latest transformations within the matrix magnify the powerful agency of a shape-shifting landscape and intensify the fragility of humans threatened by a complex dynamic of Anthropocenic processes.

Tears of the Earth

In two Eveny reindeer herding communities in northeast Siberia where I conducted research, the latest environmental transformations are manifested in a flux of the interconnected events all triggered by permafrost thaw. The sense of entanglement with which events unfold is becoming more and more pervasive as permafrost thaw drives a sequence of other destructive events, the impact of which proliferates erratically in all possible directions. Therefore, the directions the changes take become increasingly hard to predict by locals.

Since a large part of the area in which Eveny live and move is covered by boreal, coniferous forest, this particular part of the land is highly vulnerable to the impact of wildfires caused by human carelessness in the vicinity of roads constructed by the industrial sector and utilized for the transportation of natural resources. Due to prolonged periods of very dry and hot days, it is often lightning that causes fires. In the Soviet past when wildfire-fighters were well paid and had the appropriate equipment to fight large-scale fire – including helicopters and planes – professional fire-fighters played a crucial role in containing and extinguishing fires. Since all of this institutional support is no longer properly maintained, the only means Eveny have at hand is their own community efforts. Without the necessary back-up and due support, the effect of their fire-fighting remains almost minimal. But, as Adriana Petryna's recent account of Californian wildfires has shown, even with the most up-to-date state support, the models of fire-spread and technologies of fire suppression have failed to catch up with a new type of fire hurricanes. According to Petryna, the accelerated rate at which the phenomenon of wildfire overtakes the technology of its suppression is such that any human projection of its behaviour is bound to fail, with dire consequences for emergency responders (Petryna 2018: 585).

In the Siberian case, fire-fighting techniques are also constrained by the limited capacity of the fire-fighters to perceive the fire-spread in its full scale of velocity. The speed of the fire-spread varies and has a capacity for deception that local fire-fighters fail to read, even if they have indeed completed their task of extinguishing a fire properly. The fire can break out after several weeks of quiet and invisible smouldering in the thick layer of moss and set a large area of forest aflame in no time. Over the past two decades the forest fires have become an annual phenomenon and one of the decisive factors that contributes to the appearance of huge sinkholes and ravines, leaving the surface perforated. Forest fires impact the land to such an extent that ravines drop down by as much as a few dozen metres, while leaving internal layers of permafrost open and unprotected from intense heatwaves during summer. As a result, the temperature regime of internal ice structures rises significantly, intensifying further degradation of permafrost. All of the latter adds up to a considerable amount of detrimental change already going on underneath the surface layer and increases the likelihood of such phenomena as collapsing mountains, landslides and snow avalanches.

Since 2015, Eveny reindeer herders have been annually inundated by an unusual amount of precipitation and by the rapidly changing nature of floods. Quickly flooding rivers have lately become the norm rather than the exception. The speed of the development of floods has significantly increased. If in the past it would take one week of prolonged rains for a river to flood, now a river can rapidly flood within half a day. The speed with which river floods develop affects the condition of roads and migration paths used by reindeer herders, as the roads become quickly destroyed by flash floods.

Apart from the overwhelming amount of precipitation, reindeer herders attribute the changing nature of eruptive floods to the impact of forest fires, the effect of which is non-linear and multidirectional. Reindeer herders are particularly devastated to see how the pastures rich in lichen are being quickly destroyed by wildfire. An Eveny elder, Vasily Keymetinov-Bargachan, informed me that 'Eveny shamans referred to forest fires as *tor ingamta*', which translates from Eveny as 'tears of the earth'. According to Bargachan, 'the earth is crying now … it cries with forest fires as every forest fire is a tear of the earth'. Given the speed with which permafrost melts, such an analogy is not just a poetic metaphor. Comparison of fire with tears might be viewed as counterintuitive or contradicting the basic scientific laws, but this impression will be deceptive. Since permafrost-bound land consists of ground saturated with ice, the Eveny reindeer herders' observations make the connection between the frozen, ice-bound land and tears, as both consist of water as the former turns into liquid after large-scale wildfire strikes. The earth saturated with ice acts as a powerful animistic force that can respond to anthropogenic destructions with sadness and tears, just like a reindeer or a human being.

Moreover, the frozen layers of the earth turn liquid because fire destroys the layer that is hosting complex root systems branching in the soil. Acting as a natural shield for the internal frozen ground, these woven, branching roots protect permafrost from degradation. Alongside roots and branches, fire destroys the most valuable protective layer that mainly consists of lichen. The lichen layer plays quite an important role as it safeguards the temperature regime of the entire ground ecosystem. While lichen has always been a vital element of reindeer diet, it also holds a central place in what Eveny call *bilaek* – a web of mercifulness in which each element is at the mercy and care of another element.[4] According to Nikolai Neustroyev, an elder of the community of Tompo, the notion of *bilaek* implies that 'humans have always remained at the mercy of wild and semi-domesticated reindeer; reindeer have been at the mercy of lichen, which in turn has been at the mercy of the land which has stayed solid owing to mercifulness of lichen'. Since all elements in this human–non-human community have been bound by inter-reliance, their safety and continuance are determined by a symmetrical network of merciful dependence. If such an important element and crucial environmental variable as lichen is led to extinction, the entire system will experience destabilization of temperature balance, triggering further degradation of permafrost.

The disruption to the forest vegetation inflicted by wildfires simultaneously expands into the animal world, driving an escalated migration of wild species which try to escape environmental disasters in neighbouring regions. According to Eveny of Sebyan, people are now dealing with the rapidly changing behaviour of bears that do not follow established rules concerning human–bear interaction and whose behaviour is getting ever more erratic. What had maintained peaceful coexistence and properly sustained boundaries between humans and local bears is now being challenged by 'refugee bears' fleeing areas of boreal forest destroyed by fires. The challenge confronting Eveny is the unpredictability of these 'refugee bears' that do not follow conventions, rules and mutual expectations known and followed by local bears. Since bears are territorial and very defensive of the area they mark through scratching and rubbing trees, their sense of territoriality is challenged by wildfires destroying territorial boundaries. There has been a set of practices, taboos and rituals addressing the uncertainty and ambiguity of the animal world; accumulated knowledge about bears among reindeer herders does indeed revolve around this established set of rules. Features of the Circumpolar bear ceremonialism precisely point to this set of rules that shape and affect humans' relations with the bear (see Hallowell 1926; Kwon 1999; Brightman et al. 2012 and others). However, the dramatic speed with which the latest environmental changes have happened is also affecting this well-established mode of human–animal mutuality. While fleeing conflagrant forests in the Russian Far East, the bears lose the sense of what constitutes a specific territory.

When disoriented and desperate, they tend to attack people and domestic reindeer erratically.

Furthermore, the population of domestic reindeer is rapidly decreasing due to significantly increasing numbers of wolves; these constitute one of the major threats to highly valued reindeer. Wolves require constant attention from reindeer herders as they demonstrate astonishingly high levels of adaptability. According to one experienced reindeer herder and hunter, wolves adapt quickly because they are highly observant predators with a very high potential for learning. They learn from each other as they gain and transmit their knowledge and skills to young wolves quite quickly. Since they attack in packs, young wolves learn from more experienced ones when participating in attacks on reindeer. They know when to retreat in good time and know when to return and launch a collective attack on herds of reindeer. He says:

> They attack the reindeer as if they are their property. Unlike bears, they don't have any sense of social boundaries and respect for humans and reindeer. They always observe humans and know when a person has a rifle and doesn't have it. They become blunt and reckless when we don't have rifles at hand. Now they are taking the power over our reindeer as reindeer herders fail to protect them.

The unruly bears and highly insidious and masterful wolves have the potential to exceed the limits of tolerability, while stretching the human capacity for resilience too thin. Maintenance of the human capacity for resilience depends upon keeping many of the environmental variables within tolerable limits (Eriksen 2016: 126–27). It is the tolerable limit to which humans adapted while utilizing a toolbox of skills, knowledge and things accumulated by generations of experts and which provide actors with the means to engage with ever-changing conditions. When such variables as unruly bears or wolves reach the edge of a tolerable limit, i.e. becoming more dangerous and unpredictable than ever before, the situation requires an amplification of the human capacity to adjust and accommodate to whatever emerges in accordance with an accumulated fund of knowledge.

Cosmo-Geo-Ecological Knowledge

What constitutes the Eveny fund of knowledge? Reindeer herders build on their own skills and knowledge, highlighting the ever-increasing importance of a mobile lifestyle. Maintaining mobility is a vital element of their toolbox of skills which is centred on mobility and flexibility. One of the features that characterize the Eveny technique of survival has always been a special emphasis on the lightness of their material technologies and mobile infrastructure.

Easily movable tents, luggage and belongings, as well as a preparedness to move, instantly assured that people had a better chance of surviving and staying safe in the taiga. Mobility, specifically movement with their domestic reindeer, has been a predominant framework through which Eveny experience and understand the world and is a central component of their livelihoods which revolve around the seasonal cycle of reindeer migration. Reindeer, sledges, tents and skis have been the core aspects of their livelihoods; the idea of moving along one's family migration route is meaningful both to Eveny living in reindeer herding camps in the forest and to those living in small villages and urban centres.

Difficulties in getting from the villages to the reindeer herding camps and pastures and vice versa continue to condition logistical and psychological preparedness for risky situations. As one Eveny elder instructed:

> You have to travel light but make sure you bring all necessary stuff yourself. The people who are able to survive are the ones who move between camps a lot and always have a tent, a bunch of ropes, a variety of light leather and plastic bags, a reindeer skin mat to sleep on, kettle, tea, drinking mugs, axe, knife and a box of matches. All of that has to be neatly organized so that you can pack your stuff within minutes.

This emphasis on lightness, constant alertness, organization of things inside the tent and readiness to flee the onset of disaster has been shaped in response to the need to escape environmental dangers in time, including floods, landslides and forest fires.

These strategies continue to be taught to the younger generations, together with the habit of reacting calmly to any sudden environmental calamities, even if they feel panicked inside. Although Eveny develop adaptive and accommodating rather than mitigating strategies, the reindeer herders, who have hardly contributed to the causes of dramatic climate change, never turn to debates about who is responsible (and therefore should pay) for the negative consequences that people are experiencing. Instead, they focus on the survival strategies, skills and means they have at hand. Eveny environmental knowledge is concerned with understanding how to cope with dynamic transformations; rather than seeking to stabilize an ecosystem for maximum predictability as most geoscientists and engineers would do, they are more centred on devising coping strategies that build on their own patterns of mobility and observational skills. The emphasis on flexibility and alertness also highlights that a broader set of variables is required for taking a decision on a plan for action. For example, people continue to rely on divination practices centred on a ritual with a shoulder blade of a wild reindeer.[5] In the absence of any scientific predictive device, this practice attempts to generate a reading out of uncertainty. According to an experienced Eveny herder and hunter of the community of Tompo: 'One has to keep the dried shoulder blade of a recently hunted wild reindeer over the fire until one sees the first cracks. The cracks that appear on the shoulder may predict whether the disaster is on its way, from which direction the disaster may come and in which approximate form'. Unlike in southern Siberia and Mongolia, the ritual does not require a specialist diviner with the status of a respected medium for communication with the spirit world; any hunter or reindeer herder is able to make sense of the cracks according to their own individual reading. Reindeer herders carry out the divination ritual just before taking a long-distance trip, usually undertaken when their reindeer require a change of pastures. If the shoulder blade burnt before a forthcoming trip cracks along a straight line, the trip is meant to be uneventful and smooth. If the crack creates a hole in the blade, it is understood as a sign of potential misfortune that can be very hard to avert.

Techniques to predict the future include not only meticulous observations of the present, including signs appearing on a reindeer shoulder blade, but also an attempt to prevent calamity by appeasing the spirits of the land who, when properly fed and not disturbed by the loud presence of humans or their greedy behaviour, do not cause harm. People understand that the chances to contain the threat from powerful non-human forces may increase if they feed the fireplace and give the first piece of the hunted game to the land, as earth deities respond by providing benevolent protection. The ritual of appeasing the spirits of the land is aimed at containing their whims and encouraging their benign protective influence.

The whimsical nature of permafrost-bound land has been acknowledged by geoscientists. In my conversations with Russian permafrost specialists based in the regional city of Yakutsk, I learnt that they too struggle to predict the timing of shifts in permafrost. What is clear to them is that permafrost is degrading faster than natural scientists have ever estimated and the thaw is rapidly changing the topography of the land. These geoscientists – whose observations are based on scientific measuring taken over the decades – concur that the shifts inside the ice formations often follow decentring and unsystematic moves. These moves are not based on a linear, proportional relationship between cause and effect. Since such shifts are aleatory by their nature, it is never certain what direction a sequence of further changes in internal layers will take. The radius of such a shift may be short and abrupt. Alternatively, the velocity of the shift may suddenly oscillate, reach the surface layer and erupt with a landslide or mudflow. They find it increasingly hard to predict when the next disaster is likely to strike, as shifts within internal ice layers are becoming more unpredictable.

If the Big Science claims to privileged knowledge are predominantly held by mainstream institutional structures of climate science generously funded and backed up by authoritative bodies, here the scientists seem to be candid in admitting the limitations of their knowledge and lack of capacity to provide up-to-date devices for data sensing, sampling and forecasting. By offering such a perspective on the unpredictability of shifts, geoscientists were candid in highlighting that Russian geoscience is unable to provide proper monitoring of permafrost. The latter would require a long-term effort of observations and multidisciplinary research, jointly conducted by geoscientists, seismologists and glaciologists who currently lack the appropriate technology for monitoring and whose research is significantly underfunded these days. The situation with underfunding and lack of monitoring and sampling has not been unique to Russia, as a focus on permafrost and multidisciplinary, collaborative research on the cryosphere in general has not been prioritized by academia. This field of scholarly inquiry has been underfunded and understudied across all Arctic regions. Ann-Maria Virkkala and her colleagues pertinently stress that the comprehensive data and indicators of environmental changes in the Siberian Arctic and Subarctic, alongside other permafrost-bound areas in the American and Scandinavian Arctic that are likely to experience rapid permafrost thaw, are scarce (see Virkkala et al. 2019). Since these regions are under-sampled, the lack of data suggests that scientists do not understand the whole range of changes that global warming might cause, nor do they reach out to indigenous reindeer herders and hunters for any updates and observations, and if they even do or did so, the expertise and effort offered by indigenous experts are not recognized and properly documented in scientific papers.

Such monitoring was possible in the Soviet period, before the late 1980s, as geoscientific research was well funded and, in addition, involved topographical guidance by local reindeer herders whose knowledge of the landscape and survival skills always guaranteed the safe and sound completion of any geomorphological project. In Soviet Russia, geoscientists would never have dared to embark on an arduous, long-distance journey through impassable forest and risky rocks without the guidance and help of reindeer herders. Some of them openly admit that without reindeer herders' knowledge of the landscape, they would never have been able to provide monitoring of permafrost and generate scientific data on permafrost (see Alekseiev 2010). However, it was not only reindeer herders' guidance that helped geoscientists to survive the unknown and hostile terrain of northeast Siberia but also the Eveny habit of staying alert to any subtle changes and signs generated in the course of divination practices.

According to their personal recollection, while in the field scientists would never question the reindeer herders' knowledge, as the reindeer herders' consideration of potential risk scenarios and their repertoire of mitigating and adapting strategies were always wider and less constrained by scientific requirements aimed at maximizing the sense of reliability and transparency of those scenarios. In personal recollections, one permafrost scientist told me that:

> An experienced permafrost scientist, Gavrilov worked for a long time in the Siberian Arctic. He was the first who initiated the establishment of the research stations for observations of permafrost in the region. He always relied on local guides, and among them the most important people were Eveny reindeer herders. Any expedition to the field was not possible without them. At that time (around the fifties/sixties) there were zero communication devices, and no radio or telecommunication equipment to reach out for help was available. But for some reason, when he was just about to arrive in their camp, the reindeer herders were already moving towards him riding their reindeer. They would greet him and help with transportation of research equipment and heavy luggage. All the people in the camp already knew that he was coming, and cooked food and warm dry clothes were already waiting for him. What he told me is that, to ensure they are prepared to help and welcome him, the reindeer herders instructed him to do the following: before embarking on his long journey he should look in the direction his trip will take and shout forcefully in Eveny language: 'It's me Vladimir, I am on my way – I'll see you soon!' Vladimir learnt the indigenous language and was fluent in the Eveny language, as he understood that speaking Eveny was vital for his survival. People would get this message even in the most remote locations in the Arctic taiga and tundra.

At that time, when aircraft would land on frozen rivers and drop inexperienced researchers, reindeer herders were pivotal for their transportation. Reindeer herders were crucial for the scholars' adaptation in the field – reindeer herders taught them how to live and survive in local conditions.

In this particular instance the permafrost scientist describes what Eveny would call the practice of sending one's *djuluchen* towards one's destination. By announcing out loud his intention to undertake a trip, his colleague Gavrilov sent his *djuluchen* towards a camp of the reindeer herders where he was planning to arrive soon. The practice of sending *djuluchen* ('spirit that travels ahead' or 'forerunner') forward before one's travel is widespread among Eveny reindeer herders and hunters in northeastern Siberia. As I have shown elsewhere (see Ulturgasheva 2012, 2016), the concept of *djuluchen* illuminates the human potential to foreshadow one's own future by sending one's own partible component ahead of oneself into the future along the envisioned trajectory. According to Eveny, *djuluchen* is an inherent component of a human and animal personhood, which in literal translation reads as a 'shadow that falls or runs ahead of a person'.

It is a nomadic concept which signifies the partible or separable component of human personhood (some locals refer to it as 'one's travelling spirit') which departs ahead of its owner and arrives at the destination prior to the owner's actual appearance. Prior to the person's arrival, people have already heard and seen the arriving person's *djuluchen*, which is seen as a shadow that imitates the body image of the arriving person and even reproduces the movements and sounds of the person's walking around the camp and unpacking. Without even knowing that the person is travelling towards their camp, people may recognize that a specific known person will arrive in their camp sometime soon. The *djuluchen* travelling spirit awaits his or her owner, who reunites with the *djuluchen* upon his or her 'actual' arrival.

The informal recollection of how vital reindeer herders' expertise and skills of living on and from the land were for a scientist's survival illustrates that, when it comes to the question of safety, any knowledge, especially of the sort that helps people to stay safe and survive, is utilized as long as it proves to be effective. Listening and looking for the signs, including *djuluchen*, is part and parcel of the repertoire of flexibility that Eveny reindeer herders have mastered. The repertoire includes a broader set of variables required for taking a decision on a plan for action. This set of variables contains clear instances of thinking that encompass non-linear, acausal information emerging out of a rather wider field than one can access by linear, cause-and-effect thinking. In other words, this strategy draws on more than one way of knowing. By teaching the scientist how to send his *djuluchen* forward, the reindeer herders expanded his understanding of flexibility. Moreover, the account by the scientist, who has been convinced by the instrumentality and effectiveness of the practice informed by animist ways of connecting and moving, provides an example of how distinct bodies of knowledge could be activated in mutually formative and inclusive ways. I view the latter account as a rare instance of the emergence of cosmo-geo-ecological knowledge, i.e. knowledge that combines several cosmovisions in a symmetrical, synergistic manner.

But this has never been acknowledged and documented formally. The contribution of reindeer herders has never been properly recognized by official Soviet and post-Soviet accounts as evidence of the uncertainties of scientific knowledge.

What we can also learn from the instances of partnership provided above is that the collective effort aimed at surviving the extreme conditions of the Siberian Arctic compelled the humility of the scientists and their readiness to listen and follow the animist rules of engagement with the land and resulted in genuine symmetry between them and reindeer herders. According to the principles of *bilaek*, the partnership worked because the scientists knew that they were at the mercy of the Eveny and their reindeer. As soon as reciprocity in the web of mercifulness is dismissed or disrupted, the collaboration turns into plain extraction and exploitation.

Conclusion

This discussion has engaged with two distinct onto-epistemological dimensions of environmental change in the Siberian Arctic, namely, an animist cosmovision expressed through *bilaek*, i.e. a web of mercifulness and interconnectedness, and a geo-cryological world vision centred on the perception of permafrost as a scientific object and technogenic obstacle. The reindeer-morphic model of the world discussed above is central for understanding the animist cosmovision of *bilaek*. In accordance with *bilaek*, Eveny engage with and devise their strategies for dealing with the latest dynamic of climate change. In the absence of any infrastructural and state support, they continue to rely on their practical knowledge which revolves around their relations with cosmologically vital non-humans such as reindeer and lichen. For reindeer herders, the permafrost-bound land has always been a complex and dynamically interconnected ecology, highly sensitive to any environmental pressures, including the ones induced by climate change. Their responses to the latter do not privilege humans and are far from exemplifying an arrogant anthropocentrism inherent to capitalist, highly individualized societies. Their outlook is neither humano-centric nor exclusively centred on the non-human or extra-human, as equal attention to both has been crucial for devising effective responses and survival strategies.

While recognizing the importance of scholarly inquiry with a focus on bio-, techno-animacies/intimacies and the post-humanist ontology of climate change, this material has shown that an animist cosmovision is more relevant for understanding Eveny relations with environmental calamities and their responses to them. It is the animist sociality that continues to inform their current modes of adaptability and techniques of adaptation, accommodation and adjustment. The reindeer herders' perception and understanding of the permafrost, together with their responses to the latest changes, offer us an encompassing view of the animism which recognizes the centrality of non-human actors (reindeer, bears, lakes, winds, mountains, weather and permafrost) and their powerful impact on human safety and well-being. Eveny responses and strategies show that they do not divide the world into human versus the rest of nature. They do not posit a human being as a dominant figure standing at the top of an evolutionary ladder, as in a destructive type of anthropocentrism, nor do they posit human exceptionalism. Although their animist livelihood and adaptability revolve around their own safety, their understanding of safety centres on the symmetry of human and non-human elements.

This account of a collaboration between natural scientists and indigenous knowledge holders particularized how Siberian Eveny reindeer herders' knowledge of the permafrost-bound land enabled scientific research on the Siberian permafrost conducted by Soviet Russian geomorphologists. The environmental knowledge of Eveny reindeer herders, informed and shaped by animist relationality and shamanic cosmology, was critical not only for geoscientists' physical survival but also for shaping the scientists' engagement with and understanding of the Siberian cryosphere. The scientists' informal recollections and personal accounts of their research conducted in the field alongside reindeer herders provided a rare glimpse into how the reliance and dependence of geoscientists on Eveny reindeer herders' knowledge illuminate an opportunity for generating a new type of onto-epistemological knowledge missed by scientists. The inability to see the opportunity was due to a closed mindset which was unable to perceive a promising space for production of a cosmo-geo-ecological knowledge. This is the kind of knowledge that would enable a more complex, more encompassing understanding of the relational networks which are pivotal for forming future climate strategies and providing for human security.

If those instances had been properly acknowledged and documented, they could have made a difference in challenging the dominant knowledge paradigm built on exclusivity and the nature/culture divide. The discussion of the lack of recognition of the reindeer herders' expertise, aside from the lack of monitoring and under-sampling, emphasizes the limitations of the dominant modernist cosmovision exclusively centred on humans at the top of the hierarchy. This chapter partly responds to the need to pay tribute and do justice to Eveny reindeer herders' contributions to scientific studies of permafrost and partly shows how the effort of symmetrically co-mobilizing heterogeneous epistemologies is critical if science (in its plurality rather than singularity) is to respond adequately to the contemporary climate crisis. In a context where indigenous knowledge holders constantly find their views erased, or subordinated to 'more scientific' views and more dominant political agendas at national and international levels, such recognition (although informal and unpublicized) represents a much needed step towards decompartmentalization, the recalibration of knowledge production processes, and the destabilization of the science paradigm as Foucauldian power/knowledge.

Acknowledgements

This chapter is based on research funded by the Arctic Social Sciences Program at the US National Science Foundation (ARC-1424042). The final stage of this research was supported by the ERC Synergy Grant COSMOVIS/856543 under the European Union's Horizon 2020 research and innovation programme. Preliminary versions of this chapter were presented at the Departments of Social Anthropology of the University of Manchester and the University of Edinburgh, the Institute of Social and Cultural Anthropology of the University of Oxford and at the International Symposium on 'Indigenous Communities and Climate Change in North America and Russia' convened by Candis Callison at Princeton University (USA) in December 2018. I am particularly grateful to Barbara Bodenhorn for her highly thoughtful and perceptive suggestions on the earlier version of the manuscript. I extend my deepest gratitude to all Eveny interlocutors who patiently shared their time and precious insights. Egden Teken.

Olga Ulturgasheva is a Senior Lecturer/Associate Professor in Social Anthropology at the University of Manchester, UK. Over the last twenty years she has been engaged in a number of anthropological and cross-disciplinary studies exploring animism, human and non-human personhood, childhood and youth, climate change, resilience and adaptation patterns in Siberia, American Arctic and Amazonia. She is the author of *Narrating the Future in Siberia: Childhood, Adolescence and Autobiography among the Eveny* (Berghahn Books, 2012) and co-editor of *Animism in Rainforest and Tundra: Personhood, Animals, Plants and Things in Contemporary Amazonia and Siberia* (Berghahn Books, 2012). She serves as a Principal Investigator and co-Principal Investigator for two large international, collaborative research projects focusing on the dynamic of climate change in Alaska, Siberia and the Russian Far East funded by the US National Science Foundation and the European Research Council.

Notes

1. See Bodenhorn and Ulturgasheva 2016, 2017; Ulturgasheva and Bodenhorn 2016.
2. There are several types of creation myths in Eveny folklore with distinct plots and different sets of characters, both human and non-human. I have heard this version of the creation myth from several sources but it was first documented and published by Eveny folklorists, Khristofor Dutkin and Vasily Robbek (1978).
3. The analysis of radical alterity emerging out of the Amerindian ethnography of shamanic societies (Viveiros de Castro 1998; Descola 1996; Vilaca 2002) is often associated with the methodology of the 'ontological turn' (Henare, Holbraad and Wastell 2006; Holbraad and Pedersen 2018), which is heavily and continuously criticized by Eurocentric scholars. The debate revolving around the 'ontological turn' questions such fundamental concepts within anthropology as culture, ethnocentrism and reflexivity. The debate between those who advocate the ontological turn and its opponents remains to be resolved, due to the profound disagreements of both parties on the questions of difference and translation. See the examples of criticism of the 'ontological turn' by Bessire and Bond (2014), Boellstorff (2016) and Heywood (2012).
4. This discussion resonates with the account of a Canadian Métis scholar, Zoe Todd, who looked at human-fish relations in the Inuvialuit community of Paulatuuq in the western Canadian Arctic (2014) and among her native Métis in the Lake Winnipeg watershed (2016) through the concept

of refraction, i.e. 'a refraction in which we acknowledge that fish do a significant amount of labour in co-constituting our reciprocal responsibilities to one another' (2018: 68). While drawing from the writings of indigenous scholars, including the work by Canadian First Nation legal scholar, John Borrows (2014), Todd relevantly highlights that 'fish have borne witness to – and resisted – the incredible upheavals of Indigenous livelihoods, laws, language and lands over the course of the last few centuries. We need the principles of reciprocity, care, tenderness and trust that are centred in the "dynamic-but-rooted" (Borrows 2014) Indigenous legal orders in places like *amiskwaciwâskahikan*' (2018: 73).

5. Russian ethnographer Vladimir Bogoraz also documented a similar divinatory practice among the Reindeer Chukchee, who used the scapula bone of the domesticated reindeer to predict the future. He described the divination ritual as follows: 'The Reindeer Chukchee use for divination only the shoulder-blade of the domesticated reindeer. The animal, in most cases, is killed for this particular purpose ... The bone is taken raw, and the meat carefully cleaned from it. Then a small piece of burning coal is kept close to its centre. It is fanned, by means of blowing or light swinging, till the bone is carbonized, and gives the first crack. After the performance, the burned place is immediately broken through and reduced to crumbs, but the bone itself is added to the common kitchen-stock used for trying tallow ... Usually one vertical crack is formed, with various ramifications above and below' (Bogoraz 1975: 487).

References

Alekseiev, Vladimir. 2010. *V krayu vechnogo kholoda* [In the Region of Permanent Cold]. Novosibirsk: Novosibirskoye Akademicheskoye Izdatel'stvo 'GEO'.
———. 2016. *Prityazheniye Merzloi Zemli* [Appeal of the Frozen Land]. Novosibirsk: Novosibirskoye Akademicheskoye Izdatel'stvo 'GEO'.
Allen, Craig, David Breshears and Nate McDowell. 2015. 'On Underestimation of Global Vulnerability to Tree Mortality and Forest Die-off from Hotter Drought in the Anthropocene', *Ecosphere* 6(8): 1–55.
Bessire, Lucas and David Bond. 2014. 'Ontological Anthropology and the Deferral of Critique', *American Ethnologist* 41: 440–56.
Bignall, Simone, Steve Hemming and Daryle Rigney. 2016. 'Three Ecosophies for the Anthropocene: Environmental Governance, Continental Posthumanism and Indigenous Expressivism', *Deleuze Studies* 10(40): 455–78.
Bird-David, Nurit. 1999. '"Animism" Revisited: Personhood, Environment and Relational Epistemology', *Current Anthropology* 40: 67–91.
———. 2006. 'Animistic Epistemology: Why Do Some Hunter-Gatherers Not Depict Animals?', *Ethnos* 71(1): 33–50.
Bodenhorn, Barbara. 2000. 'It's Good to Know Who Your Relatives Are but We Were Taught to Share with Everybody: Shares and Sharing among Inupiaq Households', *Ethnological Studies* 53: 27–60.

———. 2004. '"He Used to Be My Relative": Exploring the Bases of Relatedness among Inupiat of Northern Alaska', in J. Carsten (ed.), *Cultures of Relatedness: New Approaches to the Study of Kinship*. Cambridge: Cambridge University Press, pp. 128–48.

Bodenhorn, Barbara and Olga Ulturgasheva. 2016. 'Northern Futures? Climate, Geopolitics and Local Realities, Executive Summary', *Northern Notes* 46 (autumn/winter): 30–35.

———. 2017. 'Climate Strategies: Thinking through Arctic Examples', *Philosophical Transactions of the Royal Society A* 375(2095): 20160363.

Boellstorff, Tom. 2016. 'For Whom the Ontology Turns: Theorizing the Digital Real', *Current Anthropology* 57(4): 387–407.

Bogoraz, Vladimir. 1975. *The Chukchee*. New York: AMS Press.

Borrows, John. 2014. 'Physical Philosophies: Freedom and Indigenous Peoples', Public talk, Pierre Elliott Trudeau Foundation Summer Institute, Osoyoos, Canada.

Braidotti, Rosi. 2009. *The Posthuman*. London: Polity Press.

Brightman, Marc, Vanessa Grotti and Olga Ulturgasheva (eds). 2012. *Animism in Rainforest and Tundra: Personhood, Animals, Plants and Things in Contemporary Amazonia and Siberia*. Oxford: Berghahn Books.

Chu, Pey-Yi. 2020. *The Life of Permafrost: A History of Frozen Earth in Russian and Soviet Science*. Toronto: University of Toronto Press.

Cruikshank, Julie. 2005. *Do Glaciers Listen? Local Knowledge, Colonial Encounters, and Social Imagination*. Seattle, WA: University of Washington Press.

DeConto, R. et al. 2012. 'Past Extreme Warming Events Linked to Massive Carbon Release from Thawing Permafrost', *Nature* 484: 87–91.

de la Cadena, Marisol. 2010. 'Indigenous Cosmopolitics in the Andes: Conceptual Reflections beyond "Politics"', *Cultural Anthropology* 25(2): 334–70.

———. 2015. *Earth Beings: Ecologies of Practice across Andean Worlds*. Durham, NC: Duke University Press.

de la Cadena, Marisol and Mario Blaser (eds). 2018. *A World of Many Worlds*. Durham, NC: Duke University Press.

Descola, Philipp. 1996. 'Constructing Natures: Symbolic Ecology and Social Practice', in P. Descola and G. Pálsson (eds), *Nature and Society: Anthropological Perspectives*. London and New York: Routledge, pp. 82–102.

DiNovelli-Lang, Danielle. 2013. 'The Return of the Animal: Posthumanism, Indigeneity and Anthropology', *Environmental Sciences* 4(1): 137–56.

Dutkin, Khristofor and Vasily Robbek. 1978. 'Myth about the Origin of the Earth and Human Being in Eveny Folklore', in N. Emelyanova and V. Petrova (eds), *Epicheskoye Tvorchsetvo Narodov Sibiri i Dal'nego Vostoka* [Epic Creativity of the Peoples of Siberia and Far East]. Yakutsk: Yakuskiy Filial Izdatel'stva SO AN SSSR.

Eriksen, Thomas Hylland. 2016. *Overheating: An Anthropology of Accelerated Change*. London: Pluto Press.

Escobar, Arthuro. 2018. *Designs for the Pluriverse: Radical Interdependence, Autonomy, and the Making of Worlds*. Durham, NC: Duke University Press.

———. 2020. *Pluriversal Politics: The Real and the Possible*. Trans. David Frye. Durham, NC: Duke University Press.

Fortun, Kim. 2014. 'From Latour to Late Industrialism', *HAU: Journal of Ethnographic Theory* 4(1): 309–29.
Hallowell, Andrew Irving. 1926. 'Bear Ceremonialism in the Northern Hemisphere', *American Anthropologist* 28: 1–175.
Haraway, Donna. 2008. *When Species Meet*. Minneapolis: University of Minnesota Press.
Hastrup, Kirstin. 2013. 'The Ice as Argument. Topographical Mementos in the High Arctic', *Cambridge Anthropology* 31(1): 52–68.
Henare, Amiria, Martin Holbraad and Sari Wastell (eds). 2006. *Thinking through Things: Theorising Artefacts Ethnographically*. London: Routledge.
Heywood, Paolo. 2012. 'Anthropology and What There Is: Reflections on "Ontology"', *Cambridge Anthropology* 30: 143–51.
Hodder, Ian. 2014. 'The Entanglements of Human and Things: A Long-Term View', *New Literary History* 45(1): 19–36.
Holbraad, Martin and Morten Pedersen. 2018. *The Ontological Turn: An Anthropological Exposition*. Cambridge: Cambridge University Press.
Howell, Signe. 1984. *Society and Cosmos: Chewong of Peninsular Malaysia*. Oxford: Oxford University Press.
———. 2016. 'The Relationality of Species in Chewong Animistic Ontology', in B.E. Bertelsen and S. Bendixsen (eds), *Critical Anthropological Engagements in Human Alterity and Difference*. New York: Palgrave Macmillan, pp. 43–63.
Jamail, Dahr. 2019. *The End of Ice: Bearing Witness and Finding Meaning in the Path of Climate Disruption*. New York: The New Press.
Kirksey, Eben and Stefan Helmreich. 2010. 'The Emergence of Multispecies Ethnography', *Cultural Anthropology* 25(4): 545–76.
Kwon, Heonik. 1999. 'Play the Bear: Myth and Ritual in East Siberia', *History of Religions* 38(4): 373–87.
Lovejoy, Thomas. 2013. 'The Climate Change Endgame', *New York Times*, 21 January 2013. Retrieved 18 March 2020 from https://www.nytimes.com/2013/01/22/opinion/global/the-climate-change-endgame.html.
MacCormack, Patricia. 2012. *Posthuman Ethics: Embodiment and Cultural Theory*. Abingdon: Ashgate.
Moore, Amelia. 2015. 'Anthropocene Anthropology: Reconceptualizing Contemporary Global Change', *Journal of Royal Anthropological Institute* 22(1): 27–46.
Morton, Timothy. 2013. *Hyperobjects: Philosophy and Ecology after the End of the World*. Minneapolis: University of Minnesota Press.
Murphy, Michelle. 2008. 'Chemical Regimes of Living', *Environmental History* 13(4): 695–703.
Nekrasov, Igor and Viktor Deviatkin. 1974. *Morfologiya kriolitozony basseyna reki Yany i sopredel'nyakh raionov* [Morphology of Cryolitozone of the River Yana and Neighbouring Districts]. Novosibirsk: Nauka.
O'Reilly, Jessica. 2016. 'Sensing the Ice: Field Science, Models, and Expert Intimacy with Knowledge', *Journal of the Royal Anthropological Institute* 22(S1): 27–45.
Pedersen, Morten. 2001. 'Totemism, Animism and North Asian Indigenous Ontologies', *Journal of the Royal Anthropological Institute* 7(3): 411–27.

Petryna, Adriana. 2018. 'Wildfires at the Edges of Science: Horizoning Work amid Runaway Change', *Cultural Anthropology* 33(4): 570–95.
Physorg. 2021. 'Russia Forecasters Warn over Siberia Forest Fires', 23 March 2021. Retrieved 25 March 2021 from https://phys.org/news/2021-03-russia-siberia-forest.html.
Povinelli, Elizabeth. 2016. *Geontologies: A Requiem to Late Liberalism*. Durham, NC: Duke University Press.
Raffles, Hugh. 1999. 'Local Theory: Nature and the Making of the Amazonian Place', *Cultural Anthropology* 14(3): 323–60.
———. 2002. *In Amazonia*. Princeton, NJ: Princeton University Press.
———. 2011. *Insectopedia*. New York: Vintage Books.
Richardson, Kathleen. 2016. 'Animism: The Uncanny Personhood of Humanoid Machines', *Social Analysis* 60(1): 110–28.
Rival, Laura. 2012. 'Animism and the Meanings of Life', in M. Brightman, V. Grotti and O. Ulturgasheva (eds), *Animism in Rainforest and Tundra*. Oxford: Berghahn Books, pp. 69–82.
———. 2016. *Huaroni Transformations in Twenty-First-Century Ecuador: Treks into the Future of Time*. Tucson, AZ: The University of Arizona Press.
Shakhova, N. et al. 2010. 'Extensive Methane Venting to the Atmosphere from Sediments of the East Siberian Arctic Shelf', *Science* 327(5970): 1246–50.
Shapiro, Nicholas and Eben Kirksey. 2017. 'Chemo-ethnography: An Introduction', *Cultural Anthropology* 32(4): 481–93.
Streletskiy, Dmitry. 2021. 'Permafrost Degradation', in W. Haeberli and C. Whiteman (eds), *Snow and Ice-Related Hazards, Risks, and Disasters*, 2nd edition. London: Elsevier, pp. 297–322.
Streletskiy, Dmitry and Nikolai Shiklomanov. 2016. 'Arctic Cities through the Prism of Permafrost', in R. Orttung (ed.), *Sustaining Russia's Arctic Cities: Resource Politics, Migration, and Climate Change*. Oxford: Berghahn Books, pp. 201–20.
Thacker, Eugene. 2005. 'Biophilosophy for the Twenty-First Century', *CTheory*. Retrieved 31 March 2020 from https://journals.uvic.ca/index.php/ctheory/article/view/14452/5294.
Todd, Zoe. 2014. 'Fish Pluralities: Human-animal Relations and Sites of Engagement in Paulatuuq, Arctic Canada', *Etudes/Inuit/Studies* 38(1–2): 217–38.
———. 2016. 'From a Fishy Place: Examining Canadian State Law Applied in the *Daniels* Decision from the Perspective of Métis Legal Orders', *TOPIA: Canadian Journal of Cultural Studies* 36: 43–57.
———. 2018. 'Refracting the State Through Human-Fish Relations: Fishing, Indigenous Legal Orders and Colonialism in North/Western Canada', *Decolonization: Indigeneity, Education & Society* 7(1): 60–75.
Tsing, Anna. 1999. 'Becoming a Tribal Elder and Other Green Development Fantasies', in T. Li (ed.), *Transforming the Indonesian Uplands*. Abingdon: Taylor & Francis, pp. 157–200.
———. 2005. *Friction*. Princeton, NJ: Princeton University Press.
———. 2011. 'Arts of Inclusion or How to Love a Mushroom', *Australian Humanities Review* 50: 5–21.

Ulturgasheva, Olga. 2012. *Narrating the Future in Siberia: Childhood, Adolescence and Autobiography among the Eveny*. Oxford: Berghahn.

———. 2016. 'Spirit of the Future: Movement, Kinetic Distribution and Personhood among Siberian Eveny', *Social Analysis* 60(1): 56–73.

———. 2017. 'Ghosts of the Gulag in the Eveny World of the Dead', *Polar Journal* 7(1): 26–45.

Ulturgasheva, Olga and Barbara Bodenhorn. 2016. 'Arctic Futures? Climate, Geopolitics and Local Realities', *Witness the Arctic: Chronicles of the NSF Arctic Science Section* 20(3): 23–30.

Vilaca, Aparecida. 2002. 'Making Kin Out of Others in Amazonia', *Journal of the Royal Anthropological Institute* 8(2): 347–65.

Virkkala, A.-M. et al. 2019. 'Identifying Multidisciplinary Research Gaps across Arctic Terrestrial Gradients', *Environmental Research Letters* 14(12): 1–14.

Viveiros de Castro, Eduardo. 1998. 'Cosmological Deixis and Amerindian Perspectivism', *Journal of the Royal Anthropological Institute* 4(3): 469–88.

Weston, Kath. 2017. *Animate Planet: Making Visceral Sense of Living in a High-Tech Ecologically Damaged World*. Durham, NC: Duke University Press.

Willerslev, Rane. 2007. *Soul Hunters: Hunting, Animism, and Personhood among the Siberian Yukaghirs*. Berkeley, CA: University of California Press.

Willerslev, Rane and Olga Ulturgasheva. 2012. 'Revisiting the Animism versus Totemism Debate: Fabricating Persons among Eveny and Chukchi of Northeastern Siberia', in M. Brightman, V. Grotti and O. Ulturgasheva (eds), *Animism in Rainforest and Tundra: Personhood, Animals, Plants and Things in Contemporary Amazonia and Siberia*. Oxford: Berghahn Books, pp. 84–119.

Wolfe, Cary. 2010. *What Is Posthumanism?* Minneapolis: University of Minnesota Press.

CHAPTER 3

She'll Do What She Needs to Do

Rachel Nutaaq Ayałhuq Naŋinaaq Edwardson

I remember when I was around nineteen or twenty, my father, who was at the time the president of our regional Tribal Council, Iñupiat Community of the Arctic Slope, addressed a living room full of visitors in town covering a story on melting sea ice. They were pushing him to tell stories as a 'Native elder', about the devastation of the Arctic due to climate change. They were fishing for the same stories we often see in media from First Nations people around the world around the devastation and difficulties they are experiencing. My father, well versed in conversing with outsiders, responded:

> What do I think of climate change? I say bring it on. As Native people we've lived sustainably and in harmony with the earth for tens of thousands of years. And then these great big countries have only taken 200 years to unsettle everything. But the earth will never lose. She'll do what she needs to do. She'll clear the slate and then she'll start again. And as that happens, as things get colder or hotter, as storms get worse and droughts go longer, we Native people, we will be the only ones to survive, because we know how to live with the earth. So I say, bring it on.

My father's summation of climate change has always brought a wry smile to my face. Not because I share all of his views of how things might play out, but because he is a beautiful, gentle man with a heart big enough to hold all the pain and trauma of his childhood as a native person, big enough to soak his seven children with love, big enough to defend the rights of our people for the past fifty years and yet still with some room in it to share a cautionary tale with those who have tried to oppress him and our people since they first arrived to exploit our lands.

I do share my father's concerns about the way in which 'modern' humans have impacted our earth. Like him, I think powerful industrialized nations need a wake-up call. Climate change may be the biggest threat facing a multitude of unprepared developed and developing nations but as an Iñupiaq woman I cannot help feeling the approach being taken by most (even the most 'progressive') of these nations appears to be not just flawed, but actively avoiding the difficult conversations about the root cause.

Carbon emissions may well be creating the environmental conditions for irreversible climate change. But are not these emissions merely a symptom of the social, political and historical conditions that fixed this crisis in place many centuries ago? We were taught as young Iñupiaq children to observe a problem and understand its root cause before arriving at a solution. Using that approach, this crisis tracks much further back than industrial pollution and therefore, in order to be sustainable, the solutions will require a much deeper and much more uncomfortable interrogation of the system and fundamental drivers that created this crisis.

Understanding What Informs Our Being

Our people, the Iñupiat from Arctic Alaska, are members of the Inuit nation that spans almost the whole of the Circumpolar North. As Iñupiaq people, we are raised to observe, on a daily and hourly basis, the weather patterns, the changes in plant growth, the changes in animal migration patterns and behaviour. Our social, political, spiritual, emotional and physical existence is tied, on a day-to-day basis, to the health of the animals and plants in the ecosystem we are dependent upon. We have thrived in one of the harshest climates on the planet precisely because our lives and laws revolve around the core principles of sustainability and subsistence. Central to our ability to live sustainably for tens of thousands of years has been our focus as a people on looking holistically, inclusively and critically at all problems.

Our epistemological and ontological truths grow first from our environment and our place in its ecosystem. Like many First Nations peoples, our long-term and complex relationship with our environment fuels our understanding (through a daily lived experience) that we come from/are of the land, ocean/waterways, air/cosmos, and animals. We do not see ourselves as masters of the land or the ocean. Our dominance over the earth is neither realistic nor part of how we exist.

There are two fundamental Iñupiaq concepts, common to all Inuit communities – *nuna*, loosely meaning land, and *siḷa*, loosely meaning air/atmosphere – which may help to illustrate these core understandings of our Iñupiaq relationship to our environment.

In the Iñupiaq dictionary, by Dr Edna MacLean, *siḷa* is translated as 'air, atmosphere, weather'. *Nuna*, in the same dictionary, is translated as 'ground, tundra, earth: inland; country, territory: a citizen's nation-state' (MacLean 2014).

Our Elders Fannie Kuutuuq Akpik and Jana Pausauraq Harcharek discuss *siḷa* as follows: '*Siḷa* is the weather. It is also the atmosphere. Here's the *nuna*, or the land, and anything from the land into the moon, the sun, the stars – that's all *siḷa*. *Siḷa* has a soul in the same way we do as people in the same way animals do.'

Alaska Fairbanks Iñupiaq instructor, Ronald Brower, speaking about the concept of *siḷa*, says:

> *Siḷa* has many meanings that I know of. One, *siḷa* is within me, I breathe in *siḷa*. And then at night I could look into the sky and I could see the stars, so they said that *siḷa* is within us and infinitely far away. It can also be our breath. *Siḷa* imparts life to all living things and all living things must have *siḷa* to be alive. So from that we then enter into the spiritual realm of *siḷa*, which is then dealing with ourselves our inner selves and how we relate to the rest of the universe around us. (Brower 2013)

In this way, the very life force that is within us is also the weather around us and the life force that fuels the universe. *Siḷa* and *nuna* are vitally important to all aspects of the self and Iñupiaq way of life. Canadian Inuit writer Rachel Attituq Qitsualik describes *siḷa* and *nuna* this way:

> How was the weather behaving? That was always our primary concern upon rising from sleep. 'Go out and see the *siḷa*,' my father would instruct. We were to scan the horizon, practicing our powers of observation. Was there anything unusual, out of place, not in keeping with the *siḷa*? What was the aspect of *siḷa*? Calm? Thunderous? Threatening? What was the color of *siḷa*, gray, red or blue? The edge of *siḷa*, the horizon, what did it tell you? Was it dark? If so, a storm was on its way. Were the clouds white on gray, or gray on white, a critical difference. It was all-important to be able to read *siḷa*. Siḷa and nuna determined your existence. It was no wonder the word siḷa also meant 'wisdom.' A person with a 'large *siḷa*'

was wise… Even today, traditional Inuit wisdom maintains that the body has its own *siḷa*. *Siḷa* is the air and we who have our own air also have a part of *siḷa* – a part of its life force'. (Qitsualik 2018)

These concepts of *nuna* and *siḷa* may seem opaque or even romantic to those inexperienced with Inuit lifestyles. However, they illustrate the intertwining of the environment with our being and explain why we come to our relationship with the earth with humility. It's in this way that the complexity of Iñupiaq political and social systems rests in a set of understandings and tools for navigating life in a balanced and respected way together and always in a sustainable way, with our particular ecosystem.

I provide this brief overview, of a small corner of my understanding of an Iñupiaq way of being, in the hope that by means of comparison, it might encourage policy makers and leaders to shed their own light on the first challenge facing their governments if they want to find real solutions to climate change. I believe the first part of that challenge is to acknowledge the 'fundamental principles' that seem to have informed how they and their ancestors (as colonizers) approached the land, the people and the resources in First Nations' territories.

I cannot speak for the experiences of other First Nations communities, so I limit myself to the experience of First Nations communities in North America and begin by framing this comparison in its most essential form, with a few extracts of how the colonizing state bodies wrote about how they approached the 'native peoples' or 'Indians' (sic) of this land.

> The dominant policy of the Federal Government toward the American Indian has been one of forced assimilation which has vacillated between the two extremes of coercion and persuasion. *At the root of the assimilation policy has been a desire to divest the Indian of his land and resources … thus freeing large amounts of additional land for the white man.* [my emphasis] (United States 1969)

> The Indians must conform to 'the white man's ways,' *peaceably if they will, forcibly if they must.* They must adjust themselves to their environment, and conform their mode of living substantially to our civilization. This civilization may not be the best possible, but it is the best the Indians can get. [my emphasis] (United States 1880)

As an Iñupiaq person who occupies the in-between spaces of Iñupiaq society and Anglo-American society I have spent most of my adult life learning about and reflecting upon the evolution of the

Iñupiaq relationship with Anglo-American society and governments since those early contact days. The settler–colonial relationship continues to inform the American Government and Iñupiaq tribal authorities continue to seek ways to maintain and assert their sovereign status.

To get underneath the 'fundamental principles' that I perceive have informed successive government's attitudes to our people, it is important to go back to the beginning. The first 'explorers' that came to our sovereign territory did not come to inhabit our land. There was no intention to live in this new environment. They came in search of resources to extract and exploit. Because of this, they presumably didn't feel the need to learn to live sustainably on our land. The 'fundamental principles' that informed their approach to our land and our people were in every way, by circumstance and intent, exploitative. As a consequence, they neither looked for nor sought out any knowledge from our people about how the animals, land, air and the waters breathe, move, respond and change.

Our value to settler colonists and states has only ever been measured by the amount of access we could provide for them to our resource rich land. This is certainly the case in Alaska and the relationship with our Iñupiaq people is, I suspect, not so different to the relationship other colonizing nations established with the First Nations' communities they encountered (Wolfe 2006). In declaring their way of being in such a way, those early colonizers declared from the outset that the environment was not something with spirit, or knowledge or any kind of integrated relationship with humans that walked within it.

Once the extent of resources on our land became apparent to the early colonists, they proceeded to set up colonies. In this process they 'claimed' the 'new land' under their legal constructs and in that process provided themselves with a 'justifiable' (albeit racist and legally unfounded) platform for the relentless exploitation and extraction of our resources back to their countries of origin. There was never and has never been a plan for sustainability. Which leads me to ask – how do these nations and decision-makers possibly think that from this foundation, with these operational settings, using tools that come from this history, they can even begin to unpick the climate crisis that this exploitation driven 'way of being' has created?

Like many First Nations people who have educated me, I look at this history that informs colonizing states and feel a degree of sympathy for them. Their origins are soaked not just in the trauma of separation from their countries of origin but in the trauma of separating from a grounded sense of being in their own countries that must have existed at some point in their history. What has been the impact of trauma on the colonizer, of entering a new territory and ignoring every fibre of the human need to feel connected to the land and waters we live within? In echoing the wisdom of Resmaa Menakem (2017), I have also wondered for many years how this trauma has been compounded by the trauma of inflicting so much pain on other communities with the sole defence being extraction and exploitation for one's own benefit.

'Ways of being and knowing', 'ontological and epistemological truths' – no matter which way you frame the language, the interrogation of colonial nations' origin stories upon the lands of First Nations peoples tells us a lot about why we are in this current climate crisis. If leaders and climate change policy thinkers were able and willing to locate the origin of climate change where it actually exists, they would be compelled to acknowledge that the political and economic drivers of their growth have always been based on an unsustainable and inhumane model that is dependent on exploitation of land, people and resources. And in acknowledging this, they would be liberated to acknowledge that their economic model of perpetual growth keeps crashing and needs an overhaul because it goes against the laws of nature and sustainability.

Understanding What Informs Our Decision-Making

For over 10,000 years (or by our own accounts more) we have learned to live together, intertwined with our environment, sustainably. Our society is grounded by four fundamental laws. The Maliġuagaksrat, or, as our cousins in Inuktitut (Canadian Arctic) call it, the Maligait, are four key laws in the Inuit world that guide everything we do (Tagalik 2009). Those four laws are:

1. Respect all living things
2. Work for the common good
3. Maintain harmony and balance
4. Continually plan for the future

These Maliġuagaksrat ground our decision-making process in a matrix that is holistic, long-term, critically conscious and consensus driven. Everything is judged against this. Our knowledge is grown from a transfer of ancestral heritage and also from a pedagogy that requires us to observe, listen, meditate and reflect upon our environment and each other. In this process we grow our relational knowledge of the earth and our people and simultaneously grow our critical consciousness.

I recall as a child being on a family hunting trip out on the Arctic Ocean in a small tin boat. It was a perfect spring day, the blue sky and water of the Arctic inviting our family to join them. We were learning to drive the boat and Dad was teaching us how to navigate the ocean and how to 'see' animals. We searched the ocean, exploring and chatting excitedly; we knew how lucky we were. After an hour or so we were many miles offshore and when we looked up, the sky had changed colour to a deep grey. We (the kids) panicked just a little at first and then progressively more as we realized we had not been watching where we were travelling. Dad calmly announced to us that we had got ourselves 'turned around'. We didn't know which way was home.

After our (the kids') attempts to work out which way to go, Dad finally spoke up and told us to turn off the motor. Confused but completely unaware of our options, we did as we were told. My father then calmly poured himself a cup of coffee, lit a cigarette and waited. He observed the sky, the wind and the water. This was his way of calling on our ancestors and listening. After about twenty minutes he cleared his throat and asked us what we saw. Not having much to offer, he asked us to look again, and more closely he directed our attention to the ocean but this time to see the current we had been sitting on top of all along. We suddenly saw that the boat had turned itself around again and there, clear as could be, was the current running at the meeting of the two oceans. We quickly made the connection to where we must be and how we could find our way home.

The point of this story is not to fuel the already problematic fetishizing of our elders and their 'wisdom', but to demonstrate how we are raised to problem solve from a position of strength and humility. Firstly, our Dad didn't panic because he knew we were not lost. We are raised to understand that we are never lost if we stay grounded in our knowledge of the land and the waters that raised us. Secondly, he knew that the answer to the problem was in listening, hearing, and being humble to the situation they were in. If we reflect on our journey, listen to all the knowledge around us, acknowledge how we got into the place we are sitting, it's easier to map back to where we want to be.

Since colonizers have arrived in our country, they have brought a decision-making lens to all our interactions that is driven by the singular focus of exploitation. This approach to their decision-making has obscured not just the way in which they engage with us, but their ability to observe, hear, reflect and find a path forward that recognizes the extraordinary knowledge base that our people bring into the room, and often ignores pathways that would be more beneficial to our collective existence on our ancestral lands.

In the spring of 2016, just two months after Shell Oil withdrew its activities from our ocean waters, ending a forty-year battle against deep-water oil extraction in the Arctic, the United States Federal Bureau of Ocean Energy Management (BOEM) arrived unannounced in Utqiaġvik, Alaska, my home town. They brought with them several hundred pages of completed environmental studies, designed and conducted by them, assessing potential impacts to the environment of a new oil lease sale in the outer continental shelf off the north slope of Alaska. They had not consulted with our tribal government about these studies or the new lease. Their stated intention on this visit was to get community feedback on the studies. The studies had not been sent to the Tribe or the community in advance, much less constructed in consultation or collaboration.

I stood in the room as an observer, behind a camera, documenting the process. There were about fifteen staff from both State and Federal Offices. They were very excited because their scientists and researchers had, for the first time, mapped seventy years into the future, further than they had ever mapped, and had extended the survey area to look at the impact of oil exploration across a few extra map-blocks from offshore. They quieted the room and were ready with pen, paper, maps and cameras to take all and any comments.

The meeting had been scheduled to last two hours, and for the first hour and a half I watched the only three Iñupiaq participants in the room desperately trying to convey, to non-First Nations policy advisors, the threat to our way of life that offshore oil development represents. The Iñupiaq participants tried to explain that to understand the impact on the whales, the people and the environment, BOEM must look at the whole habitat of the whale, the people and the environment – not just four square blocks on a map of the ocean. They explained to the government staff that what 'long-term planning' means to the Iñupiaq people is seven generations – backwards and forwards – not just seventy years.

To convey their message they had to condense (much as I am doing here for you), into a handful of sentences, what our way of life is, why it's important to us and why we are trying so desperately to hold onto it. It was and remains an impossible task but one that we seem to be endlessly engaged in with the colonial government agencies and decision-makers of the United States. Yet here were these three members of my community, once again trying to wrestle back control of yet another narrative and another decision that had the potential to completely undermine and destroy subsistence whaling, the backbone of Iñupiaq culture.

As a reader or an observer on that day, you might be forgiven for asking why, if this was so important, were there only three Iñupiaq people in the room?

Aside from arriving more or less unannounced, BOEM had visited on one of the most important days in the Iñupiaq calendar, the whalers' service, which is the official start of spring whaling. Some may surmise that this was deliberate timing on the part of the government to avoid the task of taking real feedback, navigating complex conversations, and hearing from an entire community. However, if we give the BOEM the benefit of the doubt, we can arrive at an equally disappointing but consistent conclusion: they had not thought about what they were doing in the context of the people, the land and the history we share. In a decision-making matrix that is driven to prioritize exploitation rather than collaboration and sustainability, they had applied the usual myopic or siloed approach to their process.

BOEM had applied their filters of knowledge to the issue and remit they were facing and ignored the people who might be better placed to inform how the decisions and assessments might be made. It is precisely because they are part of the United States federal government and not the Iñupiaq Community of the Arctic Slope (or a Native Village Tribe) that BOEM operates under a decision-making process that comes from and prioritizes American economic, social principles and American mandates built to sustain Anglo-centric cultural constructs.

Whether this model of exploitation of First Nations communities deliberately or accidentally silences and marginalizes First Nations 'ways of being and knowing', the effect is the same. This approach literally turns its back on an accumulated reserve of knowledge that has allowed us as First Nations people to live sustainably with each other and our environment in our regions for tens of thousands of years. The madness of it is that the same knowledge, agility of thinking and adaptation that our communities have developed over an unimaginably long period of time are the very approaches that the global community is now trying desperately to 'unearth' as the climate crisis deepens.

Understanding Our Holistic Approach

Whaling is an activity that spans the whole year, crosses all territory and draws from every aspect of our society. It not only provides physical, cultural and spiritual sustenance, it is the safety net of our whole community, our whole way of life. We could not continue whaling if we did not maintain it in a holistic (or multi-disciplinary) and long-term (or sustainable) relationship with the environment, animals and the people.

Historically whaling provided us with materials to build our houses and make the tools we needed to survive in our environment. Still today, when our whaling crews are given the gift of the whale, we are blessed with food and sustenance to feed our entire community throughout our long winters. Whaling provided and continues to provide us with ceremonial traditions throughout the year including (but not limited to) the Whale Festivals – *Nalukatak* and *Qagaruq* (celebrating a successful hunt and honouring the spirit of the whales) – the winter games (to build endurance and skills, share stories and celebrate through dance), *Kivgiq* Festival (The Messenger Feast and winter dance ceremony) and now the Easter, Thanksgiving and Christmas feasts.

Our young boys and girls become men and women through whaling and the surrounding hunting traditions. The moral compass that guides an Iñupiaq adult can be pinned largely to these continued hunting traditions. From a spiritual perspective, our understanding of the environment, the nature of the animals and our relationship to everything around us is largely, if not wholly, informed by this mutual bond we share with the animals and our environment.

In describing this relationship between the Iñupiaq and the whale, Patrick Attungana, a revered whaling captain from Tikigaq (Point Hope), Alaska said:

> We are Iñupiat on the shores of the seas... We eat the animals of the seas and of the land. We exist because of those older than we are. We live because we follow their example. Our body fluids are mixed with the blood of animals, with the oil of the animals – like the Iñupiat of old who used the same animals.
>
> From the Iñupiat of the past, a covenant has been passed down. This covenant – a group of intelligent people who have a good sense of perception is like a book to their people. They have good memories and because of them, we can hunt whales today. This holds hunting together. We want

our descendants to follow this example. Those of us who are getting older, even older than I, want our descendants to follow the teachings and to be obedient. (Attungana 1985)

This concept is hard to translate into English, but points to our people's understanding and lived reality as integrated members of an ecosystem with all the complexity that dependence and integration carries through the generations and across our society. It integrates the physical, spiritual and cultural connections to the animals that sustain us, directly through our ancestry.

In short, we could not be a whaling community if we thought in siloed, short-term ways. We could not be a whaling community if we made decisions that benefited only a few, or decisions that failed to consider the long-term consequences of our actions.

As a result of this inheritance and our worldview, many Iñupiaq people can see the profound damage inflicted on our community and our sustainable and integrated way of life when siloed thinking and a system driven by a perpetual growth model (based on resource extraction and exploitation) is applied to us. The extent of that damage and the lengths to which the government has gone to break our community's holistic connection to the lands and waters is a constant theme of our resistance.

Our holistic being, our ontology and epistemology is a continual reminder to the United States Government of their unsustainable approach to our lands and their repeated attempts to force us into 'a system designed to dissolve the Indian social structure'. In the context of the current climate crisis, now is the time for leaders and policy makers to acknowledge the strength of our system, the inherent sustainability of our way of living, rather than continuing to force us to adopt a way of living that has led the colonizer into a state of social and environmental crisis.

Our elders never stop teaching us these critical lessons. During a recent Cultural Safety workshop I was co-facilitating with one of our community organizations, I was fortunate enough to hear senior elder and community leader Rex Okakok recount the story of the revitalization of *Kivgiq*. The *Kivgiq* Festival was a central part of our community's ceremonial life. However, the impact of colonization and the epidemics saw the festival banned for many years until it re-emerged in 1988.

In the 1980s suicide amongst our young people was at troubling levels. Successive government led health campaigns targeted boredom, lack of physical activity and drugs and alcohol and in turn funded gym programmes, drug and alcohol education programmes and anti-drug T-shirts and caps, believing these were reasons for suicide amongst my generation of youth. The campaigns failed to make an impact on the crisis.

Faced with this unprecedented problem, Iñupiaq leaders convened a special commission that adopted an Iñupiaq approach to the problem and began by speaking with elders and community members. Through this process they found the root cause of the problem to be the mental health of our young people and in particular their sense of disengagement from Iñupiaq identity. Not surprisingly, a century of colonization was having a visible and highly damaging impact on our children.

In response, and following a lengthy period of consultations that neither assumed what the solution would be nor limited people to a deadline, the leaders made the unexpected decision to re-introduce the *Kivgiq* Festival. This didn't just mean redirecting money that had been previously identified for smaller government programmes. It required a holistic response across all levels and all areas of our community. Time was needed with elders, storytelling was rejuvenated, histories were re-told, family connections were strengthened, physical activity in the form of dancing, racing and sports, hunting, sewing, cooking traditions, knowledges and practices were strengthened. A range of traditions focused on Iñupiaq learning and pride for our young people were once again energized.

Because the solution was grounded in who we were as a people and our relationships to each other, our lands and waters and our histories, the *Kivgiq* Festival became self-sustaining once again. It affirmed for us that many of the answers to the trauma inflicted by colonization lay in the strength of our culture and our ability as a people to trust processes that holistically address the root cause of a problem, not just its symptoms, processes that reconnect us to each other and our lands.

Humility and the Future

Despite the violence inflicted on us, our communities have never stopped sharing and never stopped listening. It's a core foundation of our social and economic structure. It's the way we have thrived for so long in such a challenging climate. If our approach of listening and seeking out the root cause of a problem was taken by large industrialized nations, perhaps they could acknowledge that when they exported (through colonial activity) their model of exploitation into First Nations communities, it required them (as colonizers) to silence and marginalize their own humanity while violently silencing the knowledges and sciences of First Nations people (they could not silence our humanity).

In the process of silencing and oppressing our ways of being, knowing and doing, colonizing nations literally turned their backs on an accumulated knowledge bank which has allowed First Nations people to live sustainably with each other and our environment in our regions for tens of thousands of years. For leaders and policy makers struggling with solutions to climate change, perhaps it will assist them to know that we are still here. We are still living as Iñupiaq people, on Iñupiaq country with understandings of the earth that our people have drawn upon to maintain balance and respect for millennia.

We continue to plan for the future by having the humility to look to our past and understand our missteps today. We are also here resisting, waiting for the leaders and policy makers, who speak down to us, to finally come to us in the spirit of authentic collaboration. Only then can we share our critical and holistic knowledge and understandings to support the design of solutions for global problems facing our people as well as theirs.

Perhaps at some point soon, the world will be in a better position to commence an honest conversation about the climate crisis, its causes and solutions. That conversation will need to include and value the voices of peoples with critical experience and toolkits who have previously been ignored. As my father, and so many other First Nations leaders around the world, say, 'the earth will never lose, she will do what she needs to do. She'll clear the slate and start again'.

The question remains, what are we all willing to do to ensure we have a place on that earth?

Acknowledgements

I thank David Selvarajah Vadiveloo *for his unstinted support and editorial brilliance with this chapter.*

Rachel Nutaaq Ayałhuq Naŋinaaq Edwardson is an Iñupiaq/Norwegian/Sami woman from Utqiagvik, Alaska. She describes her work in film, education and community activism as being guided by sovereign grounded resistance. She is the daughter of George and

Debby Edwardson and is married to former human rights lawyer and social justice activist, David Selvarajah Vadiveloo. Together they have three joyful children.

References

Attungana, Pattrick. 1985. 'Whale Hunting in Harmony', *Alaska Native News*, 3(11).

Brower, Ronald. 2013. 'Sila and Sungauraq in Iñupiaq Culture', [Online video], Film University of Alaska Fairbanks. Retrieved 2 April 2020 from https://vimeo.com/76089154.

MacLean, Edna Ahgeak. 2014. *Iñupiatun Uqaluit Taniktun Sivuniŋit: Iñupiaq to English Dictionary*. Fairbanks: University of Alaska Press.

Menakem, Resmaa, 2017. *My Grandmother's Hands: Racialized Trauma and the Pathways to Mending Our Hearts and Bodies*. Las Vegas: Central Recovery Press.

Never Alone [Video Game]. Upper One Games and E-Line Media. 2014. Akpik Fannie Kuutuq, Harcharek Jana Pausauraq.

Qitsualik, Rachel Attituq. 2018. 'Learning to Observe, Read Sila All-Important to Inuit', *Indian Country Today*. Retrieved 2 April 2020 from https://indiancountrytoday.com/archive/learning-to-observe-read-sila-all-important-to-inuit.

Tagalik, Shirley. 2009. *Caring for Children the Inuit Way*. Prince George, BC: Canadian National Collaborating Centre for Aboriginal Health.

United States. 1969. *Indian Education: A National Tragedy, a National Challenge*. Report of the Committee on Labor and Public Welfare, United States Senate. Washington DC: United States Government Printing Office

United States. 1880. *Annual Report of the Commissioner of Indian Affairs*. Washington DC: United States Government Publishing Office.

Wolfe, Patrick. 2006. 'Settler Colonialism and the Elimination of the Native', *Journal of Genocide Research* 8(4): 387–409.

CHAPTER 4

Weathering the Storm
An Indigenous Knowledge Framework of Yup'ik Youth Well-Being and Resilience in Alaska

Stacy M. Rasmus

The Yup'ik Alaska Native world has always been a changing one, but the past century has seen not only accelerated change but an imposition of new forces transforming Indigenous landscapes and lifeways (Burch 2005; Fienup-Riordan 2000; Chance 1990; Napoleon 1996; Oswalt 2011). The swiftness and severity of the intruding colonial forces disrupted societal and relational systems and fissured people from the protective factors that once kept families and communities safe, well and strong (Berry 1985). Problems emerged that have never before been encountered. By the 1950s, family groups that once moved freely across a region the size of the state of Nevada in the lower-48 states were forced to settle into one of fifty-six village communities so that children could attend Euro-American schools (Fienup-Riordan 2000). Technologies, economies and social systems began to shift rapidly to accommodate and incorporate Western influences. Some adaptations were advantageous, such as the introduction of vaccines and Western medicines (Ayunerak et al. 2014), and others involved agency and syncretism by Yup'ik communities to incorporate elements of the new and incoming technologies and socio-cultural systems into traditional practices and belief systems (Fienup-Riordan 1991). Ultimately though, this marks a period of colonial transition where families were forced to live in settlements, children were sent out to boarding schools, and new social, economic, political and religious systems were imposed (Fienup-Riordan 2000; Rasmus, Allen and Ford 2014).

By the 1960s, young Alaska Native people began dying by suicide (Kettl and Bixler 1991), and rates have continued to increase, producing one of Alaska's most urgent public health crises. Suicide among children, adolescents and young adults in Yup'ik communities was nearly unheard of up until the establishment of statehood in 1959 (Ayunerak et al. 2014), but in the 1970s, Alaska Native suicide rates began to double every five years, with most of the increase among fifteen to twenty-five-year-olds (Allen, Levintova and Mohatt 2011). From 1960 to 1995, the suicide rate increased by approximately 500% (Shain 2016). The colonial disruptions during this time period increased conditions associated with suicide risk (e.g. substance abuse, disrupted social roles), and challenged the community-level social safety net of youth protective factors that might have moderated the effects of the traumas associated with an externally imposed, colonial change (Chandler and Proulx 2006; Chandler and LaLonde 1998; Kvernmo and Heyerdahl 2003; Wexler 2009). This cultural disruption in Alaska and across the Arctic is also associated with acculturation stress and identity struggles in young Indigenous people (Berry 1985; Kvernmo and Heyerdahl 2004; Phinney 2000) with the dislodging of age-old cultural practices, impinging on youth perceptions of Indigenous values. These imposed conditions cut youth off from traditional resilience processes (Alia 2007; Kirmayer et al. 2011; Ulturgasheva et al. 2011, 2014) with real health consequences (Bjerregaard 2001; Chandler, LaLonde and Sokol 2003; Kirmayer, Fletcher and Boothroyd 1998; O'Neil 1986).

Growing up in the Arctic and Subarctic has always come with risk and required the development of resilience and adaptative capacity building to gain the knowledge and tools for survival (Ayunerak et al. 2014; Condon 1988). The same is true today, but the terms of survival have changed. The tools and teachings once vital for livelihood, safety and well-being are falling into disuse and neglect by many of the younger generations whose daily lives have shifted focus from being out on the land, water and ice to being indoors (Oswalt 2011; Rasmus, Allen and Ford 2004). For the Elders survival meant learning to weather a storm in a *qayaq* (kayak) or boat on the sea; and teachings to 'be as a piece of wood' in the water could save a life by turning panic into calming meditation in rough waters to prevent tipping over (Fienup-Riordan and Rearden 2015). These teachings today are not finding a receptive ear in young people who do not experience the pressure to subsist as a daily requirement for survival, and instead may engage in subsistence more occasionally rather than as a daily necessity (Rasmus, Allen and Ford 2014). Yup'ik Elder Joe Phillip, interviewed by Fienup-Riordan (2020: 22), warns though that if young people 'do not hear the *qanruyun* (teachings) they will be like someone lost in a storm, like ones who don't know their whereabouts'. It is true too today that young people need to learn to weather storms, but these may not necessarily be the ones causing waves and whiteouts outside on the water and land; instead, it may be the swirling swells of emotion or freezing pangs of lonesomeness one feels on the inside that needs instruction and tools for coping and finding safe harbour.

The suicide data in Alaska makes it clear that some young people have become lost in the storm. Fortunately, there is another emerging narrative of Alaska Native strengths and resilience (Allen et al. 2014; Allen et al. 2018; Mohatt et al. 2004; Ulturgasheva, Rasmus and Morrow 2015; Wexler et al. 2014). This movement has grown stronger through a long-term research effort (Rasmus et al. 2019a) led by Yup'ik communities, and the Elders within them (Ayunerak et al. 2014), to develop solutions to end suicide and promote youth well-being through Indigenous knowledge, teachings, language and lifeways (Rasmus, Charles and Mohatt 2014; Rasmus et al. 2019b). While progress is being made to reduce disparities, there is still more research that is needed to understand newly emerging challenges, such as climate change, and to promote Indigenous knowledge frameworks and definitions of youth and community well-being.

The Yup'ik notion of 'weathering the storm' is central to this discussion as it eloquently captures the scale and dynamic of the challenges that Yupiit (pl. Yup'ik), from Elders to children, are confronted with today. It is getting stormier every year, and each new storm requires a specific set of skills and knowledge adapted in accordance with Yup'ik ways of living (*yuu'yaraq*) and teachings (*qanruyutet*). This chapter examines youth resilience and community adaptations in an era of climate change from a Yup'ik Indigenous knowledge framework that views and places these dynamic social processes within a complex universe of interlocking systems and overlapping worlds.

The first part of this chapter examines youth well-being in a Yup'ik universe, drawing from interviews and narratives with Yup'ik Elders and knowledge bearers. Well-being and resilience in a Yup'ik perspective is defined and understood within a holistic ecological worldview that interconnects humans to the environment and animals in relational and mutualistic ways. The understanding of youth well-being and resilience in a Yup'ik Indigenous framework represents an important reframing of suicide not as an individual action but as an event within systems that have become unbalanced. The second part of the chapter presents a Yup'ik Indigenous knowledge framework of youth well-being and resilience in an era of climate change and community adaptation where tides are bucked and storms are weathered in life as they are out on the land and water. This Indigenous knowledge framework is juxtaposed to an emerging One Health paradigm that advances a monolithic definition of well-being that, on the surface, appears to reflect Indigenous epistemologies that emphasize the interrelationships among human, animal and environmental welfare in the production of health. The emergence and advancement of the One Health framework on an international Arctic policy level comes at a time when Indigenous leaders and communities are calling for Indigenous-led and Indigenous knowledge-based research initiatives. The chapter concludes with an argument for the recognition and valuing of Indigenous knowledge frameworks that capture the complexity of a sentient and changeable Yup'ik universe, and explain youth well-being and resilience as arising within a cosmic harmonizing of systems and worlds constantly in flux: never quiet but always listening. Thinking with and through Indigenous knowledge frameworks can reveal more fully and meaningfully the ways in which young people are weathering storms in their lives on the lands that generations of their ancestors have walked and continue to walk in spirit behind them.

Youth Well-Being in a Yup'ik Universe

In a Yup'ik universe and epistemology (Kawagley 2000), where everything in the environment has personhood and sentience, including living beings and objects as small as a single discarded fish bone (Fienup-Riordan 2020: xxxvi), and all forms are interconnected, solutions to perturbations, such as storms, in one system (i.e. weather, social, psychological) must inherently involve all systems coming into balance and harmonizing. The balance of systems and relationships within and between systems as being the core determinant of health and well-being provides the ideological foundation for an intertidal ecological framework of youth resilience. The well-being of a Yup'ik individual is contingent on the well-being of the Yup'ik world. Any one part of this sentient and changeable universe then, such as tides on an ocean, can be observed and provides indicators into the status of human lives and social systems. As the Yup'ik universe is impacted by climate change, globalization and other economic and societal pressures, people living in traditional places and engaging in Indigenous spaces are feeling these impacts and outcomes are being reflected in human behaviours that mirror the environmental disruptions. It is a frequent saying among Yup'ik Elders today in reflections on climate change that the 'world is changing along with the people' (Fienup-Riordan 2010). The health status of Yup'ik communities today reflects how people are changing in sometimes harmful and destructive ways.

Other systems within the Yup'ik universe are also in flux and changing in ways that are potentially damaging, with melting permafrost, erosion of coastal banks, unsteady ice with less snow, and through declines in keystone species such as king salmon (Moerlein and Carothers 2012). A Yup'ik Elder interviewed by Fienup-Riordan (2020: xxvii) states, 'The weather they say is becoming a liar'. As all things are connected in a Yup'ik world, the weather system is reflecting the disturbances in the human social systems and psyches where unpredictable and inappropriate actions, such as suicide, are occurring. But these individual actions, from a Yup'ik perspective, must be considered within the historical moment and context surrounding the individual. As Fienup-Riordan (2020: xxii) notes, in a Yup'ik framework, 'Although individuals are responsible for their own actions, they cannot be expected to act appropriately if they are not in control of their land, language, and life. This assessment implies that a sector of the population has lost such a sense of control'. Suicide, in this framework, would be seen as a 'consequence of the conditions existing at the time' (ibid.); not as an individually motivated behaviour. This statement reflects a post-colonial condition when neither land nor language could be controlled and dealt with directly by Yup'ik rightsholders.

Well-being in this framework must also be consequential to existing conditions: a collective and interconnected construct. Human well-being was once more intrinsically linked to the Yup'ik universe (Ellam Yua), and to all the systems therein, particularly the animals (Fienup-Riordan 2020). The human–animal relationship is still central to the Yup'ik way of life, referred to as the *yuu'yaraq* (Ayunerak et al. 2014), but conditions today have imposed regulations and restrictions on the relationship that have strained the fundamental and relational connection (Hensel 1996). Some teachings about the animals have fallen out of everyday use and knowledge, but as Yup'ik Elder John Phillip states, 'You know how they say a person's stomach cannot change, that their efforts at subsisting cannot change' (Fienup-Riordan 2020: 22). As long as the Yup'ik world exists, the Indigenous people living within it will harvest from it, and health and well-being will always be essentially tied to it; health is in the harvest.

As reported by Fienup-Riordan (2020: xxxvi), even as the people are changing and becoming more 'Westernized', in one Yup'ik Elder's assessment, the animals 'haven't become Western, they are aware of things'. This is an essential instruction in seeding the conditions for renewal of more reciprocal relationships between humans and animals once again in the Yup'ik universe. Another Yup'ik Elder, interviewed by this author as part of a long-term research project focused on youth resilience and community adaptations, provided a related teaching that 'All animals and every game has a spirit. When you give water to that seal, the spirit of the seal will be thankful. He'll come back to that person again. I think that's a prayer' (2017, personal communication). Young people are made stronger, given protection and resilience through these teachings and through the connections they make with the animals. Stronger connections and more secure relationships to the land, animals and ways of living may in turn provide a greater sense of control and agency for young people growing up in Yup'ik communities. This is important not only for youth well-being today, but for community and cultural persistence into the future.

Systems in Harmony Listen

Current challenges that young people face today in Yup'ik communities, including suicide, can be understood as events within systems where individual actions are reflections of imbalance and perturbations within these systems. Of greatest challenge for young people today is learning how to live in equipoise within systems in flux and between overlapping worlds, where intrusive and pervading Euro-American systems have muted the resonance of Yup'ik teachings. Yup'ik teachings (*qanruyutet*) are mechanisms that contribute to community resilience and adaptive capacity and provide comprehensive instruction for living in harmony within a holistic and interconnected world of systems. These systems integrate across environmental, biological, socio-cultural, spiritual and temporal dimensions. According to Yup'ik teachings, changes observed in one spatial and temporal dimension could be extrapolated to apply meaning in other dimensions and times; this is particularly true for changes observed in the environment and/or among the animals and its meaning for human beings. An excerpt from an interview conducted with a Yup'ik Elder for a project on community adaptations to climate change provides a clear example of this systems-level translation:

> Our own Elders told us when we were growing up that the world was going to change and then go back to the way it was a long time ago before the *kassaq* (Europeans/Euro-Americans) came. They saw the *kassaq* coming and knew our Yup'ik way of life was going to change with it. Then they said, when the animals start to come down to the sea; when animals of the land like the moose and wolf, when they start to move towards the coast like they are now, the world is going to back to the way it was. And when the moose walk into the sea it will return to the way that it was when our ancestors were living their yuu'yaraq (traditional Yup'ik way of life). (2013, personal communication)

A Yup'ik universe is a changing one but its nature is not necessarily accumulative or linear in design; rather, it reflects the cycling of life, death and rebirth that is at the foundations of traditional Yup'ik cosmology (Fienup-Riordan 1995). Human beings are not at the centre of this cycling process but are instead involved in an ongoing constellation of reciprocal exchanges and engagements with animate and inanimate beings and objects that all cycle collectively. In the quote above, a moose walking into the sea is an indication of an end to one collective cycle, and the prospective of a new world beginning. Moose were not traditional inhabitants in a Yup'ik universe, and were rarely seen in the Yukon-Kuskokwim (YK) Delta and never as far as the Bering Sea coast. Moose began moving into the YK Delta a few decades ago and their population has grown exponentially over the past decade, coinciding with rapid climate changes and environmental transitions. Moose now run in small groups along the edges of Hooper Bay, Alaska on the Bering Sea coast, bringing prophesies to pass and an even greater urgency in communities racing to adapt and provide young people with the teachings and tools they will need to bridge the worlds turning.

There is also great significance and meaning in the event of terrestrial life returning to the sea as a catalyst for change and for a return to a more balanced Yup'ik universe. Yupiit are the people of the seal, and in Yup'ik oral tradition returning to the sea and travelling to the land of the sea people is regenerative and restorative (Fienup-Riordan 1995). Moose become an intrinsic part of the Yup'ik universe by returning to the sea where terrestrial and oceanic systems interact, communicate and join into interdependent relationship. The Yup'ik universe is relational and systems function like kinship networks, being reciprocal and mutualistic, at times feuding and estranged, and always growing and changing shape over passages of time. For relationships to remain healthy as for systems to remain harmonious, each within them must be heard.

In a Yup'ik world everything listens (Fienup-Riordan 2020). Seals listen, dogs listen, berries and birds listen, rocks listen; everything from a blade of grass to the wind listens. What though in a contemporary Yup'ik world is being heard? What is the land listening to when many of the people living upon it have been forced to direct their words, thoughts and actions into structures and systems of power outside the Yup'ik world? Do these structures of power listen? Then answer is often, no. Yet, there are positive developments being undertaken to empower and centre Indigenous knowledge and Indigenous people within conversations related to climate change and community health and resilience in the Circumpolar North (Bodenhorn and Ulturgasheva 2017; Marino 2015; Ray and Raymond-Yakoubian 2015; Young 2012). One strategy for opening up the 'ears' of Western world power structures to Indigenous frameworks, epistemologies and pedagogies is to demonstrate the ways in which Indigenous knowledge is foundational to many current and often deemed 'cutting-edge' scientific approaches (Jack et al. 2020).

Figure 4.1. *A small herd of moose running on the beach near Hooper Bay, Alaska. © Jan Olsen*

One example of this is seen in the emerging 'One Health' scientific paradigm that recognizes the interconnectedness of the health and well-being of people with the animals and environment (Hueffer et al. 2019). While having its origins in veterinary epidemiology and zoonotic disease research (Atlas 2013), the One Health concept has come to have particular significance in the Circumpolar North where Indigenous peoples continue to live in close relationship to the environment and the animals, and communities and traditional lifeways are threatened by rapidly changing climates (Hueffer et al. 2019). The One Health framework has been posited as a viable strategy for understanding resilience and community adaptations to climate change in the Arctic as it brings together human, animal and environmental scientists along with community stakeholders as part of regional networks (Ruscio et al. 2015). One Health research has also recently become an official foundational activity of the Sustainable Development Working Group of the Arctic Council, a seat of significant power in terms of international policy and decision-making (SDWG 2017).

On initial review, the One Health movement appears as a significant step forward in recognizing the holistic and interconnected welfare of social and biological systems in the Arctic. The One Health framework is also arguably intrinsic to Arctic Indigenous knowledge systems, a point that is recognized by those advancing the One Health paradigm (Hueffer et al. 2019; Jack et al. 2020). Yet on closer introspection, its packaging in Western scientific language and advancement by academics situated in Western systems and institutions seems to be what enabled its recent prioritization on an international platform. Those authoring and advancing a One Health framework are primarily natural scientists and medical epidemiologists, and the research agenda is generally driven by an interest in the environmental and climate change processes whereby people and social processes tend to become ancillary or anecdotal to the primary focus on biological systems (Huntington et al. 2019). Gearheard et al. noted this phenomenon when observing discussions led by Arctic Indigenous residents themselves on the meaning of ice (2013). She noted how these conversations tend to contrast with those led by scientists, where residents would prioritize the lived experiences of health and health care, economic viability and the importance of sustaining culture, language and traditional lifeways in discussing the qualities and impacts of climate change on ice.

It could also be argued that the One Health framework, as a 'constructivist' approach (Hueffer et al. 2019), may continue to privilege Western scientifically derived knowledge over Indigenous knowledge and may ultimately mute the diverse, complex and uniquely defining characteristics of Indigenous frameworks of health and resilience. From this more critical perspective, the One Health paradigm continues in a Western tradition to focus on 'cross-talk' between disciplines, communities of interest and systems. This is quite contrary to a Yup'ik worldview that listens. In a Yup'ik Indigenous framework, the focus is on listening across systems and hearing between worlds. What follows is an extended narrative from one such moment of listening to what the animals and the ocean tides are telling us, shared by an Elder in a Yup'ik community on the Bering Sea coast where young people are learning how to live in very stormy times. A Yup'ik Indigenous framework of youth well-being and resilience emerges that, on the surface, shares characteristics with the One Health approach, but goes much deeper, capturing the impermanency, complexity and egalitarity of interlocking systems in a language of the people living within them.

Weathering Storms: A Yup'ik Indigenous Framework of Youth Well-Being and Resilience

In the summer of 2016, I sat with a Yup'ik Elder in the late-night twilight on a 25-foot aluminium weld boat that floated silently on the shallow inlet waters just outside of the Bering Sea coastal community that I was visiting for fieldwork. This Elder had invited me to go boating with him to visit an old village site up the ocean coast. We had originally planned to bring a small group of young people from the community with us so that the Elder could provide teachings to the youth about their ancestral homelands and patterns of movement. On the morning of the day of the planned outing, the Elder deemed the wind too high and the waters too rough to take youth with us and so we went out on our own. The Elder had timed our outing with the tides, to leave and return when the tide was high enough to clear the shallow inlet that led from and to the village cut bank where boats can dock securely. When we returned at the scheduled time, the tide was still out and we were forced to anchor and wait for the rising waters. During the three hours that followed, this Elder told stories and reflected deeply upon the changes in the environment, the animals and the people that he was witnessing. About the tides he observed:

> It's kind of depressing, you know, when you can't count on your friends. The tides use to be our friend. We knew when to expect them. We could

count on them. Now we, it's like we don't know them anymore. They are becoming stranger and that's scary. I don't want to take the kids out.

In a sentient Yup'ik universe, tides are like people and have moods and can be fickle and unpredictable. People interact with the ocean and the tides as they would with family members and friends. Sometimes being out on the ocean and navigating tides is a loyal and happy experience, bringing good humour and connection with other fond friends such as the seals, whales and walrus. At other times the ocean and tides can become threatening and scary, evoking feelings of fear and anxiousness. In an era of rapid climate change, these times of unpredictability and fear appear to be increasing, causing, in the words of this Elder, 'depressing' feelings, and fewer opportunities for young people to learn how to live on the land and water and develop strong and trusting relationships with the ocean and its tides. The impacts of climate change on Indigenous mental health in the Arctic have until recently (Cunsolo Willox et al. 2015) been a much neglected area of study. It is clear from this Elder's narrative that the relationship between people living in coastal communities and the ocean is critical in a Yup'ik Indigenous framework of well-being and resilience. When I ask what he thinks is causing the changes in the tides, the Elder states:

> I think the weather is changing with the people. The people are becoming different and you don't know them like you use to. Like I don't know what my grandchildren do. They are into all kinds of things I never seen before. They are learning to be Yup'ik in a different world than what I grew up in.

The first sentence in the quote above is a common statement among Yup'ik Elders as it was earlier stated. Here the quote is specific to the weather but is also generally applied to all changes taking place in the Yup'ik world and universe. What is important here is the reflection of the tidal shifts that are taking place among the generations of people. This Elder, who lives in a multi-generational household with his grandchildren, can share in a physical space and still very literally not know what his grandchildren do. His grandchildren have been swept up in a tide that has pulled them into virtual spaces and expanded the Yup'ik universe into areas where he has never been, and may not want to go. The cumulative impacts of rapid change on social and environmental systems have resulted in a Yup'ik universe that is expanding in some ways, contracting in others and that needs to find ways to best get along again or adapt to these changed and changing conditions. While the Yup'ik world is changed and changing, young people still must learn how to live their ancestral life ways, as the Elder reflects:

> We need to give young people the *yuu'yaraq* teachings. Even if their minds seem like they are full of other things or we don't understand them; just like how we have to still go out even if we get stuck on a low tide and need to wait a while. We need to keep going and talk to the young ones and be willing to wait a while for their minds to open up and understand what we are trying to tell them. The world is going to go back to the way it was at the beginning and our children have to know how we survived it before there was electricity, boats and snowmachines.

It is in this quote that a Yup'ik Indigenous framework that listens becomes clearly drawn through the three passages together that explain youth resilience and risk through a maritime ecological metaphor of tides and intertidal movement. Tidal movements of the sea are indeed akin to inter-human relations that could switch from friendly and reliable to estranged and unfamiliar suddenly. The weather and tides changed drastically just like the people whom the Elder sometimes feels he cannot recognize or know and predict. Tides can exist on the ocean as they can in the minds of the young people, pulling them out and closing them off or pushing them fast to new places where a *qayaq* seems no longer necessary. There, in these new expanses of a Yup'ik universe, are young people at their greatest risk for getting lost. Swept away on angry tides, young minds are weathering storms in their lives as their ancestors did but with fewer of the teachings and tools needed to survive the rough seas and skies. In a Yup'ik Indigenous framework of youth well-being and resilience, teachings cast out a lifeline for young people lost in storms and provide tools for weathering storms inside as well as outside oneself. A Yup'ik child listens even as their mind appears closed, because everything living in a Yup'ik universe listens.

In a Yup'ik Indigenous framework learning to weather storms and navigate the tides is a metaphor and practical strategy for resilience. The suicide epidemic is one of the hardest tides that has hit Yup'ik communities, and young people are most vulnerable to being pulled out into the new expanses that have been created over time and through much imposed and ongoing change, with some eventually and tragically lost in the storm. There is hope in that tides can be navigated and storms weathered, sometimes by waiting for them to pass or come in, at other times by being proactive in tending and modifying tools to guide and protect oneself, and finally in being prepared with a toolkit to make you stronger, more resilient and capable of weathering the next storm to come.

Conclusion

It is important to continue to recognize the plurality of Indigenous frameworks for understanding health, well-being and resilience. One Health, as it is currently being operationalized (Lee and Brumme 2013), is not an Indigenous framework or decolonial approach. This does not mean there is no value in its conceptualization or advancement, particularly in environmental and biological sciences where consideration of social and cultural processes is often marginalized. Indigenous knowledge frameworks capture the complexity of a sentient and changeable Yup'ik universe, and explain youth well-being and resilience as arising within a harmonizing of relational systems that cycle through time and across tipping points or tidal points of strength and vulnerability (e.g. Ulturgasheva et al. 2014). Indigenous frameworks provide models for understanding the deeper complexities of systems and their interactions from the perspectives, and in the languages, of those living through these systems and whose health and resilience is held in balance as worlds collide and change a universe.

The Yup'ik universe, while always changing and adapting, has been weathering an unprecedented onslaught of imposing forces, from colonialism to climate change, the tolls of which are being reflected back to us most powerfully and unacceptably through young lives being lost to suicide. Work is being done and communities are taking action to heal from within and provide the teachings and the tools to young people to weather the storms and navigate the tides to safe harbour at sea as on land and in life. Understanding the suicide disparity within a Yup'ik Indigenous framework of resilience and well-being provides a perspective and a language to use that promotes hope and presents solutions for collective healing from colonial trauma. Suicide among young people may be a new event within systems in a Yup'ik universe today but storms and tides are long-standing perils to the Indigenous people living along the Bering Sea coast, and storms can be weathered and tides navigated successfully with the proper teachings and tools. In an Indigenous framework, prevention of suicide in Yup'ik communities re-engages the strengths of Indigenous knowledge and traditional practices for survival and prosperity and applies these to contemporary circumstances requiring navigation through the dangers and the rough waters of life.

Yup'ik communities are applying Indigenous knowledge and developing models of protection from suicide risk that derive from Indigenous theories and traditional values, teachings and ways of life (Rasmus et al. 2019b). While these efforts are growing, and an evidence-base demonstrating their efficacy and effectiveness to engage youth and achieve wellness outcomes is emerging (Allen et al. 2018), Alaska Native communities are still struggling to reduce persistent disparities in suicide and other related diseases of despair (e.g. Copeland et al. 2020). While the atmospheric climate undergoes rapid change in response to global population pressures, the social climate of structural racism and discrimination worldwide is not changing fast enough. Indigenous lives and ways of life continue to be lost and marginalized respectively under the dominant national regimes that are meant to care for all citizens. Standards of best practice for suicide prevention in the USA are not proving to be effective in reducing rates of suicide in Alaska Native communities, as rates have been very high and have continued to rise over the past forty years.

Clinical and mental health best practices for suicide prevention have not proven to be a fully feasible or effective solution for Alaska Native people, particularly for young people living in rural and remote communities. Alaska is a low-resource setting in a high-income country, and Alaska Native people are guaranteed rights to health care based on the 1971 Alaska Native Claims Settlement Act legislation. Structural barriers and racial inequities impact health care access and service delivery in Alaska, and rural communities are very often cut off from continuity of care and must rely on community-level resources to protect young people and build resilience from within. The limited resources available to provide services that are preventative and strengthening to Alaska Native youth would be better leveraged by providing support to Tribes at the community level to enact strategies that build on Indigenous knowledge and frameworks and promote well-being and resilience. The COVID-19 pandemic has made this point even more clearly as communities have locked down and flight service companies have reduced routing and flights to rural villages. During this time many Yup'ik communities have turned towards traditional subsistence practices as a self-determined measure to ensure food security and promote good health. Some communities have also directed a portion of their US federal COVID-19 relief funds and community grants towards hunting, fishing and gathering activities. In an Indigenous framework,

Yup'ik communities are weathering the storm of the pandemic, drawing from the same community and resilience resources that protect young people from suicide. There is enduring hope and sustainability in an Indigenous resilience framework where the tides will turn, the storms will pass and the people will always remain.

Acknowledgements

I extend my deepest gratitude and respect to the Yup'ik Alaska Native communities who have partnered and shared generously in this work. It has been a rare privilege to learn from Indigenous knowledge bearers who have weathered many a storm and come through stronger. Seeing these strengths carry on and pass down to young people inspires hope, even in stormy times, *quyana*. I appreciate the editors of this volume, Dr Olga Ulturgasheva and Dr Barbara Bodenhorn, for their tireless energies in organizing an Arctic panel at the Royal Anthropological Institute and following through on this publication. Finally, I am so grateful to my long-time research collaborator, Dr Olga Ulturgasheva, for providing the title to this chapter and working so closely with me to recognize and draw out the deep Indigenous literal and metaphorical meanings in 'weathering the storm'. This chapter would not have been possible without Dr Ulturgasheva's support, and I have learned so much through our exchanges and collaborations with Yup'ik and Eveny Indigenous communities, *alagda*.

This research was supported by the National Science Foundation Award#1207894 and Award#1424042. Additional support was provided by P20RR061430, National Center for Research Resources, National Institutes of Health. The content is solely the responsibility of the author and does not necessarily represent the official views of the NSF or the NIH.

Stacy M. Rasmus, PhD, is a Research Associate Professor and Director of the Center for Alaska Native Health Research at the University of Alaska Fairbanks, USA. Dr Rasmus has worked with American Indian and Alaska Native (AIAN) communities for over two decades and has built an international programme of research focusing on the promotion of Indigenous strengths, well-being and resilience in Alaska, the Arctic and the Pacific Northwest. Dr Rasmus is trained in the social and behavioural sciences with specific expertise in the translation of Indigenous knowledge and practice into health interventions that are community-driven and culturally-centred.

References

Alaska Department of Health and Social Services. 2015. *Top Five Leading Causes of Death by Age Group, Alaska*. Juneau, AK: Division of Public Health.

Alaska Native Epidemiology Center. 2017. *Alaska Native Health Status Report: Second Edition*. Anchorage, AK: Alaska Native Tribal Health Consortium.

Alia, Valeria. 2007. *Names & Nunavut: Culture and Identity in the Inuit Homeland*. New York: Berghahn Books.

Allen, James, Marya Levintova and Gerald Mohatt. 2011. 'Suicide and Alcohol-Related Disorders in the U.S. Arctic: Boosting Research to Address a Primary Determinant of Health Disparities', *International Journal of Circumpolar Health* 70(5): 473–87.

Allen, James et al. 2014. 'People Awakening: Collaborative Research to Develop Cultural Strategies for Prevention in Community Intervention', *American Journal of Community Psychology* 54(1–2): 100–11.

———. 2018. 'Multi-Level Cultural Intervention for the Prevention of Suicide and Alcohol Use Risk with Alaska Native Youth: A Nonrandomized Comparison of Treatment Intensity', *Prevention Science: The Official Journal of the Society for Prevention Research* 19(2): 174–85.

Atlas, Ronald. 2013. 'One Health: Its Origins and Future', *Current Topics in Microbiology and Immunology* 365: 1–13.

Ayunerak, Paula et al. 2014. 'Yup'ik Culture and Context in Southwest Alaska: Community Member Perspectives of Tradition, Social Change, and Prevention', *American Journal of Community Psychology* 54(1–2): 91–99.

Berry, J.W. 1985. 'Acculturation among Circumpolar Peoples: Implications for Health Status', *Arctic Medical Research* 40: 21–27.

Bjerregaard, Peter. 2001. 'Rapid Socio-Cultural Change and Health in the Arctic', *International Journal of Circumpolar Health* 60(2): 102–11.

Bodenhorn, Barbara and Olga Ulturgasheva. 2017. 'Climate Strategies: Thinking through Arctic Examples', *Philosophical Transactions, Series A, Mathematical, Physical, and Engineering Sciences* 375(2095): 20160363.

Burch, Ernest. 2005. *Alliance and Conflict: The World System of the Inupiaq Eskimos*. Calgary, Canada: University of Calgary Press.

Chance, Norman. 1990. *The Inupiat and Arctic Alaska: An Ethnography of Development*. New York: Holt Rinehart & Winston.

Chandler, Michael and Christopher Lalonde. 1998. 'Cultural Continuity as a Hedge against Suicide in Canada's First Nations', *Transcultural Psychiatry* 35(2): 191–219.

Chandler, Michael and Travis Proulx. 2006. 'Changing Selves in a Changing World: Youth Suicide on the Fault-Lines of Colliding Cultures', *Archives of Suicide Research* 10: 125–40.

Chandler, Michael et al. 2003. 'Personal Persistence, Identity Development, and Suicide: A Study of Native and Non-Native North American Adolescents', *Monographs of the Society for Research in Child Development* 68(2): vii–viii, 1–130.

Condon, Richard. 1988. *Inuit Youth: Growth and Change in the Canadian Arctic*. New Brunswick, NJ: Rutgers University Press.

Copeland, William et al. 2020. 'Associations of Despair with Suicidality and Substance Misuse Among Young Adults', *JAMA Network Open* 3(6): e208627. https://doi.org/10.1001/jamanetworkopen.2020.8627

Cruikshank, Julie. 2006. *Do Glaciers Listen?: Local Knowledge, Colonial Encounters, and Social Imagination*. Vancouver: UBC Press.

Cunsolo Willox, Ashlee et al. 2015. 'Examining Relationships Between Climate Change and Mental Health in the Circumpolar North', *Regional Environmental Change* 15: 169–82.

Fienup-Riordan, Ann. 1991. *The Real People and the Children of Thunder: The Yup'ik Eskimo Encounter with Moravian Missionaries John and Edith Kilbuck*. Norman, OK: University of Oklahoma Press.

———. 1995. *Boundaries and Passages: Rule and Ritual in Yup'ik Eskimo Oral Traditions*. Norman, OK: University of Oklahoma Press.

———. 2000. *Hunting Tradition in a Changing World: Yup'ik Lives in Alaska Today*. New Brunswick, NJ: Rutgers University Press.

———. 2007. *Yuungnaqpiallerput/The Way we Genuinely Live: Masterworks of Yup'ik Science and Survival*. Seattle, WA: University of Washington Press.

———. 2010. 'Yup'ik Perspectives on Climate Change: "The World is Following Its People"', *Études/Inuit/Studies* 34: 55. 10.7202/045404ar.

———. 2020. *Nunakun-gguq Ciutengqertut/They Say They Have Ears Through the Ground: Animal Essays from Southwest Alaska*. Fairbanks, AK: University of Alaska Press.

Fienup-Riordan, Ann and Alice Rearden. 2015. *Ellavut/Our Yup'ik World and Weather: Continuity and Change on the Bering Sea Coast*. Seattle, WA: University of Washington Press.

Gearheard, Shari, Henary Huntington and Lene Kieslen Holm. 2013. *The Meaning of Ice: People and Sea Ice in Three Arctic Communities*. Hanover, NH: International Polar Institute.

Hensel, Chase. 1996. *Telling Our Selves: Ethnicity and Discourse in Southwestern Alaska*. Oxford and New York: Oxford University Press.

Hueffer, Karsten et al. 2019. 'One Health in the Circumpolar North', *International Journal of Circumpolar Health* 78(1): 1607502.

Huntington, Henry, Mary Carey and Charlene Apok. 2019. 'Climate Change in Context: Putting People First in the Arctic', *Regional Environmental Change* 19: 1217–23.

Jack, Joe et al. 2020. 'Traditional Knowledge Underlies One Health', *Science* 369(6511): 1576.

Kawagely, Oscar. 2000. *A Yupiaq Worldview: A Pathway to Ecology and Spirit*, 2nd edition. Long Grove, IL: Waveland Press Inc.

Kettl, Paul and Edward Bixler. 1991. 'Suicide in Alaska Natives, 1979-1984', *Psychiatry* 54(1): 55–63.

Kirmayer, Laurence, Christopher Fletcher and Lucy Boothroyd. 1998. 'Suicide among the Inuit of Canada', in Antoon Leenaars et al. (eds), *Suicide in Canada*. Toronto: University of Toronto, pp. 187–211.

Kirmayer, Laurence et al. 2011. 'Rethinking Resilience from Indigenous Perspectives', *Canadian Journal of Psychiatry* 56(2): 84–91.

Kvernmo Siv and S. Heyerdahl. 2003. 'Acculturation Strategies and Ethnic Identity as Predictors of Behavior Problems in Arctic Minority Adolescents',

Journal of the American Academy of Child & Adolescent Psychiatry 42(1): 57–65.

———. 2004. 'Ethnic Identity and Acculturation Attitudes among Indigenous Norwegian Sami and Ethnocultural Kven Adolescents', *Journal of Adolescent Research* 19(5): 512–32.

Lee, Kelley and Zabrina Brumme. 2013. 'Operationalizing the One Health Approach: The Global Governance Challenges', *Health Policy and Planning* 28(7): 778–85.

Marino, Elizabeth. 2015. *Fierce Climate, Sacred Ground: An Ethnography of Climate Change in Shishmaref, Alaska*. Fairbanks, AK: University of Alaska Press.

Moerlein, Katie and Courtney Carothers. 2012. 'Total Environment of Change: Impacts of Climate Change and Social Transitions on Subsistence Fisheries in Northwest Alaska', *Ecology and Society* 17: 10.

Mohatt, Gerald et al. 2004. '"Tied Together Like a Woven Hat": Protective Pathways to Alaska Native Sobriety', *Harm Reduction Journal* 1(1): 10.

Napoleon, Harold. 1996. *Yuuyaraq: The Way of the Human Being*. Fairbanks, AK: Alaska Native Knowledge Network.

Nelson, Edward. 1983. *The Eskimo about Bering Strait*, 2nd edition. Washington, DC: Smithsonian Institution Press.

O'Neil, John. 1986. 'Colonial Stress in the Canadian Arctic: An Ethnography of Young Adults Changing', in Craig Janes, Ron Stall and Sandra M. Gifford (eds), *Anthropology and Epidemiology: Interdisciplinary Approaches to the Study of Health and Disease*. Vol. 9. Dordrecht: D. Reidel Publishing Company, pp. 249–74.

Oswalt, Wendall. 2011. *Bashful No Longer: An Alaskan Eskimo Ethnohistory, 1778-1988*, 2nd edition. Norman, OK: University of Oklahoma Press.

Phinney, Jean. 2000. 'Identity Formation across Cultures: The Interaction of Personal, Societal, and Historical Change', *Human Development* 43(1): 27–31.

Rasmus, Stacy M., James Allen and Tara Ford. 2014. '"Where I Have to Learn the Ways How to Live": Youth Resilience in a Yup'ik Village in Alaska', *Transcultural Psychiatry* 51(5): 713–34. https://doi.org/10.1177/1363461514532512.

Rasmus, Stacy M., Billy Charles and Gerald Mohatt. 2014. 'Creating Qungasvik (a Yup'ik Intervention "Toolbox"): Case Examples from a Community-Developed and Culturally-Driven Intervention', *American Journal of Community Psychology* 54(1–2): 140–52.

Rasmus, Stacy M. et al. 2019a. 'With a Spirit that Understands: Reflections on a Long-Term Community Science Initiative to End Suicide in Alaska', *American Journal of Community Psychology* 64(1–2): 34–45.

———. 2019b. 'The Qasgiq Model as an Indigenous Intervention: Using the Cultural Logic of Contexts to Build Protective Factors for Alaska Native Suicide and Alcohol Misuse Prevention', *Cultural Diversity & Ethnic Minority Psychology* 25(1): 44–54.

Ray, Lily and Julie Raymond-Yakoubian. 2015. 'A Bering Strait Indigenous Framework for Resource Management: Respectful Seal and Walrus Hunting', *Arctic Anthropology* 52: 87–101. 10.3368/aa.52.2.87.

Ruscio, Bruce et al. 2015. 'One Health – A Strategy for Resilience in a Changing Arctic', *International Journal of Circumpolar Health* 74: 27913.

Shain, Benjamin. 2016. 'Suicide and Suicide Attempts in Adolescents', *Pediatrics* 138(1): e20161420.

Sustainable Development Working Group. 2017. *One Health; Operationalizing One Health in the Arctic*. Tromsø: Arctic Council Secretariat.

Ulturgasheva, Olga, Stacy Rasmus and Phyllis Morrow. 2015. 'Collapsing the Distance: Indigenous Youth Engagement in a Circumpolar Study of Youth Resilience', *Arctic Anthropology* 52(1): 60–70.

Ulturgasheva, Olga et al. 2011. 'Navigating International, Interdisciplinary, and Indigenous Collaborative Inquiry: Phase 1 in the Circumpolar Indigenous Pathways to Adulthood Project'. *Journal of Community Engagement and Scholarship* 4(1), 50–59.

Ulturgasheva, Olga et al. 2014. 'Arctic Indigenous Youth Resilience and Vulnerability: Comparative Analysis of Adolescent Experiences across Five Circumpolar Communities', *Transcultural Psychiatry* 51(5): 735–56.

Wexler, Lisa. 2009. 'Identifying Colonial Discourses in Inupiat Young People's Narratives as a Way to Understand the No Future of Inupiat Youth Suicide', *American Indian and Alaska Native Mental Health Research Journal* 16(1): 1–24.

Wexler, Lisa et al. 2014. '"Being Responsible, Respectful, Trying to Keep the Tradition Alive": Cultural Resilience and Growing Up in an Alaska Native Community', *Transcultural Psychiatry* 51(5): 693–712.

Young, Kue T. (ed.). 2012. *Circumpolar Health Atlas*. Buffalo, NY: University of Toronto Press.

Chapter 5

Journalism in Canada's Northern Territories
Digital Media, Civic Spaces, Indigenous Publics

Candis Callison

Every so often the Arctic makes news around the world as scientific research organizations release reports about the state of sea ice extent in the Arctic Ocean. For those who pay attention to climate change news and science, there is a feeling of routine in seeing what the latest variability entails. Text-based descriptions and short stories generally accompany maps that depict the top of the world with a white amorphous blob of frozen Arctic Ocean in the centre of land masses labelled Russia, Canada, Alaska, Greenland and Europe. Outlines on the map show where previous sea ice extended to in prior years. In 2007, media and communications scholars labelled the attention to and panic about sea ice loss a 'media event' as media organizations paid more attention to the depicted losses that were framed as a palpable example of climate change (Christensen, Nilsson and Wormbs 2013). Sea ice loss has continued in a steady but non-linear decline with very little media attention being paid to the peaks and valleys that span the more than a decade of sea ice changes that have occurred since then.

Most global publics outside the Arctic know the Arctic through media representations like this: periodic reports that generate spasmodic concern from journalists, editors and their audiences. Meaning is prescribed by scientists and, sometimes, political or industry figures – rarely by Indigenous and/or Arctic-based experts.

Attention spans and southern media representations are no different in countries like Canada where 40 per cent of its land mass is in the Arctic and robust public and private media can be found in northern and southern Canada (Stoddart and Smith 2016; Callison and Tindall 2017). Even when it comes to covering climate change, Stoddart and Smith in a study of national newspapers in Canada found that 'the Arctic is not central to Canadian news about climate change' despite the Arctic being one of the main reasons the rest of the world should pay attention to Canada (2016: 326).

Given that media representations play an outsized role in public perceptions of and about the Arctic, and the Arctic plays a sometimes outsized role in representing impacts related to a future with climate change, the burden on journalists to 'get it right' in their stories about the Arctic is perhaps outsized as well. The few scholars who have studied national and international media coverage are highly critical of the ways in which the Arctic is rarely represented and often portrayed using problematic, repetitive tropes (Callison 2017; Callison and Tindall 2017; Pincus and Ali 2016; Roosvall and Tegelberg 2013; Stoddart and Smith 2016). This chapter draws on this literature, and on multi-year, multi-method research into journalism in Canada's northern territories to argue that regional media across the Arctic provide a differentiated resource for 'new narratives that put communities back into the calculus of risk and decision-making' (Bravo 2009). In so doing, regional media sources provide a stark contrast to the framing of climate change as a global crisis and instead situate climate change as part of many ongoing challenges that communities are engaged in and navigating – and able to navigate.

Journalism in northern Canada contributes to a civic space that includes stories about resilience, multiple ways of knowing and living with climate change, and locates climate change as something that is happening to people, animals, lands and oceans that are in relationships with one another. Understanding the Canadian Arctic as operating within a settler-colonial framework that underpins these relations and hierarchies of knowledge historically and in the present is essential to the doing of journalism and engagement with Indigenous publics. Further, digital media is enabling an increasingly robust civic space, shifting journalistic practices, and amplifying voices from communities – and it's widely available to global audiences through digital platforms like Facebook and Twitter. Digital media potentially affords a newly broad, diverse reach for voices and journalism that originate in the Arctic where regional discourse about regional problems with global significance might be co-produced.

This chapter first explores the ways in which Arctic voices have been framed in Canadian and international media, and then offers an overview of findings related to an ongoing research project that began in 2015 and focuses on regional journalism across the Canadian North. Very few studies have looked closely at journalistic practices and/or regional media in the Canadian or other parts of the Arctic, and none since the emergence of a hybridized media landscape (Chadwick 2013; Picard 2014) that includes radio, television, newspapers both in print and digital editions, and widely-used digital platforms like Facebook and Twitter.[1] The Arctic Journalism project has sought to understand the changing dynamics of doing journalism in and about northern Canada, situating the challenge of telling stories about the Arctic within a framework that considers the sedimentation of relations in the region, environmental changes and spasmodic global attention, and new digital possibilities for agency, accountability and self-representation.

Media Framing of the Arctic: Vulnerability and Opportunity

Climate change has to a great degree been represented as a global crisis, and the Arctic is usually framed as both metonymic of this crisis and a kind of first wave of its impact with faster rising temperatures and catastrophic effects that are reshaping Arctic lands, waters, ways of life and visions for the future. Janet Roitman has pointed out that labelling something as a 'crisis' is a 'distinction that produces meaning' (2013: 82). While that distinction and meaning-making process also depends to some degree on the context, platform, vernacular and audience (Callison 2020), crisis as framework defines both problems and solutions in particular ways – 'permitting and enabling certain narrations and giving rise to certain questions, but not others' (Roitman 2013: 5). Labelling climate change a global crisis thus has distinct stakes, and is likely to produce, amplify and torque power relations, even as it purports to offer solutions that reflect global care and concern (Callison 2021; Jasanoff 2010).

Concurrent with the rise of climate change as global crisis has been the emergence of the Arctic as a region, and site for citizenship. Martello has argued that global climate science is both 'shaping and being shaped by a new kind of citizen, namely the Arctic citizen' and that these citizens, and in particular Indigenous peoples, are represented as at risk, lacking agency, and as keepers of traditional ecological knowledge (2004: 107). Bravo has further suggested that these narratives that 'emphasize the power of global climate systems to threaten northern communities, do so largely at the cost of masking the voices of northern citizens themselves' (2009: 258). While neither Martello or Bravo offer an analysis of Arctic citizens as publics or civic spaces that include robust media, this chapter offers a consideration of both. Media at all levels (regional, national, international) are challenged to reflect the multi-faceted expert-driven and voiced problem that is climate change, and confront the ways in which the Arctic and its publics have been and might be represented as recipients of and first responders to climate change. Regional media offer distinct approaches to these challenges in part because their publics are Arctic and majority Indigenous. Indigenous, it is worth noting, is a term that should also imply diversity in terms of languages, cultures and colonial histories across the Arctic as is true in any other region impacted by European imperialism in the last several centuries.[2]

Despite the Arctic being a relatively new construct in political and organizational terms, it is and has been animated by a long history and sedimentation of media representations that range from the lone polar bear or other charismatic mega-fauna to the resourceful Indigenous hunter or 'primitive noble survivor' and the scientist in search of data, notoriety as an 'explorer', and/or usually, both (Alia 1999; Cruikshank 2005; Fienup-Riordan 1995; Sangster 2016; Stoddart and Smith 2016). What has been added to these associations with climate change coverage is the notion of vulnerability – both in terms of the Arctic being a recipient of the world's toxic pollutants and climate change, which within this broader context might be seen as not a 'new' crisis, but another major ill resulting from industrial development in the South (Watt-Cloutier 2015; Callison 2017).

Who is considered resilient and likely to succeed in fast-changing climates, and who is represented as more or less vulnerable or at risk layers on to national narratives and frames for military and industrial development. It is in this sense that dual and duelling narratives emerge between global phenomena and regional experience where vulnerability is inextricably linked with risk and reward in a system with newly configured and always likely winners and losers. This is reflected in Pincus and Ali's (2016) study of English-language media coverage of the Arctic tracked via Google News. They find that coverage of the Arctic has been on a steady increase since 2006. The three common frames they identify are related to a future with climate change where vulnerability is transmuted to opportunity: 1) a 'race for the Arctic'; 2) a 'new Cold War' between the US and Russia; and 3) conflict between oil interests and environmental groups. Certainly, 2013 Greenpeace activism and the Russian response explains the prominence of the third frame, but it also speaks to the ways in which the Arctic becomes a proxy for other issues even while these other issues are also caught up in projections of what a future with climate change might present.

This tension between vulnerability and opportunity is echoed in Canadian media frames as well, but with some significant differences. Stoddart and Smith (2016) studied Canada's two national newspapers between 1997 and 2010, and find the Arctic is framed as both an 'unchanging wilderness' and as having immense extractive resources (oil, gas and minerals). The issues that emerge are that the Arctic is being transformed by climate change, climate change is harming polar bears, and that new shipping routes are now open in the Arctic (2016: 326). These narratives and frames are, they point out, 'overwhelmingly done by news workers, media corporations, and economically and politically privileged news sources in southern Canada, and consumed by a predominantly southern Canadian news audience' (2016: 321). Such frames are, Stoddard and Smith additionally point out, inherently limiting because they efface differences in responsibility, unequal risks, vulnerability and adaptation. Climate justice provides an alternative frame, in their analysis, because it represents local and regional voices from the Arctic such that multiple experiences and perspectives, as well as pathways towards resilience, become visible (see also Roosvall and Tegelberg 2018).

Scale and agency are persistent problems in media coverage of the Arctic in part because 'the Arctic has often been framed as a kind of canary, bellwether, or proxy for the present and direct impacts of climate change', ignoring 'underlying challenges and particularities related to social histories, complex ecological interactions, and power relations' that are specific to the region and its citizens (Callison 2017). Bravo has relatedly pointed out that the larger climate change narrative 'is built exclusively on the language of scientific expertise and physical causation, and is not equipped to deal with politically, economically, legally and socially complex responses' (2009: 259). So, while climate change is global in scale and transcendent in its configuration, chronic crises in the region, like the ongoing impacts of colonialism, remain unexamined (Callison 2014; Marino 2015; Whyte 2018). Bodenhorn's response to this representational dilemma is enormously useful when she states that while the Arctic might be a good proxy for climate change, Indigenous peoples in the Arctic cannot be considered in a similarly reductive way (quoted in Diemberger et al. 2012). Instead, Bodenhorn and Ulturgasheva (2017) argue that Indigenous peoples have adapted and conceived of their ecosystems as always evolving, and that northerners must be represented as the experts on the North. What climate change entails must be understood in and on Arctic terms, with Indigenous knowledges and experiences.

Climate Justice and Beyond: Reporting on Climate Change and Arctic Communities in Canada

Scholars who have looked closely at climate change have suggested that both media coverage and scholarship need to account for power relations, and 'report in a way that reflects agency, climate justice, and multi-scalar multi-cultural perspectives' (quote from Callison 2017; see also Olausson and Berglez 2014; Roosvall and Tegelberg 2018). Boykoff and Yulsman (2013) further note that 'the cultural politics of climate change are situated, power-laden, mediated, and recursive in an ongoing battlefield of knowledge and interpretation'. This 'battlefield' becomes that much more challenging when considering the sedimentation of representations related to the Arctic, the emergent frames of vulnerability and opportunity that reflect persistent problems of scale and agency, and the long history of mis- or non-representation of Indigenous people and communities in Canadian media. Despite the prominence of leaders like Sheila Watt-Cloutier and the presence of the Inuit Circumpolar Council at major transnational and international organizations and meetings, Canadian national print media have not tended to include the Arctic and Indigenous people in reports on climate change (Stoddart and Smith 2016; Watt-Cloutier 2015).

This challenge is evident in media analyses of the last two prominent UNFCCC COP meetings in Copenhagen and Paris. Roosvall and Tegelberg (2013) looked at the framing of Indigenous people in four Canadian and Swedish newspapers during COP 15 meetings in Copenhagen in 2009, and found coverage to be very sparse (7 out of 419 articles). Canada's national newspaper, *The Globe and Mail*, featured 129 articles on COP 15, and not one of these articles featured or quoted Indigenous people. At COP 21 in Paris in 2015, my research team similarly found that neither national paper quoted northern Indigenous people and the Arctic was only once the focus of COP 21 coverage. The public broadcaster (CBC) and regional media and one international newspaper featured and quoted Indigenous people, however.

This discrepancy is not entirely out of character for print media in particular and mainstream media in general. Media have been pointedly criticized in Canada for their historic and ongoing complicity with colonialism (Alia 1999; Anderson and Robertson 2011; Lambertus 2004; Meadows and Avison 2000).[3] As Callison and Tindall (2017) point out, this is reflected in the lack of media coverage of climate change impacts in Canada that either include or focus on Indigenous peoples' experiences. Colonialism in Canada has meant that Indigenous lands were annexed with and without treaties, and human rights abrogated through federal policies that mandated enclosure, displacement, forced assimilation through multiple means, prohibition of language and culture, flexible inscription of identities, and removal of livelihoods and legal recourse (see, for example, Coulthard 2014; Simpson 2014). Climate change, similar to many Indigenous people globally, is 'intertwined with the structuring realities of colonialism that amplify existing vulnerabilities and risk' (Callison and Tindall 2017; see also Cochran et al. 2013; Marino 2015; Whyte 2013; Wildcat 2013).

Situating climate change alongside colonialism and including Indigenous perspectives presents a complex challenge in part because, as Roosvall and Tegelberg (2013) found, Indigenous people in the Arctic are often framed as hero-witnesses or victim-witnesses of climate change, and this is particularly true for Inuit. The heroic part is related to traditional knowledge which is portrayed as a potential global and scientific resource. Stoddart and Smith (2016) note however that traditional knowledge is always juxtaposed alongside scientific knowledge such that legitimacy and authority must be verified. In contrast to either the victim or hero, they look to Arctic communities and groups like the Inuit Circumpolar Council (ICC) as intervening voices that destabilize global and national media frames and represent the Arctic as a region that is full of communities that may suffer disproportionately (see also Callison 2014; Watt-Cloutier 2015).

Regional Media, Journalistic Practices, Digital Publics

Scholarship on climate change and media has not tended to juxtapose regional media with national and international media coverage, and as noted earlier, nor has scholarship that looks at the emergence of forms of Arctic citizenship tended to consider the role or function of journalism and Arctic-based media (Bravo 2009; Martello 2004). Yet, the civic imaginary and the role of media in civic life and imaginations have become increasingly important for those who study digital media more generally (Baiocchi et al. 2014). And as Callison and Young (2020) point out, scholars who have looked at the impacts of technological changes that have deeply affected journalistic routines, practices and norms have not tended to also consider persistent critiques of journalism related to gender, race and colonialism. This chapter thus makes a contribution by considering journalism as an aspect of civic life across a region with many distinct Indigenous communities and where digital technologies are shifting the role of journalism and journalistic practices.

Further, building on Callison (2017), this chapter considers diverse Indigenous peoples across the Canadian Arctic as publics whose responses, engagement and expectations shape the contours of regional coverage of climate change. Indigenous people have most often been thought of as subjects for coverage and/or research as opposed to contributors to and users of public knowledge in civic spaces (Bravo 2009). While John Dewey's 1927 construction of the public is one of an imagined, functional myth that fulfils the needs of the state and the media by virtue of its homogeneity, more recent conceptions of the public by Science and Technology Studies (STS) scholars suggest the public might better be considered in terms of 'the sheer diversity, partiality, teeming conflict, flux, and potential incoherence of real, identifiable components' (Ellis et al. 2010). Between the generalities and specificities of publics and their concerns, there is a productive tension and one that serves the functions of media in tangible ways when journalists talk about 'serving the public'. And as Callison (2017) argues, 'this is certainly applicable in thinking of Indigenous people as a kind of abstracted category and as a set of diverse peoples with distinct histories, beliefs, experiences, and knowledges'.

It is also, however, where science and media often stumble. In science, 'publics have been imagined and almost "pre-constituted" by scientific projects and science communication endeavors without an attentiveness' to wider commitments and diversities of concerns (Callison 2017). What this means is that certain notions of race, indigeneity and gender are naturalized as are categories for knowledge and processes for decision-making that involve scientific information (see, for example, Haraway 1989; Irwin and Wynne 2004; Jasanoff 2010; Miller and Edwards 2001; Reardon 2005; TallBear 2013; Whyte 2013; Wildcat 2013). Ellis et al. pointedly conclude that 'experiments in democratizing science have ironically served to reinstate the authority of science by subtle means involving erasure of the very publics being invited to participate' (2010: 8). Bravo further critiques scientific Arctic reports like the ACIA as 'intended for use by managerial elites' and experts who are part of the technocracy of scientists and bureaucrats who benefit from claiming the Arctic is in a crisis due to climate change (2009: 269).

Is journalism doing better? Journalism has traditionally been considered as a means of and for accountability where reporters stand in as surrogates for diverse publics, holding governments and other societal institutions accountable and providing information that citizens need in order to make decisions (Schudson 2001; Ward 2004). Yet, journalism has also struggled to adjust to newly participatory publics and digital tools and competing or symbiotic platforms that have given way to a state of self-declared crisis related to subsequent unprecedented economic and organizational restructuring in the news industry (Picard 2014). As Zelizer points out, such crisis declarations in journalism overlook 'the fact that crisis has different drivers in different locations' (2015: 13). The Arctic provides a key example of this when considering a 2017 report by the Public Policy Forum in Canada on the state of media that lamented the rise of digital media and platforms like Facebook and Twitter. While cognizant of the new demands on journalists and restructuring of news organizations, this chapter, in contrast, views digital platforms as tools that enable wider regional audience participation and a potentially global platform to comment on and counter dominant frames and narrative constructions of vulnerability, risk and crisis in the Arctic.

As journalism faces its own industry and practice-related challenges and crisis, reporting in and from the Arctic as a region presents a gauntlet for journalistic practice in part because of how digitally connected and geographically dispersed Arctic publics and communities are. Journalism is critical in terms of providing information at a time of ongoing social, political and environmental change even while Arctic publics and leaders are increasingly vocal on platforms like Twitter and Facebook. For example, after the Paris Agreement failed to mention the Arctic, current ICC Chair Oglalik Eegeesiak took to Twitter to declare, 'countries failed' even while world leaders and many NGOs – and much of Twitter – were celebrating the Agreement as a milestone in climate negotiations. An Arctic-focused online news outlet, RCI Eye on the Arctic (an online news source operated by CBC), interviewed Eegeesiak in the aftermath and quoted her as explaining her position this way in Quinn (2015):

'[The agreement] was historic, yes,' said Okalik Eegeesiak, chair of the Inuit Circumpolar Council (ICC), the organization that represents the world's approximately 155,000 Inuit living in Canada, Greenland, Russia and the United States.

'[But] Inuit and Saami peoples wanted to have more recognition and respect for Arctic peoples,' she said in a phone interview. 'There is some mention of Indigenous peoples and our rights and our role in climate change [issues] but there isn't much commitment to work with us.'

RCI was the only English-language news outlet to follow up on Eegeesiak's dissent and to register a response from leaders of Indigenous people in the Arctic. All of the media coverage our research team tracked during the COP 21 ignored the lack of mention of the Arctic in the Paris Agreement, even while several pointed out the mention of Indigenous knowledge and peoples. However, it is not merely a representation issue as Eegeesiak strongly points out. Instead, what is at stake is a recognition of the power relations and a desire to collaborate on solutions – 'to work with us'.[4]

Another relevant example stems from the still ongoing hashtag #sealfie, also on Twitter, where images of 'Inuit, young and old, wearing sealskin clothing in traditional and contemporary designs in photos' were posted in response to renewed efforts by anti-sealing environmental groups (Rodgers and Scobie 2015: 92). Rodgers and Scobie conclude that the movement utilized a tactical approach to 'interrupt historical attempts to marginalize their participation in the debate' (2015: 92; see also Arnaquq-Baril 2016). This stands in contrast to the relatively recent listing of the polar bear as an endangered species where Inuit voices were rarely heard in national or global media despite many Inuit communities and organizations having stated in regional media that this listing damages their economies, and distracts from more significant aspects of climate change (Callison 2014; Stoddart and Smith 2016; Wright 2014).

Adaptation to and creative uses of digital media amongst northern Indigenous communities are built on a long tradition of tactical use of media for self-determination and self-representation that began in the 1970s (Alia 1999; Anderson and Robertson 2011; Arnaquq-Baril 2016; Callison and Hermida 2015; David 2012; Ginsberg, Abu-Lughod and Larkin 2002; Hafsteinsson and Bredin 2010; Hansen and Poisey 1991; Rodgers and Scobie 2015; Roth 2005). The development of regional media is intimately intertwined with political developments across the Circumpolar Arctic that resulted in multi-lingual news and current affairs shows on radio and television on CBC North, the formation of the Inuit Broadcasting Corporation, TV North, Northern Native Broadcasting, and eventually Aboriginal Peoples Television Network (APTN) (Alia 1999; David 2012; Roth 2005). Alia (1999) has also observed that many Indigenous political figures in Canada's North began as journalists.

Calls for self-determination and platforms for self-representation are intimately related to climate change in ways that move climate justice beyond a recognition of disproportionate effects in the Arctic (Bravo 2009). Whyte considers Indigenous concerns about climate change as being centred on 'collective continuance', which he defines as 'a community's fitness for making adjustments to current or predicted change in ways that contest colonial hardships and embolden comprehensive aims at robust living' (2014: 602). Whyte argues that 'the ecological challenges of climate change are entangled, or coupled, with political obstructions' and societal institutions can either create more constraints or opportunities for Indigenous communities intent on their collective continuance (2013: 521). As a societal institution, media – at regional, national and international levels – have 'a role to play in holding societal institutions accountable for both constraints or opportunities' (Callison 2017). This chapter further argues that journalists also have a role to play in facilitating multiple perspectives, Indigenous knowledges and Arctic-led pathways towards resilience and adaptation. The following sections will provide a brief background on the ongoing research project that animates this chapter.

Background: Arctic Journalism Project

The Arctic Journalism project benefits from Anthropology, Science and Technology Studies, and Media Studies approaches that treat media as both material culture and cultural material (Boczkowski and Lievrouw 2007), and journalism as a set of norms and practices that have emerged within distinct cultural and historical contexts and are rapidly evolving alongside the adoption of digital, collaborative and participatory forms of media (for example, see Deuze and Witschge 2018; Schudson 2001; Singer et al. 2011; Ward 2004). Anthropologies of media and journalism scholarship have both used ethnographic methods to look closely at journalistic practices in and across the profession or at specific organizations (for example, Callison and Young 2020; Usher 2013). My approach follows an 'open system' and collaborative approach to ethnographic research in order to understand the complex, layered social processes at work in a vastly interconnected and increasingly global web of social realities (Fortun 2003; Marcus and Fischer 1999). Marcus and Fischer (1999) and Fischer (2009) suggest that multi-sited ethnography, collaboration with informants, reflexivity, and juxtaposition of and close attention to the circulation of media and other representations are the key tools for revealing micro and macro levels of socio-historical contexts and connections (see also Marcus 2000).

The Arctic Journalism project has become a long term project that has so far included a year-long content analysis of regional, national and international coverage, analysis of media and social media related to COP 21 in Paris, and nearly fifty ethnographic interviews and multi-sited fieldwork with Indigenous and non-Indigenous journalists serving Canada's northern territories. This chapter primarily focuses on an overview of ethnographic fieldwork conducted in 2016 with northern journalists. Other publications are under review or planned and the research website, arcticjournalism.com, remains periodically active.

As a Journalism School professor and an anthropologist, I have also sought to contribute to Arctic journalism and innovate methodologically by collaborating with and training Master of Journalism students in basic ethnographic methodologies in order to participate in this project.

Three students hired at the beginning of their Masters programme were required to complete part of their twelve-week internship in an Arctic newsroom. These students eventually lived and reported from Iqaluit, Yellowknife and Whitehorse for four to six weeks each. They kept field notes to varying degrees, published blog posts about their experiences on the research site, and participated in conducting ethnographic interviews with me in the territory they had worked in as interning journalists. In addition, four other alumni who worked briefly as Research Assistants when this project was beginning (but too late to do their internship as part of the project) went on to work in northern newsrooms and later were interviewed for the project in their capacity as working journalists.

The three students who did their journalism internship in the North and conducted ethnographic interviews with me afterwards offered multiple insights that have been helpful in characterizing the methods pioneered for this research. All students noted that it was important for them as students to do their internships in the territories because they wanted to be 'grounded' in what it was like to do news in the North. However, they also noted that they 'couldn't see outside the newsroom' they were interning in until they did the ethnographic interviews. For example, they couldn't imagine what the perspective was of other journalists working in other newsrooms, and the process of interviewing so many others about journalistic practices and the role of journalism in the North and South.

Journalism in Northern Canada: Facebook Territories?

When we began this research project, we wanted to understand what some of the differences between regional, national and local journalisms looked like. What we found confirmed the findings of much of the scholarship cited above. For example, we found international media and National Canadian media we studied are less likely to mention Indigenous groups whether reporting on climate change or resource extraction than regional media. Regional media mentions Indigenous peoples in nearly 50 per cent of articles; international media mention Indigenous people in less than 7 per cent of articles; and Canadian media mentions Indigenous peoples in almost 30 per cent of articles.[5] When we looked at a specific event like COP 21 in Paris, regional media quoted Indigenous people in 67 per cent of their stories whereas in Canada only the CBC quoted Indigenous people in national coverage.[6] Regional media covered the event with more varied sources and stories as well.

Our research questions for regional journalists focused on 1) what approaches regional journalists utilized, 2) changes to journalistic practices as a result of digital media, and 3) how they work with and think about engaging audiences that are significantly Indigenous in Canada's northern territories. Newspapers, regional radio and television – what would be considered mainstream media in the South – are based in the capitals of the territories: Iqaluit in Nunavut, Yellowknife in the Northwest Territories (NWT), and Whitehorse in the Yukon. The offices we visited to interview journalists ranged from mobile trailers, a log cabin on a lake, corporate offices above a mining company's headquarters, CBC stations and other dedicated print newspaper buildings with a press in the lower floor, and other kinds of shared office spaces.

Most journalists do the majority of their reporting outside the capital via telephone, and, in the last several years, increasingly via social media as well due to budgetary concerns and constraints. Almost anywhere in the Circumpolar Arctic is expensive to get to, and expensive to stay in as well – for travellers of any kind, including journalists (and researchers). Canada is no exception, although Nunavut has many more small communities than the other territories that are accessible only by plane and possibly by boat in the summer and icebreaker in the winter. Only the major cities have the infrastructure to support short-term guests, and even then, a city like Iqaluit (the smallest capital of the eastern-most Canadian territory of Nunavut), with a population of over 7,000, is limited in its ability to accommodate visitors, and prices for food and lodging are high.[7] Yellowknife and Whitehorse are larger and comparable in size, with populations of over 19,000 and 25,000 respectively.

All three northern territories have Arctic and sub-Arctic regions within their jurisdiction. Unlike Alaska (next to the Yukon) with a population of over 700,000, territorial populations in Canada are smaller, between 34,000 and 44,000 each. In Nunavut, Indigenous people constitute over 86 per cent of the population, nearly 53 per cent in NWT, and over 23 per cent in the Yukon. Created in 1990 as part of a land and governance settlement with Inuit, Nunavut was formerly a part of NWT.

Media is predominantly English across the territories, but in Nunavut, most media put some of their programming or publication in Inuktitut as well. NWT and the Yukon have multiple Indigenous languages with some print publications and broadcast programming in these languages. The dividing line between these territories and the provinces below them is quite porous linguistically and culturally. For example, CBC reporters in Northern Quebec broadcast in Inuktitut.

The public broadcaster CBC is the largest media employer across northern Canada. It has enormous influence as well as the most resources for coverage of breaking news and the constant opportunity to feed stories to national and broadly regional audiences (i.e. across all three territories). CBC is also the only multi-lingual news source delivering programming in several Indigenous languages, and it is one of the few news organizations to employ a high number of Indigenous journalists. Print publications also publish some stories in Indigenous languages, but there were, at the time of our research in 2016, no Indigenous people working as journalists for print publications, much like newspapers in southern Canada (see Hinchey 2022 on new efforts to develop journalism training and recruitment in the NWT).

Many news organizations and journalists in Southern Canada have resented and/or fear the changes that have come with digital media in part due to the economic restructuring that has occurred in the industry as a result (see Public Policy Forum, 2017). This was not something our research team encountered among northern journalists. Instead, Facebook in particular was considered a major shift in thinking about the public as participatory, and a new space for civic engagement. Many called it 'essential' and a 'game-changer', and others said they 'live and die' by Facebook and that their territory was 'Facebook Territory'. This also had some relation to labour issues, where newer journalists were less likely to use Facebook because they didn't yet have the well developed social networks to draw on – something that usually changed rapidly with time spent reporting. And certainly, some journalists used Facebook much more than others.

Part of the rationale offered in all territories for the meteoric rise of Facebook use is the geographic distances between communities. Prior to Facebook, many journalists did regular phone-ins to communities to find out 'news' and get pictures. The contrast between news organizations is stark on this point. For example, CBC was and remains the news organization with the biggest budget to travel to communities (an investment of thousands of dollars per trip) whereas most newspapers have no travel budget and depend on phone and social media as conduits to the communities. Images were something many journalists mentioned as being a major addition from digital media (no more developing and dark rooms), and were widely available from Facebook-enabled audiences. CBC has pages for each territory and one for the North, and often posts pictures taken in communities. These are incredibly popular with audience members who are on Facebook.

Social media and phone-ins are thus more essential to some organizations, but all increasingly rely on them as budgets continue to decline, especially at the CBC. Facebook also makes a general phone-in less necessary and a follow-up phone call more likely. Some mentioned the challenge of verification and getting past 'mere gossip', both pre- and post-Facebook. One journalist described accessing Facebook as 'swimming through sewage'. However, most journalists who had been in the North for some time were likely to use it for contacting sources, story ideas, distribution, circulation, and direct and indirect feedback. How much a story or photo is liked or shared provides a kind of barometer of how well stories resonate and reflect community concerns and priorities, but this also proves challenging when that barometer becomes a more formal metric.

Facebook dependence and usage is very dependent on organizational priorities and workplace norms. Who runs the Facebook page says a lot about what kind of tool it is thought to be and what kind of priority it requires. A few organizations use it as a marketing tool while others have editors to run the page and use it as a news and distribution tool. At the time we were doing fieldwork in mid- to late 2016, CBC was pushing a 'digital-first' strategy. They were actively experimenting with new ways of using technology such as casing and methods that would allow journalists to use their smart phones in -50 degrees Celsius.

Because there is no audience tracking like there would be in southern media markets, some journalists suggested that an emphasis on 'measurables' offered through social media likes and shares and website traffic was highly problematic. For example, one journalist asked how to compare Twitter at 2,000 followers out of a population of 30,000 versus 40 call-ins on a lunchtime show? Some journalists said their news shows were well listened to according to their in-house surveys, but generally, without some investment in audience research, it is hard to compare traditional broadcast and print with Facebook and Twitter.

The general rule of thumb in all territories however was that Twitter was used by residents in the capitals while Facebook was used by everyone in the capital and in communities. Despite spotty satellite Internet connections, or maybe because of limited Internet, many communities used Facebook to keep in touch with other individuals and with the news of the world outside their community; e.g. if you have limited Internet connection time, you're going to go to the site that offers you the most efficient means for meeting your information, news, entertainment and/or social needs. That Facebook is a privately controlled platform with no accountability of its own rarely came up in conversations with journalists; its use as a public utility only surfaced in concerns about, for example, changes to how you could direct message sources – a Facebook-wide change that had occurred in the weeks before our interviews in mid-2016.

Approaches to digital and social media were in a state of rapid evolution during our fieldwork. First, journalists discussed how it changed their own storytelling practice, as they were spending less time in the field doing reporting and more time sending out content to 7–10 spots on different platforms e.g. Twitter, Facebook, audio news and shows, TV news and shows, websites. CBC reporters in particular – across the North – described the daily challenge of gathering enough content to service all the 'mouths to feed'. Some privately suggested that the quality of radio and TV coverage was being eroded in order to increase social media content and traction while others loved the opportunity to put more content up and get immediate feedback. Second, it is still difficult to tell how much Twitter and Facebook metrics affect which stories go up and which stories get told. Some journalists expressed concern about what the future holds should informal metrics become standards, i.e. will some kinds of stories still get published if they don't get more than 500 hits? Third, the few news outlets that have been slow to adapt to Facebook and online audiences are still working out exactly how to respond to a rapidly evolving public and media landscape. Their participation will likely have some impact as will more reliable Internet connections.

Climate Change and Arctic Identity

All of the journalists we interviewed said that climate change is always 'in the background' or 'part of life', and interrelated to many stories. However, it's not a news item or news category in its own right in the North. News that features or focuses on climate change has to be driven by local events – it needs to be 'practical' and 'relevant to everyday life'. When it is discussed, climate change is framed as happening in the present and not in the distant or abstract future. Indigenous journalists in Nunavut, NWT and the Yukon were quick to point out that traditional knowledge is a major element of how they cover anything related to climate change. They are likely to turn to knowledgeable elders and hunters to substantiate or understand scientific findings rather than the other way around.

Some CBC journalists noted that national interest has shifted as well; for example, 'it used to be that if you had climate change or a polar bear in a story, it would go national'. All journalists offered varying and persistent critique of southern coverage of the North, with one editor describing the 'national reach' of Canadian newspapers as 'a joke', because the North is often passed over. Scholarship, as noted earlier, has also found that the North is not covered by newspapers even when it comes to climate change. A greater concern among some was the persistent ways in which stories about trauma, in particular youth suicide, seemed to garner attention and awards. It is a serious issue, but when it is one of the only stories that reaches the South, it perpetuates stereotypical views of northern communities and youth.

The difference in reporting on climate change and the response to how southern media covers, ignores and frames the North reflect both a highly localized and regionalized sense of news values and civic space. So, even while journalists might draw boundaries between territories and/or between themselves and an Arctic identity, they all saw themselves as northern. Distinctive northern news values varied from organization to organization, but most agreed that northern news organizations had a responsibility and/or obligation to reflect or cement what it means to be a northerner, even if what that means varied from territory to territory and between capital cities and far flung communities. Many journalists spoke of a deeper accountability in terms of how they covered and framed issues, and a deeper connection to the stories they were telling.

In one of the territories, a morning radio news show provides a vital example of what it means to both contribute to and cultivate civic space in that territory and across the North. First, linguistically, the show seamlessly moves back and forth between Inuktitut and English. The show's then producer and host both told me that which language gets used depends on who the guest/expert is and the topic. Inuktitut has several dialects so that factors into their consideration as well.

The producer had at that time worked in media for eighteen years. Originally trained as a teacher, she raised her family and lived in many communities in Nunavut and Northern Quebec. As a producer, she is responsible for about eleven hours of programming per day, the majority of which is in Inuktitut. When we asked her what media she pays attention to, she said: 'Facebook. Social Media. That's where I get most of my sources. I get messages because I've been in this business so long; you get trust from people'. Facebook in a sense provides the scaffolding and platform that makes existing social networks visible and enables a closer sense of connection and representation. And she said that it isn't just existing connections that matter, but the chance to represent community concerns and practices to each other and anyone else who happens to visit the page:

> We got into social media right away. We can tell that with our Facebook page and our Twitter that it's quite popular. And our web page is quite popular. I'm assuming, and I don't know because we don't ask, that the reason we're popular is we're unique. We showcase Arctic images. We showcase our traditional lifestyle. I know there's anti-sealing thoughts everywhere, every time you see a dead baby seal. But we post them. This young guy's first seal. Because it's our culture. It's our food. We eat it every day.

The station's social media presence offers a grounded and community view of what life looks and feels like across the North in part because of its audience and its journalists who come from communities across the territory. The host described his own start in broadcasting as beginning when he was fourteen in a small fly-in community (a familiar term across the North for communities that are not reachable via permanent roadways). He pitched a show for youths his own age in his community, and was given a regular spot. He said he 'fell in love' with radio. Eventually, when a job came up for a reporter who could speak both English and Inuktitut, he said he called the station manager 'for five months until he gave in and gave me the job'. The host went on to work for the same station twice for four-year stints, and was a widely admired host until he left several years ago.

The host said that the International Polar Year research projects are what really got their show doing a lot of stories on climate change, but they covered it with a difference:

> It [IPY] brought in a lot of researchers to the North so, talking to these researchers and then the results, what they've seen, what they've observed and then we try to balance that with what Inuit are seeing. More so now whenever we talk about climate change, it's really driven by people who are looking into it. Or if there's a major change happening that people in communities are observing then we'll talk to them.

The deep connection that journalists have with communities is perhaps more visible with Facebook than it has ever been, and the priority even with a global issue like climate change is to understand how it is elaborated within the communities who are experiencing change. It is in this sense that journalism contributes to a civic space that revolves around resilience and multiple ways of knowing and living with climate change. Daily life is represented as people, animals, lands and oceans that are in relationship with one another, whether that entails sealing or climate change.

Conclusion: Arctic Civic Spaces and Journalisms

This chapter builds on calls from scholars to consider civic spaces in the Arctic, to understand Indigenous peoples as publics, and to critique and offer alternative representations of and for Arctic communities. Scholars have continually found that journalism from southern Canada and internationally has tended to ignore, misrepresent or narrowly represent both Arctic concerns and Indigenous peoples. And while this research continues to find such gaps, it also examines approaches to regional journalism alongside national and international news coverage of the Arctic in order to bring to the fore the stark differences evident in coverage, choice of experts and treatment of Indigenous sources and experts. In its attention to Indigenous people as publics, northern and Arctic journalism in Canada offers stories of resilience in the face of change, Indigenous knowledges framed as vital expertise, and historical and cultural understandings of relations between humans, non-humans, lands and waters that impact the discourse on risk, vulnerability, adaptation and other issues related to governance and resource development.

As digital media has begun to shape and shift journalistic practices, journalists working across Canada's North provide exemplary insights into how Facebook in particular might be utilized to enhance journalistic practices and how it is rapidly becoming a vital civic space for public engagement. Because the North has often relied on a hub-and-spoke type structuring in its media, where capitals function as centres of information flow, what social media does is make these relations between geographically dispersed communities and journalists in the hub visible. Crucially too, social media allows for bi-directional distribution where journalists can amplify voices and images from communities, and communities' responses to journalistic coverage increase a sense of accountability to and engagement with its publics. What this offers in terms of understanding climate change on Arctic terms is a relational view of how communities are adapting to and prioritizing environmental change even as they deal with chronic crises related to colonialism and the last several decades of rapid social change that affect all aspects of daily life. As approaches to and uses of social media are likely to continue to evolve, so too are configurations of civic space, Indigenous publics and what constitutes 'good' journalism on and from the Arctic, offering increasing opportunities in digital media spaces to interact with Arctic representations and news co-produced on Arctic terms.

Acknowledgements

My thanks to Alfred Hermida, Tony Penikett and Kathryn Gretsinger for their support and collaboration on the grant that led to the Arctic Journalism project. My thanks also to the research assistants (now UBC journalism alumni) that have contributed so much to this project over the years, especially Peter Mothe, Alexander Kim and

Lauren Kaljur who completed their internships in northern newsrooms, and those who supported the project at various early and late stages: Garrett Hinchey, James Thomson, Maura Forrest, Emily Blake, Ricardo Khayatte, and Anya Zoledziowski.

Candis Callison is the Canada Research Chair in Indigenous journalism, media and public discourse and an Associate Professor at the University of British Columbia, jointly appointed to the School of Journalism, Writing and Media and the Institute for Critical Indigenous Studies. She is the co-author of *Reckoning: Journalism's Limits and Possibilities* (Oxford University Press, 2020) and the author of *How Climate Change Comes to Matter: The Communal Life of Facts* (Duke University Press, 2014). Candis is a citizen of the Tāłtān Nation (located in what is now northwestern British Columbia) and is a regular contributor to the podcast, *Media Indigena*. Prior to her academic work, she worked as a journalist in Canada and the United States. Candis holds a PhD in History, Anthropology and Science, Technology and Society from MIT.

Notes

1. For Canada, see Alia (1999) for a study of media in Canada's North, and a later study (2009) of international Indigenous journalism and activism that includes some digital media. See Roth (2005) and David (2012) on the rise of Aboriginal People's Television Network and Sangster (2016) on postwar film and representations of northern Indigenous people. See Daley and James (2004) for a study of Indigenous communities and mass media in Alaska.
2. See Callison (2017) for an overview of literature pertaining to how Indigenous has come to be defined and mobilized in various transnational arenas, including in the discussions leading up to the United Nations Declaration on the Rights of Indigenous People (UNDRIP).
3. See also Hirji and Karim (2009), Mahtani (2008), Henry and Tator (2002), Fleras and Kunz (2001) for how mainstream media in Canada have represented other minorities as well as Indigenous peoples in either a negative or stereotypical light and/or excluded these perspectives and voices altogether.
4. I also discuss this in Callison (2016).
5. From September 2013 to September 2104, we analysed coverage of the Arctic in regional, national and international newspapers. We chose regional sources that were accessible online (*Nunatsiaq News*, NNSL newspaper chain that publishes community paper in NWT and Nunavut, *Northern Journal* which is now closed, the *Whitehorse Star*). We did not track coverage by the CBC because of the way their websites make it difficult to categorize,

i.e. whether a story was regionally produced or not. For national news, we analysed the coverage of *The Globe and Mail, National Post,* and *Toronto Star.* For international news, we analysed the coverage of *The New York Times, The Wall Street Journal, The Guardian, The Financial Times.*

6. For COP 21 in 2015, we analysed coverage of the Arctic from November 28 to December 14 though the actual COP21 dates were November 30 to December 12 in order to catch any coverage that might have begun early or followed the event. The news sources we analysed are *Nunatsiaq News, Whitehorse Star, Northern Journal* (now closed), CBC News (regional and national were more easy to distinguish on an event basis), *The Globe and Mail, National Post, Toronto Star, The Guardian, Wall Street Journal,* and *New York Times.* We also concurrently analysed the hashtag #Arctic on Twitter, and published and tweeted our results on our arcticjournalism.com blog. A research assistant also travelled to Paris to report for the blog and *Open Canada,* a news website.

7. Tourism in these cities and beyond is an extremely expensive and newly expanding proposition that only a few ever get to experience, and tourism is usually quite removed from or only gestures at a deep understanding of the context and history of place. For example, when the Crystal Serenity, the first luxury cruise ship, went through the Northwest Passage in the summer of 2016, passengers paid a minimum of USD$21,000 for a spot aboard. Concerns were raised about where the ship might stop since the population aboard was likely to overwhelm any of the Inuit hamlets that dot the fjords and inlets along the way. The hamlet where it did stop spent months preparing for the Serenity's passengers to disembark. See CBC News 2016.

References

Alia, Valerie. 1999. *Un/Covering the North: News, Media, and Aboriginal People.* Vancouver: UBC Press.

Alia, V. 2009. 'Outlaws and Citizens: Indigenous People and the New Media Nation', *International Journal of Media & Cultural Politics* 5(1–2): 39–54.

Anderson, Mark and Carmen Robertson. 2011. *Seeing Red: A History of Natives in Canadian Newspapers.* Winnipeg: University of Manitoba Press.

Arnaquq-Baril, Alethea. 2016. *Angry Inuk.* Toronto: National Film Board of Canada.

Baiocchi, G. et al. 2014. *The Civic Imagination: Making a Difference in American Political Life.* Boulder, CO: Paradigm Publishers.

Bennett, Lance and Alexandra Segerberg. 2013. *The Logic of Connective Action: Digital Media and the Personalization of Contentious Politics.* Cambridge: Cambridge University Press.

Boczkowski, Pablo. 2014. 'Steps Toward Cosmopolitanism in the Study of Media Technologies: Integrating Scholarship on Production, Consumption, Materiality, and Content', in T. Gillespie, P. Boczkowski and K. Foot (eds), *Media Technologies: Essays on Communication, Materiality and Society.* Cambridge, MA: MIT Press, pp. 53–76.

Boczkowski, Pablo and Leah A. Lievrouw. 2007. 'Bridging STS and Communication Studies: Scholarship on Media and Information Technologies', in E.J. Hackett, O. Amsterdamska, M. Lynch and J. Wajcman (eds), *The Handbook of Science and Technology Studies*. Cambridge, MA: MIT Press, pp. 949–77.

Bodenhorn, Barbara and Olga Ulturgasheva. 2017. 'Climate Strategies: Thinking through Arctic Examples', *Philosophical Transactions of the Royal Society A* 375(2095): 20160363.

Boykoff, Maxwell and Tom Yulsman. 2013. 'Political Economy, Media, and Climate Change: Sinews of Modern Life', *Wiley Interdisciplinary Reviews: Climate Change* 4(5): 359–71.

Bravo, Michael. 2009. 'Voices from the Sea Ice: The Reception of Climate Impact Narratives', *Journal of Historical Geography* 35(2): 256–78.

Callison, Candis. 2014. *How Climate Change Comes to Matter: The Communal Life of Facts*. Durham, NC: Duke University Press.

———. 2016. 'Beyond COP21: Collaborating with Indigenous People to Understand Climate Change and the Arctic', *L'Internationale Online*. Retrieved June 2016 from https://www.internationaleonline.org/research/politics_of_life_and_death/75_beyond_cop21_collaborating_with_Indigenous_people_to_understand_climate_change_and_the_arctic.

———. 2017. 'Climate Change Communication and Indigenous Publics', *Oxford Encyclopedia of Climate Change Communication*. Retrieved October 2017 from http://climatescience.oxfordre.com/page/climate-change-communication/.

———. 2020. 'The Twelve-Year Warning', *Isis* 111(1): 129–37.

———. 2021. 'Refusing More Empire: Utility, Colonialism, and Indigenous Knowing', *Climatic Change* 167(3): 1–14.

Callison, Candis and Alfred Hermida. 2015. 'Dissent and Resonance: #Idlenomore as an Emergent Middle Ground', *Canadian Journal of Communication* 40(4): 695–716.

Callison, Candis and David Tindall. 2017. 'Climate Change Communication in Canada', *Oxford Encyclopedia of Climate Change Communication*. Retrieved October 2017 from http://climatescience.oxfordre.com/page/climate-change-communication/.

Callison, Candis and Mary Lynn Young. 2020. *Reckoning: Journalism's Limits and Possibilities*. Oxford: Oxford University Press.

CBC News. 2016. 'First Stop Ulukhaktok: Crystal Serenity Cruise Ship Sails into N.W.T.', *CBC News North*. Retrieved 31 August 2016 from http://www.cbc.ca/news/canada/north/crystal-serenity-cruise-ulukhaktok-1.3736984.

Chadwick, Andrew. 2013. *The Hybrid Media System: Politics and Power*. Oxford: Oxford University Press.

Christensen, Miyase, Annika Nilsson and Nina Wormbs (eds). 2013. *Media and the Politics of Arctic Climate Change: When the Ice Breaks*. New York: Springer.

Cochran, P. et al. 2013. 'Indigenous Frameworks for Observing and Responding to Climate Change in Alaska', *Climatic Change* 120(3): 557–67.

Coulthard, Glen S. 2014. *Red Skin, White Masks: Rejecting the Colonial Politics of Recognition*. Minneapolis: University of Minnesota Press.

Cruikshank, Julie. 2005. *Do Glaciers Listen? Local Knowledge, Colonial Encounters, and Social Imagination*. Vancouver and Seattle: UBC Press and University of Washington Press.

Daley, Patrick and Beverly James. 2004. *Cultural Politics and the Mass Media: Alaska Native Voices*. Champaign, IL: University of Illinois Press.

David, Jennifer. 2012. *Original People. Original Television: The Launching of the Aboriginal Peoples Television Network*. Ottawa: Debwe Communications.

Deuze, Mark and Tamara Witschge. 2018. 'Beyond Journalism: Theorizing the Transformation of Journalism', *Journalism* 19(2): 165–81.

Dewey, John. 1927. *The Public and Its Problems*. New York: Ohio University Press.

Diemberger, H. et al. 2012. 'Communicating Climate Knowledge', *Current Anthropology* 53(2): 226–44.

Ellis, Rebecca, Claire Waterton and Brian Wynne. 2010. 'Taxonomy, Biodiversity and Their Publics in Twenty-First-Century DNA Barcoding', *Public Understanding of Science* 19(4): 497–512.

Fienup-Riordan, Ann. 1995. *Freeze Frame: Alaska Eskimos in the Movies*. Seattle, WA: University of Washington Press.

Fischer, Michael M.J. 2009. *Anthropological Futures*. Durham, NC: Duke University Press.

Fleras, Augie and Jean Kunz. 2001. *Media and Minorities: Representing Diversity in a Multicultural Canada*. Toronto: Thompson Publishing.

Fortun, Kom. 2003. 'Ethnography In/Of/As Open Systems', *Reviews in Anthropology* 32(2): 171–90.

Ginsberg, Fay, Lila Abu-Lughod and Brian Larkin. 2002. *Media Worlds: Anthropology on New Terrain*. Berkeley and Los Angeles: University of California Press.

Hafsteinsson, Sigurjón and Marian Bredin. 2010. *Indigenous Screen Cultures in Canada*. Winnipeg: University of Manitoba Press.

Hansen, William and David Poisey. 1991. *Starting Fire with Gunpowder*. Montreal: National Film Board of Canada.

Haraway, Donna. 1989. *Primate Visions: Gender Race, and Nature in the World of Modern Science*. London: Routledge.

Henry, Frances and Carol Tator. 2002. *Discourses of Domination: Racial Bias in the Canadian English Press*. Toronto: University of Toronto Press.

Hinchey, Garrett. 2022. *Reclaiming Our Narrative: A Roadmap to Local Participation in N.W.T. Media*. Toronto: The Gordon Foundation. Retrieved 16 March 2022 from https://gordonfoundation.ca/resource/garrett-hinchey-policy-research/.

Hirji, Faiza and Karim Karim (eds). 2009. 'Race, Ethnicity, and Intercultural Communication' [special issue], *Canadian Journal of Communication* 34(4).

Irwin, Alan and Brian Wynne (eds). 2004. *Misunderstanding Science? The Public Reconstruction of Science and Technology*. Cambridge: Cambridge University Press.

Jasanoff, Sheila. 2010. 'A New Climate for Society', *Theory, Culture & Society* 27(2-3): 233–53.

Kunuk, Zacharias and Ian Mauro. 2010. *Qapirangajuq: Inuit Knowledge and Climate Change*. Igloolik Isuma productions. Retrieved 1 December 2017 from http://www.isuma.tv/inuit-knowledge-and-climate-change.

Lambertus, Sandra. 2004. *Wartime Images, Peacetime Wounds: The Media and the Gustafsen Lake Standoff*. Toronto: University of Toronto Press.

Mahtani, Minelle. 2008. 'The Racialized Geographies of News Consumption and Production: Contaminated Memories and Racialized Silences', *GeoJournal* 74: 257–64.

Marcus, George. 2000. *Para-Sites: A Casebook Against Cynical Reason*. Chicago: University of Chicago Press.

Marcus, George and Michael Fischer. 1999. *Anthropology as Cultural Critique: An Experimental Moment in the Human Sciences*. Chicago: University of Chicago Press.

Marino, Elizabeth. 2015. *Fierce Climate, Sacred Ground: An Ethnography of Climate Change in Shishmaref, Alaska*. Anchorage, AK: University of Alaska Press.

Martello, Marybeth Long. 2004. 'Global Change Science and the Arctic Citizen', *Science and Public Policy* 31(2): 107–115.

———. 2008. 'Arctic Indigenous Peoples as Representations and Representatives of Climate Change', *Social Studies of Science* 38(3): 351–76.

Meadows, Michael and Shannon Avison. 2000. 'Speaking and Hearing: Aboriginal Newspapers and the Public Sphere in Canada and Australia', *Canadian Journal of Communication* 25(3): 347–65.

Miller, Clark and Paul Edwards. 2001. *Changing the Atmosphere: Expert Knowledge and Environmental Governance*. Cambridge, MA: MIT Press.

Olausson, Ulrika and Peter Berglez. 2014. 'Media and Climate Change: Four Long-Standing Research Challenges Revisited', *Environmental Communication* 8(2): 249–65.

Picard, Robert. 2014. 'Twilight or New Dawn of Journalism?', *Digital Journalism* 2(3): 273–83.

Pincus, Rebecca and Saleem Ali. 2016. 'Have You Been to "The Arctic"? Frame Theory and the Role of Media Coverage in Shaping Arctic Discourse', *Polar Geography* 39(2): 83–97.

Public Policy Forum. 2017. *The Shattered Mirror: News, Democracy and Trust in the Digital Age*. Retrieved March 2017 from http://www.ppforum.ca/publications/shattered-mirror-news-democracy-and-trust-digital-age.

Quinn, Eilis. 2015. 'Arctic Missing from Paris Climate Agreement', *RCI Eye on the Arctic*. Retrieved 1 January 2016 from http://www.rcinet.ca/eye-on-the-arctic/2015/12/21/arctic-missing-from-paris-climate-agreement/.

Reardon, Jenny. 2005. *Race to the Finish: Identity and Governance in an Age of Genomics*. Princeton, NJ: Princeton University Press.

Rodgers, Kathleen and Willow Scobie. 2015. 'Sealfies, Seals and Celebs: Expressions of Inuit Resilience in the Twitter Era', *Interface* 7(1): 70–97.

Roitman, Janet. 2013. *Anti-Crisis*. Durham, NC: Duke University Press.

Roosvall, Anna and Matthew Tegelberg. 2013. 'Framing Climate Change and Indigenous Peoples: Intermediaries of Urgency, Spirituality and de-Nationalization', *International Communication Gazette* 75(4): 392–409.

———. 2018. *Media and Transnational Climate Justice: Indigenous Activism and Climate Politics*. Bern: Peter Lang Publishing Group.

Roth, Lorna. 2005. *Something New in the Air: The Story of First Peoples Television Broadcasting in Canada*. Montreal: McGill-Queen's Press-MQUP.

Sangster, Joan. 2016. *The Iconic North: Cultural Constructions of Aboriginal life in Postwar Canada*. Vancouver: UBC Press.
Schudson, Michael. 2001. 'The Objectivity Norm in American Journalism', *Journalism* 2(2): 149–70.
Simpson, Audra. 2014. *Mohawk Interruptus: Political Life across the Borders of Settler States*. Durham, NC: Duke University Press.
Singer, J.B. et al. 2011. *Participatory Journalism: Guarding Open Gates at Online Newspapers*. Malden, MA and Oxford: John Wiley & Sons.
Stoddart, Mark and Jillian Smith. 2016. 'The Endangered Arctic, the Arctic as Resource Frontier: News Media Narratives of Climate Change and the North', *Canadian Review of Sociology* 53(3): 316–36.
Strong, Walter. 2018. 'What Will the Arctic Indigenous Wellness Project do with its $1M Arctic Inspiration Prize?', *CBC News North*. Retrieved 1 February 2018 from http://www.cbc.ca/news/canada/north/2018-arctic-inspiration-prize-1.4513445.
TallBear, Kim. 2013. 'Genomic Articulations of Indigeneity', *Social Studies of Science* 43(4): 509–33.
Usher, Nikki. 2013. 'Marketplace Public Radio and News Routines Considered: Between Structures and Agents', *Journalism* 14(6): 807–22.
Ward, Stephen. 2004. *The Invention of Journalism Ethics: The Path to Objectivity and Beyond*. Montreal: McGill-Queen's Press (MQUP).
Watt-Cloutier, Sheila. 2015. *The Right To Be Cold: One Woman's Story of Protecting Her Culture, the Arctic and the Whole Planet*. Toronto: Penguin Canada.
Whyte, Kyle P. 2013. 'Justice Forward: Tribes, Climate Adaptation and Responsibility', *Climatic Change* 120(3): 517–30.
———. 2014. 'Indigenous Women, Climate Change Impacts, and Collective Action', *Hypatia* 29(3): 599–616.
———. 2018. 'Indigenous Science (Fiction) for the Anthropocene: Ancestral Dystopias and Fantasies of Climate Change Crises', *Environment and Planning E: Nature and Space* 1(1–2): 224–42.
Wildcat, Daniel. 2013. 'Introduction: Climate Change and Indigenous Peoples of the USA', *Climatic Change* 120(3): 509–15.
Wright, Shelley. 2014. *Our Ice Is Vanishing/Sikuvut Nunguliqtuq: A History of Inuit, Newcomers, and Climate Change*. Montreal: McGill-Queen's Press (MQUP).
Young, Mary Lynn and Candis Callison. 2017. 'When Gender, Colonialism, and Technology Matter in a Journalism Startup', *Journalism*. Retrieved 20 December 2017 from https://doi.org/10.1177/1464884917743390.
Zelizer, Barbie. 2015. 'Terms of Choice: Uncertainty, Journalism, and Crisis', *Journal of Communication* 65(5): 888–908.

Chapter 6

People of the Cryosphere
A Cross-Regional, Cross-Disciplinary Approach to Icescapes in a Changing Climate

Hildegard Diemberger and Astrid Hovden

Living with Icescapes

The icy landscape in front of me was overwhelming in all its glittering whiteness; I was carefully putting one foot after the other with caution, as I was told. I was five, and it was my first experience on the glacier. I had seen glaciers many times before, bivouacking next to the icy waters of the lakes at their front but also casually looking at the patterned blue and white face of the Alpine giant that was a reassuring yet distant presence overlooking the place where I was born. But this time, it was different; it was the first time on the ice. The grown-ups had tied me with a reassuring rope like every other member of the team, and I was carefully walking between them. Nothing felt threatening. The murmur of the water, the beautiful icy sculptures we were walking by created an intriguing, enchanting presence. I was told not to go close to crevasses, they could be dangerous. I understood. I looked from a distance at those cracks in the ice with their infinite shades of blue. They were fascinating. At one point, I saw a smallish one. It looked harmless. It was almost a baby crevasse, I thought. It was not too far from our trail, so I ventured in its direction to look at it; I wanted to look into its depth, from a safe distance, I considered. I walked a few steps as far as the rope allowed. It was enticing. The grown-ups were clearly slightly distracted as this was easy terrain, and I seemed to be following in their footsteps as I was told. So I walked those few steps quickly, just to give a peep into the icy depth. Suddenly, the reassuring icy terrain I was walking on cracked under my feet, and I fell, not much, into the azurine depth and landed on a small ice bridge. The rope promptly pulled me out of my predicament. Those few seconds, though, with the icy breath of the glacier rising from its depth, the murmur of the water running somewhere under my feet, and the sheer possibility of being swallowed by the gaping chasm will stay with me for the rest of my life. So will the trust and admiration for the people who pulled the rope and who knew how to read the glacier, its terrain, as well as the vagaries of the weather that could transform an enchanted landscape into a confusing and treacherous whiteness where cloud and fog merged with the icy terrain. But how did they know what they knew? And how did they anticipate the immediate and the long-term future of this landscape?

When presenting the oral version of this chapter, Hildegard Diemberger recalled her earliest experiences with ice in the Alps as these have informed her later academic interest in the Himalayas. She returned to this image again and again many years later, reading as an anthropologist about the icy breath of *sila* in Greenland so beautifully described by Kirsten Hastrup (2012: 227–30) or tinkering with the question 'do glaciers listen?' asked by Julie Cruickshank (2005) in her exploration of Athapaskan cosmology. She also returned to her childhood experiences with icescapes when sharing stories of icy encounters with the people of the Himalaya she lived with whilst studying their mountain landscapes. What had become a common theme by then, though, was the anxiety that disappearing icescapes were eliciting in the people who lived with them – the message that the vanishing ice, the swelling glacial lakes, the receding snowlines on mountains were conveying to people living next to them in the Alps, the Himalaya or the Arctic. The constantly changing icescapes were undergoing transformations that seemed out of kilter with past experiences of variability.[1] Moreover, people were trying to make sense of all this in many different ways. If walking is a mode of knowing, the intimate relationship with icescapes seemed to give access to one of the many souls of this 'animate planet' (Weston 2017) and its tribulations. It is this profound interest in icescapes and the people living with them that drew Hildegard and Astrid together.

Born in rural Norway, where the embodied knowledge of dealing with snow and ice is part of everyday life, Astrid developed a passion for the Himalayas. During her fieldwork in the Limi Valley in northwestern Nepal, she had direct experience of a glacial lake outburst flood that caught the village of Halji, washing away several fields and houses and threatening to destroy the eleventh-century local Buddhist monastery. Hildegard and Astrid found themselves together asking questions about the rapid transformations of these landscapes and how changing icescapes, and the experience of people living with them in different geographical locations across the world, seem to resonate with each other.

In this chapter, we look at the Tibetan plateau and the Himalayas, focusing mainly on an area in northwestern Nepal where agro-pastoral communities have been increasingly threatened by glacial lakes outburst floods. On the basis of ethnographies and historical sources, we explore the ways in which the study of Himalayan regions can be set in dialogue with that of the Circumpolar North. In both instances, the mediation between local and scientific knowledge, cultural constructions of risk, and community action in contexts that are particularly vulnerable to climate change-related hazards seem to emerge as features of the social life of the cryosphere – that area where by virtue of high altitude or high latitude, ice is a formative and formidable force in people's lives. What emerges through this comparison is that ice is the focus of different epistemic, moral and affective frameworks within cosmopolitical ecologies shaped by human and non-human actors.

The Social Life of the Cryosphere in a Changing Climate

Climate change narratives have been increasingly informed by a range of terms that have travelled across disciplines, literary genres and cultural contexts. Most prominently, the notion of the 'Anthropocene', defining human impact on the globe in geological terms, from its original use within the natural sciences, has become a key concept that powerfully spans the social and natural sciences to address a range of threats at the planetary scale. In a similar way, a range of notions has emerged to bring together non-contiguous places in geographies of climate change that advocate cross-regional, cross-disciplinary approaches.

The notion of the 'cryosphere' (from the Greek κρύος *kryos*, 'cold', 'frost' or 'ice' and σφαῖρα *sphaira*, 'globe, ball'), mentioned above, is used in the natural sciences[2] to refer to areas of the world where water is predominantly in the solid state and has increasingly been used in narratives of 'climate change' that bring together people living at high altitude with people living at high latitude.³ Proximity to ice formations affected by rising temperatures and vulnerability to changing weather patterns impacting livelihoods are some of the most striking common denominators. People inhabiting these areas have learned since time immemorial to observe and deal with their ever-changing icescapes – precious reservoirs of locked-in freshwater, a crucial element in local climate systems, the terrain on which to walk but also the source of a wide range of risks and hazards. These icescapes seem to have been recently undergoing unprecedented transformations and have become local and global proxies for climatic transformations.

As highlighted in a number of publications, in the study of the cryosphere, the human and social dimension have been neglected, and a genuine cross-disciplinary approach is called for: 'To understand these dynamic intersections between people and the cryosphere, it is crucial to integrate disciplines, to talk across boundaries, and to embrace concepts and methods applicable to coupled natural-human social-ecological systems' (Huggel, Carey, Clague and Kaab 2015). The notion of the 'Third Pole,' originally connected to a history of adventure and exploration (Dyhrenfurth 1953), has been mobilized by natural scientists and development agencies (e.g. International Centre for Integrated Mountain Development)⁴ as the area on the planet with the largest accumulation of ice outside the Poles to promote an integrated approach to environmental challenges from conservation to responses to climate change (Qiu 2008; Huettmann 2012). The concept of the 'Three Poles' links the Himalaya-Karakorum-Hindukush Region to the North and the South Pole as drivers of regional and global weather systems as well as indicators of global processes. The inclusion of the 'Third Pole' in the International Polar Year (2007–2008) ensured that these icescapes were seen as connected on the global stage. The history of this concept is currently being explored in the framework of the project 'The Third Pole as a Geographical Imaginary: its Historical, Cultural and Political Roots' (PI Michael Bravo), Department of Geography, University of Cambridge.

The Arctic includes an extraordinary cultural and historical diversity and different modes of engaging with icescapes. While the skills of living on ice deployed by people who live in the extreme North relying on hunting skills are quite unique, more similarities can be seen between people who inhabit permafrost environments at high latitude and high altitude and between transhumant pastoralists living next to mountain glaciers. Even more, similarities can be found among communities who are making a living, combining and recombining ancient skills with new technologies, materials and opportunities. Whatever the livelihood, however, they all share the fact that they live in places where ice matters and where small differences in temperature have a big impact. A reflection of this common feature is the fact that images of their predicaments are often used to illustrate the vulnerability of environments to climate change.

Just as island people far removed from one another are increasingly brought together by a shared sense of emergency linked to rising sea levels (and sometimes take joint action on the global stage), people of the cryosphere can be seen as linked by comparable experiences of human responses to vanishing ice. New geographies of 'climate change', therefore, raise important questions: in what ways is it fruitful to explore anthropologically notions such as the 'cryosphere', which have originated within the natural sciences but have developed a sort of social life on the global stage? In what ways is the 'cryosphere' part of an Anthropocene that seems increasingly messy, fractured and shaped by new geographic configurations?

A first approach can be identified as, broadly speaking, phenomenological. It revolves around the idea of 'sensing icescapes', exploring the wide range of sensory and conceptual experiences that are involved in knowing ice and snow: glacier views and snow lines, crackling ice and roaring avalanches, as well as the cold breath of crevasses and seracs or the life-supporting taste of unlocked fresh water – all these features are deeply connected to wider cosmological frameworks. Drawing inspiration from or resonating with Basso's ethnography of 'lived topography' (Basso 1996), this approach is both pragmatic and poetic and can be seen reflected not only in songs and tales but also in practical ways of going about life in the Arctic as well as in the Himalaya, in the Andes or the Alps. It is often also linked to profound affective reactions to landscape transformations in moral geography that is interpreted at multiple levels so as to anticipate nature both in the short and long term – sometimes with prophetic implications (see, e.g., Sehnalova 2019: 216–82; Diemberger, Hovden and Yeh 2015: 249–71; more generally see also Ingold 2000; Cruickshank 2005).

A second approach revolves around the political economy and political ecology of these regions, addressing the threats to ecosystems and livelihoods due not only to exposure to erratic weathers patterns, vanishing ice, radical changes in the permafrost and glacial lake outbursts but also to the increasing dependence of communities from national and multinational organizations which often support strategies for the adaptation to climate change while simultaneously promoting the exploitation of natural resources and more centralized governance (see, e.g., Yeh 2014: 61–74; Bravo and Rees 2006: 205–15).

A third approach focuses on the way in which people of the cryosphere have become proxies for global processes so that images of human livelihoods threatened by vanishing polar ice juxtaposed to those of retreating mountain glaciers in the Himalaya, the Andes or the Alps are deployed in global narratives potentially informing various forms of environmental activism. A vocabulary informed by the ways in which humans relate to the uncertainty of specific environments and the spiritual qualities of places can acquire new global relevance: from *tendrel* (*rten 'brel*) indicating interconnectedness of all phenomena in Tibetan Buddhist landscapes (see, e.g., The Karmapa 2017) to *imaka* meaning 'perhaps, maybe', framing Greenland's narratives of human life's icy settings (see below) and linking them to broader ideas of 'anticipation' (Nuttall 2010: 21–37).

These different dimensions are not mutually exclusive, and they instead inform each other. Perceptions rooted in local day-to-day observations and cosmological frameworks blend with a wide range of global scientific narratives and technological infrastructures that reach remote sites in bits and pieces, creating new 'assemblages' (see Makley 2014: 233); they are engaged with or not by the different epistemic communities involved in decision-making. The 'cryosphere' emerges thus as a site of flows and frictions (Tsing 2004) within global connections, where encounters are driven by different agendas, situated contingencies and cultural specificities in a variety of competing 'scale-making projects' and zones of 'awkward engagement'. Practical issues of access to and engagement with icescapes and their surrounding shape distinctive forms of 'remoteness' co-created by global processes (see also Saxer and Anderson 2019). Both poetic and prosaic, powerful and vulnerable, life-supporting and life-destroying, ice defines this zone of engagement as a powerful agent shaping all kinds of human interaction, narratives and theories of the environment far beyond being an actor in the Latourian sense (see Hastrup 2012: 227).

Moral, Poetic and Prophetic Icescapes

People living on or close to icescapes have learned how to read the ice and the snow. From testing the consistency of different ice or snow, noting distribution patterns, to observing the changing snowline on mountains, all of these experiences shape what Ingold (2000) calls the 'dwelling perspective' of those who relate to this environment on a daily basis.

For the Canadian North, Julie Cruickshank's fascinating exploration of the Athapaskan 'ecological epistemology', *Do Glaciers Listen?* (Cruickshank 2005), shows that glaciers were perceived as sentient and animate entities, prepared to respond to human behaviour. In a similar way, Himalayan and trans-Himalayan mountains covered in snow and ice can actively engage in social relations and be perceived at multiple levels. As 'owners of the land' (*sadag, sa bdag*), they protect specific territories, granting fertility and prosperity to all living beings.[5] They can be brothers, sisters, fathers, mothers or even ancestors, and they are often married to adjacent lakes. Erratic weather and environmental disasters are often attributed to a disturbed relationship with these landscape spirits, often described in a cumulative way as *lha lu* (*lha klu*), i.e. ranging from the gods of the sky and the high mountains above (*lha*) to the spirits of the underground and the waters (*lu*) (see also Salick, Byg and Bauer 2012: 447–76, as well as Diemberger, 2021). Albeit converted to Buddhism in the process of the Buddhification of Tibetan landscapes, they are still the masters of places.

Empirical knowledge that provides the basis for walking competently on ice, avoiding treacherous terrain, assessing snow cover to deploy a strategy to look after domestic animals in case of storms, or estimating risks involved in glacial lakes bursting and flooding human settlements or encampments often combines with poetic perspectives that make these landscapes into a sort of canvas for visual, aural and tactile narratives with moral and even prophetic undertones – the stories that capture the spiritual sense of place.

Mt Kailash, a mountain that is sacred to several Asian religions and whose relevance cuts across several national boundaries, is a powerful example.[6]

Located in a mountain range that constitutes the headwaters of great rivers departing in all cardinal directions, it epitomizes the importance of ice and snow for human survival. A popular prophecy tells that at the beginning of time, the peak was white like a conch shell. In the middle time (now), it is striped like a *zi* stone, and at the end of time, it will be black like a piece of charcoal.[7] Local dwellers, mystics who have come from afar, and pilgrims all gaze in awe at his mighty presence – a lord of the place who also provides a powerful sense of time.

Figure 6.1. Mount Kailash with prayer flags. © Hildegard Diemberger

From Buddhist and Hindu perspectives a worldly embodiment of the cosmic mountain and seat of powerful deities, Mt Kailash alias Gang Tise is historically also understood as the embodiment of a more localized spiritual entity called Ge khod who used to protect the regional kingdom of Shangshung and its rulers (according to some local views, the name Tise can be translated in the Shangshung language as 'water-god').[8] Once integrated into the Tibetan empire in the seventh century, Mt Kailash became famous as one of the protecting deities of Tibet, the Land of Snow (lit. Gangjong, Gangs ljongs), together with a number of other mountain deities scattered across the Tibetan plateau. Through visual connection, it has the power to hallow, purify and even send off the dead exposed to its blessing via this visual connection on the top of high passes in its vicinity. Mt Kailash in the west, Chang Targo in the north and Nyanchen Thanglha in the northeast are considered to be three brothers married to the big lakes at their feet, whilst also being listed among the nine most famous Tibetan protectors of the world, the *sipa lha gu* (*srid pa lha dgu*).

Towering with glittering whiteness above boggy permafrost plains and high-altitude grasslands inhabited by Tibetan nomads with their Yak herds, Nyanchen Thanglha is one of these powerful protecting deities located further to the east, just north of Lhasa. Despite being located in a particular geographical area, this snow-capped mountain is worshipped across the Tibetan plateau and among the Buddhist communities of the Himalayas. An eleventh-century manuscript telling the story of how it was converted to Buddhism by the spiritual master Padmasambhava reveals that this snow mountain not only actively resisted its taming but did so by unleashing storms:

> All the strong winds said: 'let's see the fight against the Buddhist master [Padmasambhava]'. The Buddhist master boiled the carcass of a bull in a copper cauldron, then he put his foot on top of it and made it disappear. Then, a cloud appeared on the snowy top of Thanglha in the middle of the month of winter. Wild flashes of lightning and thunderclaps came. Hail and round snowflakes fell [from the sky]. From then onwards, the area in that direction was brought into subjection [by the Buddhist master] and, even though they went on fighting [the winds] were meeker than before. (*dBa' bzhed* folio 11)

Nyanchen Thanglha, like all the other sacred snow mountains protectors of Tibet, have indeed been masters of the weather as well as of all what makes human living possible on the Tibetan plateau. They kept these features after being subdued and converted to Buddhism by spiritual masters – but were hierarchically downgraded to 'worldly deities' (in contrast to higher Buddhist deities 'beyond the world').[9]

As a powerful male mountain deity, Nyanchen Thanglha is married to the heavenly lake at its feet, the female Namtsho (lit. 'sky-lake'), and they both protect the well-being of the place and its dwellers. This cosmological union has a remarkable resonance with climatological research carried out in the same area. A recent study of the microclimate around Mt Nyanchen Thanglha and Lake Namtsho (Nam Co) by atmospheric scientist Hans F. Graf, in the framework of the project Atmosphere - Ecology - Glaciology Cluster in the frame of TiP (DFG SPP 1372) 'Tibetan Plateau: Formation, Climate, Ecosystems', has shown that landscape features such as mountains and lakes are interconnected in shaping the local moisture circulation system, which drives the local weather and influences the local effect of the monsoon (see also Diemberger and Graf 2012: 233–34). Precipitation – its quantity, quality and timeliness – is key for vegetal and animal life in this terrain. Creating a feedback loop, deforestation and degradation of grassland also have an impact on weather, potentially aggravating the effects of global warming (see also Marin 2010: 162–76 for similar phenomena in the Mongolian setting). Local and global human impacts on climate are thus interconnected in multiple ways, and people who live in these environments are not only affected by but capture these entanglements in their innumerable observations.

The shepherd and the scientist look at the same mountain and its snow cover with different eyes but both sense that it reflects the well-being of the place. Different types of environmental knowledge that conceptualize environmental interconnectedness in different but not incompatible ways can dovetail and interfold. It is the politics of cultural mediation that may enable or disable negotiation, shaping the 'partial connections' (Strathern 2004) that link actors taking decisions about these landscapes against the background of very different epistemological traditions and potential ontological incommensurability.

Nyanchen Thanglha is both a local proxy for the understanding of wider environmental processes from a climatological perspective and the embodiment of a powerful spirit involved in human destiny since time immemorial. It has related to people inhabiting its land through mediums, divination practices (involving the shoulder blade of animals, mirrors, dice, birds and many other types of divination popular on the Tibetan plateau and across Inner Asia), as well as written and oral narratives (see Maurer, Rossi and Scheuermann 2019).

Figure 6.2. *Oracle possessed by the Mountain Nyanchen Thanglha.*
© *Carlo Meazza*

He is the lord of domestic and wild yaks, and the passage above seems to evoke animal sacrifice, a common ritual practice through which human communities on the Tibetan plateau related to their mountain spirits before their conversion to Buddhism. As a mighty mountain and a powerful mountain god, it has been reimagined and reframed many times according to different traditions, with scientific understandings being just one of the many layers of interpretation. The negotiation of different perspectives has a long history and is not binary, i.e. traditional vs. modern, local vs. global, sacred vs. secular.

According to a common trope, the Buddhification of landscape deities involved the reform of animal sacrifice and its transformation into the offering of an effigy or the setting free of an animal. However, in some areas, animal sacrifice persisted up to very recent times or even the present day. This is the case of Mt Takyong, a peak in southwestern Tibet considered to be an emanation of Nyanchen Thangla's brother, Chang Targo, the lord of the northern plain, worshiped by the nomads of Porong. Until 1959 he used to receive the sacrifice of a white sheep during New Year celebrations. On that occasion, the local ruler of Porong and a ritual specialist called an Aya used to climb up the mountain to a particular sacred spot where the sacrifice took place. The Aya priest read the entrails of the animal to give forecasts on the weather, health and challenges for the following year and called for good fortune and prosperity for the land, its people and its leaders. Subsequently, the animal was cooked and shared with the whole celebrating community. A prophecy linked the appearance of the mountain to the well-being of the land: as long as the dark reddish mountain kept its white tip (a small permanent ice field), there would be prosperity. If this disappeared, disaster would strike. In many ways, this echoes the narrative about Mt Kailash mentioned above and is probably a widespread trope based on both local observation and transmitted traditions from elsewhere.

Arguing against a clear-cut distinction between moral and ecological climate, Diemberger (2012) has suggested elsewhere that this understanding of climate is also highly political. According to the manuscript mentioned above (the *dBa' bzhed*, corroborated by other sources), a range of disastrous weather events and calamities prompted the consultation of diviners which in turn led to a political regime change and eventually to Buddhism becoming Tibet's state religion in the eighth century. Weather divination, both in terms of revealing the deeper meaning of past events and anticipating future ones, is thus a practice endowed with considerable power. As such, it is politically sensitive and predicated on a shared understanding of what constitutes authoritative knowledge; unsurprisingly, it can also be contested either as a superstitious practice from a secularist perspective or, more often, through a distinction between 'good' divination and 'bad' divination. Following a view that does not challenge the validity of divination as such, bad divination can be criticized in opposition to good divination; the latter is associated with a process that is carried out according to recognizable protocols for the wider good rather than for particular interests and manipulation. In his study on Tibetan divination, Rolf Sheuermann comments:

> From a Buddhist doctrinal stance, spirit-mediumship should be considered as being inferior to most other methods as the information received is not based on a person of authority, such as a dharma guardian or *dharmapāla* that is believed to have transcended the world (*'jig rten las 'das pa'i srung ma*), but on a worldly deity (*'jig rten pa'i lha*) or worldly *dharmapāla* (*'jig rten pa'i srung ma*). As Réne de Nebesky-Wojkowitz noted, 'none of these high-ranking guardians of religion would condescend to interfere with more or less mundane affairs by speaking through the mouth of a medium', and a prediction cast by a spirit-medium invoking a worldly deity is deemed fallible since its source of information is not trustworthy. Such a deity may either have its personal motive to cast a

> wrong prediction or its capacity of foreknowledge is flawed or limited. On the contrary, the majority of Tibetan cleromantic practices involve invocations of the blessing and inspiration of the Buddha, revered Buddhist deities, and/or Buddhist masters, which is meant to guarantee the efficacy of the divination. The assumed efficacy of the practice is grounded in the doctrine of *pratītyasamūtpāda* or dependent arising, the notion that things do not manifest randomly but occur due to an interplay of causes and conditions. (Maurer, Rossi and Scheuermann 2019: 163)

Whatever the process, as we shall see below, divination is still involved in decision-making in times of crisis (often related to extreme environmental events that characterize this region), allowing for a system of reflection and scenario thinking that is not easily dismissible in simplistic terms. Historical sources and ethnographic examples from Tibet and beyond show that divination practices can turn out to be powerful tools in making choices and achieving consensus within a community.

Despite but also thanks to their subordination to Buddhist authority, landscape deities have continued to reflect the intimate relationship between humans and the place they live in for centuries. They are not too dissimilar to the Tirakuna or Earth Beings described by De La Cadena (2015),[10] and are often central to divination practices that can be found across Asia and can be understood in the framework of environmental cosmopolitics involving non-human and/or other-than-human actors (see Sneath 2014; Sneath and Turk 2021). These deities are often conceptualized in terms of kinship relations. They can be married couples, mothers, fathers, children, brotherhoods and sisterhoods as well as ancestors and they are profoundly relational among themselves and towards the beings inhabiting their land (humans included). These features remained, whilst being continuously re-invented and re-enacted, after the Buddhification of Tibetan landscapes. In contrast to the South American settings, they have been integrated into politico-religious formations rather than suppressed by ontologically more rigid frameworks such as colonial Christianity.

As Mt Nyanchen Thangla is married to Lake Namtsho, so Mt Kailash is married to the sacred lake at its feet, Mapham Yumtsho. Consisting of a mountain and lake dyad, this site is endowed with a sanctity that is recognized far beyond the region itself, as witnessed by the millions of pilgrims who visit it every year. It is thus not surprising that prophecies linked to this mountain have acquired a global profile, linking it to the destiny of the world.

Living with Icescapes under Threat

Whilst the prophetic narratives revolving around Mt Kailash point towards a distant future, the immediate one is often a site of contestation. As the mountain is a popular site for tourism, the rapid development of infrastructure projects, with the construction of a road replacing the ancient pilgrimage route around the mountain, has elicited strong emotional responses, both positive and negative. In addition, the increasing accessibility of this area rich in a wide range of minerals (including gold and rare earths) has promoted mining activities, which are even more likely to raise both cosmological and environmental issues in ways that resonate with what is happening in the Arctic. In this context, extreme climatic events are part of a much wider set of issues and transformations, with which they are often entangled, as we shall see below.

Not far from Mt Kailash is the massif of the Gurlha Mandata – a sacred peak whose relevance is much more local but which still dominates the horizon and is central to the lives of numerous communities in the western Tibetan borderland where the state borders of China, India and Nepal meet.

On the afternoon of 30 June 2011, a glacial lake in the Gurla Mandhata massif burst, and a flash flood thundered down the Limi valley towards Halji village, triggering severe landslides. Houses, fields, pastureland and village infrastructure were swept away as the riverbank disintegrated and the river approached the eleventh-century monastery at the heart of the village.

Flash floods are not new to the villagers, and the villages surrounding the mountain have maintained records of their management of floods and other environmental challenges over many centuries. However, the recent flood came with unprecedented strength, raising new questions about risk management and the dilemma of whether the village needs to be relocated at the cost of abandoning the monastery. Also new is the degree to which and the way in which religious authorities are responding, and the still limited but increasing awareness of the association of these disasters with anthropogenic climate change. This is occurring at the same historical moment in which motorable roads, telephone connections and new governance modes are arriving, changing the community's long-held perceptions of and responses to environmental hazards.

Astrid was in the village when the Glacial Lake Outburst Flood (GLOF) occurred and captured in images and writing the drama and its aftermath. Taken by surprise by these events (she was involved in

Figure 6.3. Glacial lake outburst flood in Limi. © Astrid Hovden

a different type of research), she observed how the local community responded to this challenge, drawing on different types of knowledge and expertise. Some of the strategies deployed on that occasion built on the social memory of the community; others drew on forms of knowledge (technical, scientific and political) that were perceived as new and unfamiliar and were associated with 'new' links to state and international agencies that were mobilized in the wake of this emergency. Located at the very margin of the country, an area which has a long history of self-sufficiency and a relatively disconnected local administrative system, the GLOFs have functioned as essential drivers for the community to reach out to the Nepali state and INGOs for support (see also Diemberger, Hovden and Yeh 2015: 249–71 and Hovden, in press).

In the aftermath of the flood, the villagers climbed up the valley to assess the glacier the flood had come from. They also involved in their evaluation of the situation foreign researchers with an interest in the area, while building protections according to locally transmitted knowledge and a combination of old and new technologies as well as organizing a religious service in the local monastery as a ritual response. Village meetings and informal decision-making processes involved people with very different views on the event, its causality and the appropriate way to deal with it, while the participation of higher-level administrators brought a regional perspective to bear. On specific divisive issues, divination contributed in finalizing decisions.

In Limi, divination remains an important resource for decision-making and for the negotiation of a consensus in the community around a particular course of action. Local ancestral mountain deities are appeased ritually and play an important role in local perceptions and practices of the environment as well as weather/climate, but it is the Buddhist divinized historical figure Achi Chokyi Dronma/Drolma who is the main spiritual reference for important decisions. She was the grandmother of Jigten Gonpo (1143–1217), the founder of the Drigyung Kagyu sect of Tibetan Buddhism that is followed by the local monastery. The title *achi* (grandmother), however, gives her the aura of a female ancestor, and in fact, she also has a secret name that links her to one of the great ancestral clans of the Tibetan empire. Associated with specific sites of worship in the landscape as well as divination practices that take place in the monastery, she has been consulted in all momentous decisions of the community – including the negotiation with the Chinese authorities when the Limi people were invited, with very generous offers, to become part of the Chinese controlled Tibet. According to local accounts, Achi gave a negative response to what seemed an enticing offer to a very poor agropastoralist community, and people followed her advice (for details on the history and politics of this area, see Hovden, in press; see also Yeh 2019).

Achi is consulted on all kinds of issues including those that concern the environment and the management of environmental risks and hazards. This process of consultation is one of the main instances in which different knowledge regimes are combined when debating causality and taking decisions on responses (see Hovden and Havnevik 2021). Whether the disaster is explained as a disturbance of *lha lu* spirits or an unusual accumulation of snowmelt, Achi seems to be able to mediate and unify people around a common strategy (in most cases), which often involves specific concrete actions in the landscape as well as ritual responses.

This process of mediation makes it possible to work out a course of action, drawing on a range of knowledges that may come from very different epistemological traditions. In practice, potentially non-reconcilable ontological assumptions do not necessarily matter: it is the negotiation between real-life actors who may navigate different forms of knowledge that turns out to be the determining factor in what can be seen as a 'cosmopolitical ecology' of practice (see also Kuyakanon, Diemberger and Sneath 2021). Relevance and processes of attribution matter in different ways and may shift over time.

After repeated floods, it seems that the ice formations in the glacier have slightly shifted, and the drainage channels are no longer blocked in winter so that no supraglacial lake is currently forming in spring (Kropáček et al. 2015). Thanks to the new flood defences, good glaciological fortune and the efficacious ritual response, the village, with its eleventh-century monastery, seems to be enjoying some respite. But for how long? And what about the many other places affected by similar circumstances?

The Social Life of the 'Cryosphere': Local and Global Connections

Events such as the Glacial Lake Outburst Flood (GLOF) witnessed by Astrid are necessarily localized and their causality complex so that any attribution to wider climatic trends remains a matter open to interpretation and negotiation. At the same time, they constitute powerful images, epitomizing a sense of threat made acute by the awareness of 'climate change'. They can therefore be framed within wider narratives of climate change at the global level, as reflected for example in a recent article in Al Jazeera, 'Climate Change Threatens 1,000-year-old Monastery in Remote Nepal' (by Neema Vallangi, 24 January 2019). Framing environmental disasters in terms of climate change or global environmental threats is also reflected in calls for increased responsibility towards the planet by religious leaders such as the Dalai Lama. In one of his many statements to this effect, he pointed out that:

> Global warming has brought changes in climate, including making perennial snow mountain melt, thereby adversely affecting not only human beings but also other living species. Older people say that these mountains were covered with thick snow when they were young and that the snows are getting sparser, which may be an indication of the end of the world. The harmful effect on the atmosphere brought about by emissions in industrialised countries is a very dangerous sign. (The Dalai Lama XIV 2009: 6)

And elsewhere, he highlights how we need to learn from the processes we are witnessing: 'Our Mother Earth is now teaching us a critical evolutionary lesson – a lesson in universal responsibility. On it depends on the survival of millions of species, even our own' (The Dalai Lama XIV 2009: 22).

For the Limi community, the voice of environmentalist Buddhism is embodied by the head of the Drigung Kagyu sect, the 37th Drikung Kyabgon Chetsang Rinpoche, who lives in India but has close links to the Limi monastic community. Deeply aware of global environmental challenges, he established projects such as 'The Go Green & Go Organic project' whose main purpose is 'to revive the Himalayan and Tibetan Cultures and to protect the nature, animals, birds, and environment of the Himalayan Mountains'.[11]

Karmapa Urgyen Tinley Dorje addresses global environmental concerns in his book *Interconnected: Embracing Lie in our Global Society*. As the editorial introduction points out:

> The title of this book … makes use of the term 'interconnected' rather than 'interdependent' precisely to draw attention to the human affective dimension of our interdependence, in contrast to the external phenomena more often referenced by the term 'interdependence'. The Karmapa uses the term 'interconnectedness' and 'interdependency' almost interchangeably, and the Tibetan term itself (*rten cig 'brel pa byung pa*) is a compound that includes the terms that denote dependence and connection. (Karmapa 2017: 4)

The notion of interconnectedness highlights not only interdependence of all worldly phenomena but also affective relationship. It seems thus to embrace multiple scales. It also underpins the way in which the ancient human relationship with landscape features as spiritual entities was accommodated within Buddhist cosmologies as truth could be perceived at multiple levels depending on the position of the beholder (within the distinction of conventional truth and ultimate truth associated with enlightenment). A more abstract notion of interconnectedness interfolds therefore with a situated affective relationality linking people to places.

The framing of landscape features in terms of kinship/relatedness/mutuality of being suggests a possible convergence of the anthropology of the environment and the anthropology of kinship and care. Beyond the Himalaya, this is powerfully reflected, for example, in Pope Francis' reference to San Francis of Assisi's Canticum creaturarum or Cantico di Frate Sole ('song of brother sun') in his *Laudato si* encyclical addressing the global environmental crisis. Whether it is 'brother sun' (It. *frate sole*), 'sister moon' (It. *sora luna*) and 'sister mother earth' (It. *sora madre terra*), or Tibetan landscape features such as the earth foundation mother (*sashi ama*) or mountains and lakes as mother/father/sister/brother, etc., addressing natural features in terms of kinship does not necessarily express an ontological claim but rather a relational and affective way of being in the world. It is telling that the subtitle of the encyclical is 'on the *care* of our common home' (my italics). In an oddly similar way, we find the same kind of language, for example, in funding schemes of the UK Research Councils promoting 'care for the future'.

In 2019, glaciers on different mountains across the globe were mourned as if they were dead or dying relatives, such as the glacier Okjokull in Iceland.[12] A flurry of requiems for glaciers across the Alps was organized by a variety of environmental organizations and local agencies. Christian and other rituals were repurposed to address this new issue, demonstrating a profoundly affective relationship to the landscape. Wide-ranging coverage in the press and social media has secured popular participation beyond the limited groups of mountain lovers who actually went to the glacial basins where the glaciers used to be to commemorate their demise with music and prayers.[13] In light of the disappearance or quasi disappearance of these majestic ice formations, people have been rediscovering their affective relationship to these landscapes. Looking at what is left of the Lys glacier on Mt Rosa, not far from where I was born, I couldn't help thinking about Julie Cruickshank's question, 'Do Glaciers

Listen?' (Cruickshank 2005), elicited by the glacial landscapes of Mt Saint Elias in British Columbia. The sad look of mountain peaks stripped of their whiteness reminded me of a Tibetan song I heard in the Himalaya declaring that 'the honour of the mountains is the snow', which inspired a collaborative article on climate change in the Himalaya (see Diemberger, Hovden and, Yeh 2015: 249–71). These images also brought to mind inspiring conversations with, and a debt of gratitude towards, scholars such as Veerabhadran Ramanathan[14] and Charlie Kennel,[15] who have not only engaged scientifically with specific issues such as the impact of black carbon on mountain glaciers or the link between greenhouse gasses and climate change, but have also been promoting a dialogue across the sciences and with representatives of a range of religious traditions in the hope of promoting engagement towards common aims in caring for life on this planet.

Conclusion: The 'Cryosphere' as a Site of 'Friction' and 'Affection'

Both the polar areas and the Himalayan region drive global and regional climate, influencing respectively El Nino phenomena and the monsoon. These icescapes therefore have both a local and a global relevance that is difficult to assess due to the complexity of the phenomena involved but is undeniable. Like the Circumpolar North, the Himalayan region (as are other sites of the high-altitude cryosphere) is central to global processes driven by climatological factors and by entirely human needs and desires. People living on or next to these icescapes also share the fact that they are considered marginal in relation to current nation-states but are interconnected through regional networks that transcend national boundaries, reflecting historic links and shared ecologies so that looking at the Circumpolar North or the Himalayan region in this light offers a different perspective on conventional geopolitics. These regions are part of the cryosphere which can be looked at as a unified system whilst taking into account the specific environmental conditions and cultural vocabulary with which people respond to them.

The cryosphere therefore emerges as a particular site of encounter of different epistemic communities and an opportunity for interdisciplinary and cross-disciplinary exploration. Addressing the challenges of interdisciplinarity, Marilyn Strathern observed that:

> The reason we have sometimes been looking in the wrong place is that we have been so focused on incommensurability, on the difficulties disciplines have as discrete entities in 'talking' to one another, that we do not see what we all know, namely that they are all alike in thinking that they have this problem. (Strathern 2006: 93)

Drawing from her experience in Papua New Guinea, she brings together the notion of 'transplant' from two different contexts as a constructive way forward:

> the re-contextualisation of items of knowledge to create new knowledge and the transferring of plants or children from one clan land to another ... what that rendering of 'transplant' adds is the notion of generativity that comes from the way plants are thought to flourish precisely because of their outside origins. (Strathern 2006: 89)

Developing her argument on useful knowledge she comments: 'Perhaps in the heat generated over interdisciplinarity, rather than taking differences between disciplines as our starting point, we might look to a critical distinction between research and management practices, and these are seen as "interfolding" rather than collapsing' (Strathern 2006: 95).

As illustrated in the case of Limi, when urgent decisions need to be taken all available forms of knowledge are likely to be mobilized. Within this management logic, ontological and epistemological differences that may be cause for clashes may also offer ground for creative 'transplants', enabling localized solutions and creative re-combinations. In environments where small differences in temperature can have a great impact, shaped by the constant fluctuation of water between the solid, liquid and gaseous state, humans relate to the environment they live in through innumerable contingent decisions with which they respond to regular variability and exceptional extreme events. In this process, different forms of knowledge and moral frameworks, different scales and temporalities are brought to bear within cosmopolitical ecologies shaped by human and non-human actors. As in the Arctic, in the Himalaya, 'human life takes place under the breath of ice. Depending on where one is, it may be a more or less permanent presence, but it is always on the horizon' (Hastrup 2012: 227). As Kirsten Hastrup suggests, ice is its own argument and a powerful agent shaping all kinds of human interaction, narratives and theories of the environment far beyond being an actor in the Latourian sense.

Perceptions rooted in local day-to-day observations and cosmological frameworks blend with a wide range of global scientific narratives and technological infrastructures that reach remote sites in bits and pieces, creating new 'assemblages' (see Makley 2014: 233) and reflecting the different epistemic communities involved in decision-making. The 'cryosphere' emerges as a site of flows and frictions (Tsing 2004) within global connections, where encounters are driven by different agendas, situated contingencies and cultural specificities, and where practical issues of access and engagement make it also part of a distinctive form of 'remoteness' co-created by global processes (see also Saxer and Anderson 2019).

Against this background, attitudes that recognize the spiritual character of landscapes and the relevant human affective relationships with their features can be seen as an ontological provocation in light of rational scientific assumptions about nature and the world. However, if one moves beyond the question of unreconcilable ontological claims to appreciate the relationality of such positions, they can be seen as fruitful ways for mobilizing human and non-human communities around shared goals. As such they can operate at multiple levels and can be translated across epistemological boundaries.

Studying the social and cultural life of the cryosphere may therefore offer new perspectives for cross-regional, cross-disciplinary research linking arctic futures to that of comparably vulnerable environments in the world. Methodologically, the cryosphere may offer a framework for comparative projects focusing on the human, non-human and other-than-human engagement with icescapes. Exploring embodied knowledge, including verbal and non-verbal communication relating to ice and snow, creates opportunities for controlled comparative exercises that have the potential to de-centre the anglophone world or at least promote a critical engagement with it.

When discussing the workshop, Hildegard Diemberger recalled:

> As a mountaineer, my father travelled from his native Alps to many mountains in the world and to the Arctic. He loved and still loves Greenland's icescapes. From his travel in 1966, he brought home three Greenlandic words: tesa, susa, imaka. As he understood them in Umanak on the West coast of Greenland, their meaning was: tesa, it has happened, it is past; susa, don't worry; imaka, maybe. When telling his story, with a smile he seemed to evoke the infinite creative possibility of uncertainty that he learnt when sharing his experience of ice with Greenlandic friends across language barriers.

Acknowledgements

This chapter reflects the result of research and impact activities that took place over many years and many projects, most recently the international collaborative project 'Himalayan Connections: Melting Glaciers, Sacred Landscapes and Mobile Technologies in a Changing Climate' ('Himalconnect'), based at the University of Oslo and the University of Cambridge (The Research Council of Norway, Norglobal scheme, project n 274491), a stakeholder workshop supported by the Global Challenges Research Fund of the University of Cambridge (GCRF, project n G 102647) and the Newton Trust Fellowship Scheme.

Hildegard Diemberger is the Research Director of Mongolia and Inner Asia Studies Unit (MIASU) at the University of Cambridge and a Fellow of Pembroke College. Trained as a social anthropologist and Tibetologist at Vienna University, she has published numerous books and articles on the anthropology and the history of Tibet and the Himalaya as well as on the Tibetan-Mongolian interface, including the monograph *When a Woman becomes a Religious Dynasty: The Samding Dorje Phagmo of Tibet* (Columbia University Press, 2007), the edited volume *Tibetan Printing – Comparisons, Continuities and Change* (Brill, 2016) and the English translation of two important Tibetan historical texts (Austrian Academy of Science, 1996, 2000). She has designed and coordinated a number of research projects funded by the UK Arts and Humanities Research Council, the British Academy, the Newton Trust, The Research Council of Norway, the Austrian Science Fund and the Italian National Research Council.

Astrid Hovden is an Associate Professor in Religious Studies at UiT – The Arctic University of Norway. Her main research interests include lived religion, social history, as well as climate change adaptation, explored through various published and forthcoming works. She has conducted several long-term ethnographic fieldwork projects on both sides of the Himalayas. Currently, she is part of the research project 'Himalayan Connections: Melting Glaciers, Sacred Landscapes and Mobile Technologies in a Changing Climate' funded by the Research Council of Norway.

Notes

1. Snowstorms, droughts, floods are all phenomena that have shaped the life of human beings in the Himalayas and on the Tibetan plateau since time immemorial. They are not new. What seems to be unprecedented – as in so many other parts of the world – is the perceived variation in frequency and intensity of these events.
2. This term is most prominently connected to Antarctic explorations and the study of snow and ice-crystals by the Polish scientist A.B. Dobrowolski, considered to be the first cryospheric scientist (see Barry, Jania, and Birkenmajer 2011). He 'defines the cryosphere – from the Greek word krios meaning icy cold – as a zone extending from the upper part of the troposphere, where ice crystals occur in clouds, to the base of the permafrost … He introduced the concept of the cryosphere as a special part of the lithosphere, closely connected to the hydrosphere and the atmosphere. He also proposed the recognition of cryology as a separate science dealing with the solid phase of water in all its aspects, of whatever origin, and recommended that it form a part of physical geography', *AB Dobrowolski – The First Cryospheric Scientist – And the Subsequent Development of Cryospheric Science* (PDF Download Available). Retrieved 23 March 2018 from https://www.researchgate.net/publication/228519645_AB_Dobrowolski-the_first_cryospheric_scientist-and_the_subsequent_development_of_cryospheric_science.
3. See, for example, conferences organized with this focus: 'High Altitudes meet High Latitudes: Globalizing Polar Issues', https://www.mountainresearchinitiative.org/news-page-all/112-global-news/1051-high-altitudes-meet-high-latitudes-globalizing-polar-issues (last accessed 6 March 2022); 'Vanishing Ice: Inquiring about the Past and Acting for the Future in the European Alps and the Arctic', convened in June 2014 in the Department of Social Anthropology of Aberdeen University.
4. The International Centre for Integrated Mountain Development (ICIMOD) is a regional intergovernmental learning and knowledge sharing centre serving the eight regional member countries of the Hindu Kush Himalaya. See http://www.icimod.org/ (last accessed 6 March 2022).
5. This category of spirits is widespread across Inner Asia, e.g. 'lus savdag' can be found in the Mongolian context (see also Sneath and Turk, in press). They have also been used as the basis for claims of legal personhood of topographic features (Studley 2018).
6. It is currently located in the Tibet Autonomous Region of the People's Republic of China, but the relevant sacred geography extends over northwestern Nepal and North India. It also has a wider global spiritual relevance.
7. The Bonpo spiritual master Lopon Tenzin Namdak mentioned this prophecy to Charles Ramble as reoccurring in ancient scriptures and being topical and evocative in relation to current global challenges.
8. Given how little is known of the Shangshung language and also how extensively it has been mythologized in later Bonpo traditions, the historical accuracy of this translation remains problematic. However, for the sake of this chapter, the mere fact that this explanation has become part of the

commentary elicited by the name of the mountain remains significant. I heard it several times from Tibetan Bonpo scholars, especially during a conference on Shangshung that took place in Lhasa in June 2018.
9. Local deities (mainly mountain gods) were integrated into the Buddhist framework through the binary classification of worldly deities (jigs rten pa'i lha/jigs rten pa'i 'das pa'I lha). The first instance of this distinction appears in the inscription that declared Buddhism the state religion of the Tibetan empire at the time of the construction of the first Buddhist monastery in the eighth century. At that time, these local deities were invited as witnesses to the event.
10. 'Earth Beings' is the translation of the word *tirakuna*, composed of the word land and the plural Quechua suffix *–kuna*. They are sentient entities that are mountains, rivers, lagoons and other visible marks of the landscape and that are in mutual relationships of care with the Runakuna.
11. http://www.fao.org/mountain-partnership/members/members-detail/en/c/98621/; http://www.drikung.org/their-holiness/hh-kyabgoen-chetsang (both last accessed 6 March 2022).
12. The funeral of the Iceland glacier had wide-ranging media coverage; see, for example, the BBC article 'Iceland's Okjokull glacier Commemorated with a Plaque' by Toby Luckhhurst, 18 August 2019; https://www.bbc.co.uk/news/world-europe-49345912 (accessed 22 September 2019). It also saw a sustained engagement by the anthropologists Cymene Howe and Dominic Boyer, who produced a documentary on the subject.
13. See, for example, Gressoney, veglia funebre per il ghiacciaio del Lys: 'Ricordiamo ciò che di buono ci ha lasciato', 27 September 2019; https://video.repubblica.it/edizione/torino/gressoney-veglia-funebre-per-il-ghiacciaio-del-lys-ricordiamo-cio-che-di-buono-ci-ha-lasciato/344599/345181 (accessed 22 September 2022).
14. Veerabhadran Ramanathan, Edward A. Frieman Endowed Presidential Chair in Climate Sustainability Scripps Institute of Oceanography, University of California, San Diego, has contributed to a wide range of research topics in atmospheric science. He was one of the scholars involved in the scientific debate at the Vatican Academy that provided the background for the Pope's Encyclical.
15. Charles Kennel, former director of the Scripps Institute of Oceanography, has been a regular visiting fellow at Cambridge where he promoted disciplinary engagement on climate change.

References

Barry, Roger G., Jania Janek and Krzysztof Birkenmajer. 2011. 'A. B. Dobrowolski – the Frst Cryospheric Scientist – and the Subsequent Development of Cryospheric Science', *History of Geo- and Space Sciences* 2: 75–79.
Basso, Keith. 1996. *Wisdom Sits in Places: Landscape and Language Among the Western Apache*. Albuquerque, NM: University of New Mexico Press.

Bravo, Michael and Gareth Rees. 2006. 'Cryo-politics: Environmental Security and the Future of Arctic Navigation', *The Brown Journal of World Affairs* 13(1): 205–15.
Cruickshank, Julie. 2005. *Do Glaciers Listen? Local Knowledge, Colonial Encounters and Social Imagination.* Vancouver: University of British Columbia Press.
XIV Dalai Lama (2009) 'Universal Responsibility and the Climate Emergency' in J. Stanley, D. Loy and Gyurme Dorje (eds), *A Buddhist Response to the Climate Emergency.* Somerville: Wisdom Publications.
De la Cadena, Marisol. 2010. 'Indigenous Cosmopolitics in the Andes: Conceptual Reflections Beyond 'Politics', *Cultural Anthropology* 25(2): 334–70.
———. 2015. *Earth Beings: Ecologies of Practice across Andean Worlds.* Durham, NC and London: Duke University Press.
Diemberger, Hildegard. 2012. 'Deciding the Future in the Land of Snow: Tibet as an Arena for Conflicting Knowledge and Policies', in K. Hastrup (ed.), *The Social Life of Climate Models.* London: Routledge, pp.100–27.
———. 2021. 'When *Lha Lu* Spirits Suffer and Sometimes Fight Back: Tibetan Cosmopolitics at a Time of Environmental Threats and Climate Change', in Riamsara Kuyakanon, Hildegard Diemberger and David Sneath (eds), *Cosmopolitical Ecologies Across Asia: Places and Practices of Power in Changing Environments.* London: Routledge.
Diemberger, Hildegard and Hans F. Graf. 2012. 'Snow-Mountains on the Tibetan Plateau: Powerful Proxies across Different Modalities of Climate Knowledge in Communicating Climate: Proxies, Processes, Politics', *Current Anthropology* 53(2): 233–35.
Diemberger, Hildegard, Astrid Hovden and Emily Yeh. 2015. 'The Honour of the Snow-Mountains is the Snow: Tibetan Livelihoods in a Changing Climate', in Christian Huggel, Mark Carey, John Clague and Andreas Kaab (eds), *The High-Mountain Cryosphere – Environmental Changes and Human Risks.* Cambridge: Cambridge University Press, pp. 249–71.
Dyrenfurth, Günter. 1953. *To the Third Pole.* London: W. Laurie.
Hastrup, Kirsten. 2012. 'The Icy Breath: Modalities of Climate Knowledge in the Arctic', in 'Communicating Climate: Proxies, Processes, Politics', *Current Anthropology* 53(2): 227–30.
Hovden, Astrid. In press. *Limi, the Land in-between: The Art of Governing a Buddhist Frontier Community in the Himalaya.* Leiden: Brill.
Hovden, Astrid and Hanna Havnevik. 2021. 'Balancing the Sacred Landscape: Environmental Management in Limi North-Western Nepal', in Riamsara Kuyakanon, Hildegard Diemberger and David Sneath (eds), *Cosmopolitical Ecologies Across Asia: Places and Practices of Power in Changing Environments.* London: Routledge.
Huettmann, Falk. 2012. *Protection of the Three Poles.* London and New York: Springer.
Huggel, Christian, Mark Carey, John Clague and Andreas Kaab (eds). 2015 *The High-Mountain Cryosphere – Environmental Changes and Human Risks.* Cambridge: Cambridge University Press.
Ingold, Tim. 2000. *The Perception of the Environment: Essays on Livelihood, Dwelling and Skill.* London: Routledge.

Karmapa, The. 2017. *Interconnected: Embracing Life in Our Global Society*. Somerwille: Wisdom Publications
Kropáček, J. et al. 2015. 'Repeated Glacial Lake Outburst Flood Threatening the Oldest Buddhist Monastery in North-Western Nepal'. *Natural Hazards and Earth System Sciences* 15: 2425–37.
Kuyakanon, Riamsara, Hildegard Diemberger and David Sneath. 2021. *Cosmopolitical Ecologies Across Asia: Places and Practices of Power in Changing Environments*. London: Routledge.
Makley, Charlene. 2014. 'The Amoral Other - State-Led Development and Mountain Deity Cults among Tibetans in Amdo Rebgong', in E. Yeh and C. Coggins (eds), *Mapping Shangrila*. Seattle, WA: University of Washington Press, pp. 229–54.
Marin, Andrei. 2010. 'Riders Under Storms: Contributions of Nomadic Herders' Observations to Analysing Climate Change in Mongolia', *Global Environmental Change* 20(1): 162–76.
Maurer, Petra, Donatella Rossi and Rolf Scheuermann. 2019. *Glimpses of Tibetan Divination, Past and Present*. Leiden: Brill.
Nuttall, Mark. 2010. 'Anticipation, Climate Change, and Movement in Greenland', *Études/Inuit/Studies* 34(1): 21–37.
Qiu, Jane. 2008. 'The Third Pole: Climate Change is Coming Fast and Furious to the Tibetan Plateau', *Nature* 454(24): 393–96.
Salick, Jan, Anja Byg and Kenneth Bauer. 2012. 'Contemporary Tibetan Cosmology of Climate Change', *Journal for the Study of Religion, Nature & Culture* 6(4): 447–76.
Saxer, Martin and Ruben Anderson. 2019. 'The Return of Remoteness: Insecurity, Isolation and Connectivity in the New World Disorder', *Social Anthropology* 27(2): 140–55.
Sehnalova, Aanna. 2019. 'Powerful Deity or National Geopark?: The Pilgrimage to A-myes-rma-chen in 2014/2015, Transformations of Modernisation and State Secularism, and Environmental Change', *Inner Asia* 21: 216–82.
Sneath, David 2014. 'Nationalising Civilisational Resources: Sacred Mountains and Cosmopolitical Ritual in Mongolia', *Asian Ethnicity* 15(4): 458–72.
Sneath, David and Elisabeth Turk. 2021. 'Knowing the Lords of the Land: Cosmopolitical Dynamics and Historical Change in Mongolia', in R. Kuyakanon, H. Diemberger and D. Sneath (eds.), *Cosmopolitical Ecologies Across Asia: Places and Practices of Power in Changing Environments*. London: Routledge.
Strathern, Marilyn. 2004. *Partial Connections*. New York: Altamira.
———. 2006. 'Useful Knowledge', *Proceedings of the British Academy* 139: 73–109.
Studley, John. 2018. 'The Ritual Protection of Indigenous Sacred Natural Sites on the Tibetan Plateau and the Optimisation of Lay Participation', *Journal for the Study of Religion, Nature & Culture* 12(4): 354–83.
Tsing, Anna. 2004. *Friction: An Ethnography of Global Connection*. Princeton, NJ: Princeton University Press.
Yeh, Emily. 2014. 'The Rise and Fall of the Green Tibetan – Contingent Collaborations and the Vicissitudes of Harmony', in E. Yeh and C. Coggins

(eds), *Mapping Shangrila*. Seattle, WA: University of Washington Press, pp. 205–28.
———. 2019. 'The Land Belonged to Nepal But the People Belonged to Tibet': Overlapping Sovereignties and Mobility in the Limi Valley Borderland', *Geopolitics* 26 (3): 919–45.
Yeh, Emily, Yonten Nyima, Kelly Hopping and Julia Klein. 2014. 'Tibetan Pastoralists' Vulnerability to Climate Change: A Political Ecology Analysis of Snowstorm Coping Capacity', *Human Ecology* 42(1): 61–74.
Weston, Kat. 2017. *Animate Planet: Making Visceral Sense of Living in a High-Tech Ecologically Damaged World*. Durham, NC and London: Duke University Press.

CHAPTER 7

Risky Decisions, Precarious Moralities
The Case of Autumn Whaling in Barrow, Alaska

Barbara Bodenhorn

Foreword

In the spring of 1997, I was in Fairbanks, along with Mike Pedersen (Science Officer for the Arctic Slope Native Association) at an NSF sponsored conference on 'the Human Impact of Global Warming in the Arctic'.[1] As we were sitting outside in the spring sunshine taking a break, Mike received the message that an ice calving event had stranded 147 whalers on the ice just off Barrow. To make matters worse, the spring conditions had generated dense fog, creating zero visibility. By that evening we had heard everyone had been recovered safely – made possible largely by state-of-the-art Search and Rescue helicopters and the fact that virtually all of the whaling boats were equipped with GPS – and heaved a collective sigh of relief. Once back in Barrow, I began to hear different sorts of conversations; mixed in with expressions of gratitude for the technologies that had hastened rescue, I also heard from whaling captains who said, 'Of course we didn't go out; I had been watching those cracks for weeks!' (which I understood) and, more puzzling for me, 'We didn't go out because the wind had dropped'. What I did not know then but know now was that wind and water currents at this time of year flow in opposite directions. If the wind stops, the water has the force to lift great chunks of ice from its short-fast ice base and set it adrift in the open water. Thus began my interest in how Iñupiaq whalers assess uncertain conditions when faced with the urgent need to make decisions in response. Faced with the same conditions and generally equipped with similar environmental knowledge, individual whaling captains had made quite different decisions about whether or not to venture out onto the ice with their crews. I was also hearing about the same decisions that had been made on different sets of information. My first opportunity to explore these issues in detail came during the following autumn whaling season. In the present chapter I consider decisions taken about the conduct of whaling at the collective level by the Barrow Whaling Captains' Association, at the crew level and by individuals. In doing so, I explore the myriad of grounds on which people were explicitly talking about why they made one decision or another: moral (cosmological), social, political, economic; and the ways in which they took multiple possible consequences into consideration. It is, I feel, a perfect illustration of the extent to which the challenges described in this volume contain within them 'constellations of risk'.

Introduction

As just mentioned, this chapter traces some of the multi-layered reasons Iñupiaq whalers articulated for the strategies they followed in the conduct of the 1997 autumn hunt. I use this material to consider several still influential models of risk that were reviewed in the Introduction. My main point is straightforward, but bears emphasis: at the level of policy, single-stranded cause and effect models of risk may well inform the basis on which policies are generated and deployed. At the level of daily practice, as this material reveals in striking detail, what constitutes 'a risk', what its possible consequences might be, and what alternative choices of action are considered possible all draw on multiple models.

In the following pages, I look at how (some) Barrow whalers talked to me about the shifts in whaling practices that took place during the 1996/97 autumn whaling seasons. The language in which whalers discuss the strategies they collectively developed reveal, in Douglas and Wildavsky's (1982) words, different orders of 'goods' and 'bads' that were taken into account. It illustrates how what often might appear as cost-effective conditions in cultural terms do not necessarily lead to predictable decisions.

At the time of the 1997 ice calving event, the 'techno/scientific/realistic' approach to risk was dominant in scientific circles, as we mentioned in the Introduction. Certainly, when I asked whaling captains either why they had gone out or not, a certain number replied in terms of the material technology under their control. But as we shall see, in my experience it was never taken as the single authoritative form of explanation.

We discussed Douglas and Wildavsky in the Introduction, but I want to reiterate one of their quotes here because it is so apropos to the discussion to come: 'fear of risk coupled with the confidence to face it has something to do with knowledge and something to do with the kind of people we are'. Different people worry about different things. '[T]o organise [in the face of perceived risk] means to organise some things in and other things out' (Douglas and Wildavsky 1982: 8). These processes of identifying risk, of assessing it and creating strategies with relation to its perceived implications are all bound up in considering 'goods' and 'bads' which are moral and consequently always both cultural and political.

The material to come can be useful to think in a number of ways. With reference to the 'expert/lay divide' as explored and critiqued by Wynne (1996), Iñupiat are quite aware of the political traps in the definition of their knowledge as 'not scientific' – traps that can be analysed quite easily with Foucauldian notions of power/knowledge. Iñupiat often act strategically in that awareness. At the same time, however, it is important that we recognize different domains of knowledge that are not necessarily in opposition to each other. Iñupiaq knowledge categories include the recognition of *taiguaqti*, or 'readers' whose expert abilities to read the environment are connected to their ability to tell what they know to others. The morality of sharing information is, according to Raymond Neakok, Sr, 'one of the rules'.[2] In many ways, Iñupiat do not set up barriers between 'our' and 'their' knowledge and are quite keen to learn what whale biologists think, without ever assuming their own knowledge of whale behaviour is somehow 'less'. As I have said, Iñupiaq discussions draw on more than one order of knowing and they take place at institutional and individual levels.

I find myself in sympathy with Douglas and Wildavsky: we need to keep in mind 'rules into which a vision of the good life can be translated' (1982: 175) before thinking about how these may or may not be framed with reference to physical or moral dangers. The good life, according to the vast majority of Iñupiat with whom I have spoken since 1980, is defined through hunting in general and whaling in particular. In contrast to the US Declaration of Independence with its assertion of an individual's self-evident entitlement to 'life, liberty and the pursuit of happiness', this good life is not expressed in a language of rights, but as a social relationship articulated as a responsibility to other humans but also, crucially, to the animals on whom Iñupiat depend. As we shall see, this generates quite a different sort of language of risk than many of the examples drawn on in the literature cited in the Introduction. Equally, it makes a difference that Iñupiat are both egalitarian and value individual autonomy in ways that are quite distinct from the mainstream society surrounding them. Thus, Douglas and Wildavsky's distinctions that we noted earlier, between egalitarian and hierarchical social organization as factors that will generate different definitions of risk, and different strategies for dealing with it, are ones to take into consideration. But those factors need to be further contextualized. What we have just touched on are the seeming contradictory values of collective responsibility and individual autonomy. I make a distinction between the sort of possessive individualism that assumes all value can be owned as private property and the kind of individualism that assumes all beings have autonomy; that whales and caribou give themselves up to hunters they deem worthy; that babies choose when to be born; and that the decisions one makes should be thoughtful because they carry weight in the world. Those distinctions play a role when precarity is demanding attention.

Similarly, the Foucauldian approaches mentioned above make important points that are relevant to the decisions Iñupiat whalers make. The extent to which the actions they take are subject to various forms of oversight and regulation, which generate local versions of oversight and regulation, is a central aspect of contemporary whaling. Yet to frame these decisions purely as expressions of governmentality would simply be to miss a great number of points. By the same token, it is of course important to realize the weaknesses inherent in assuming hazards are 'out there' floating free of culture in some way whereas risks are socially and culturally defined. The danger, once again, is to fall into a kind of descriptive language that implies everything is constructed and therefore of the same order.

The discussions I shall not enter into are those about 'modernity'. Iñupiat today are dealing with thoroughly capitalist and governmental institutions on a daily basis. They do so with great determination to 'do it their way' which at times includes thoroughly capitalist and governmental actions. I have been struck in much of the current risk literature at the extent to which many anthropological discussions of the last several decades – about contemporaneity of peoples, and about the difficulties with assuming 'the Enlightenment Project' is an all-encompassing social fact of modernity – seem to be entirely ignored. The multiple sorts of discussions Iñupiat engage in when talking about whaling remind me in fact of Latour's (1993) opening remarks in *We Have Never Been Modern*. Discussing an article about Antarctica and the ozone layer, he says, 'The same article mixes together chemical reactions and political reactions (and disagreements between chemists and meteorologists). A single thread links the most esoteric sciences and the most sordid politics, the most distant sky and some factory in the Lyon suburb' (1993: 1). His argument concerns what he calls 'the proliferation of hybrids'. Mine simply tries to untangle the different modes these discussions assume.

Nor am I going to explore the question of untranslatable categories. Iñupiat exist in a world in which official languages of risk have defined their whaling negotiations since 1978 at least when the International Whaling Commission declared that subsistence whaling should cease because it endangered the bowhead population. Their efficacy depends on being able to interpret others' concerns and being able to communicate about their own. For the moment at least I find it useful to accept the separation of 'hazard' and 'risk'. As a working definition I shall modify the BMA definition slightly and suggest hazards are recognized dangers to social goods; the risk is the potential negative consequence.

Thinning ice, thus is a hazard; the risks may include the dangers faced by crews wanting to bring a whale up on the ice, or the likelihood that hunters will not be able to find harbour seal who habitually give birth to their young at the ice edge. What I do not include as a core part of my definition is the notion of calculability. Some of the decisions whalers make – about the best time to begin autumn whaling for instance – are clear instances of complex calculations involving multiple factors. Others – such as the possibility of whales withholding themselves if people are not properly generous – cannot be subjected to the same calculus.

The Ethnography

The general framework for this discussion is set out in two ways. First, with the help of information provided by North Slope elders, we consider how rules about the proper conduct of whaling influence Iñupiaq social life in general and look at the potential consequences of ignoring them. We then turn to the formal organization of whaling, examining the different institutional levels at which whaling strategies are discussed and implemented.

'Iñupiaq Food Is Social Food' – Whaling as a Way of Organizing the Social

The social organization of whaling is often talked about in terms of its division of labour: how people organize themselves to hunt, butcher, distribute and share the whale. This is an exceedingly important part, but nonetheless only a part, of the story.

'I am Iñupiaq; I eat Iñupiaq food' is an equation that I have heard many times over the years – in many contexts and by many different people. But it is not just the nature of the food itself that is so important. 'Iñupiaq food is social food', Fannie Akpik said one evening in the autumn of 1997. And indeed, that is very literally true in many cases. People who may be forced to eat Iñupiaq food on their own – in hospital rooms for instance – talk of how incomplete that experience is. What makes it social, however, is not just that it tastes better when you can eat it together, but that it is a consequence of many social relationships – between humans, between humans and animals and among animals themselves.

It is common to hear that whales may give or withhold of themselves.[3] In the women's session of the 1991 Elders' Conference, organized by the Iñupiaq History, Language and Culture Commission,[4] Ida Koonuk spoke of this explicitly: 'The bowhead is a very distinguished mammal', she said. 'It can give itself up, which can make it very easy for the captain and crew, or it can withhold itself from another captain and crew and can be struck and lost' (IHLC 1991a: 12). The gift relationship between whales and humans is a social one that depends on two other kinds of social behaviour: generosity among humans and communication among the whales themselves. Kirk Oviok, from Point Hope, remembered his own upbringing:

> Like my aunt said, the whales have ears and are more like people. The first batch of whales seen would show up to check which ones in the whaling crews would be more hospitable to be caught. Then the whales would come back to their pack and tell them about the situation stating, 'we have someone available for us', ... This is what my wife and I have heard from my aunt Negovanna. I firmly believe this is true, that whales have ears. (IHLC 1991b: 4–5)

This is echoed by Mary Aveoganna, from Barrow. 'Always be ready with hospitality', she instructed, 'so the whale will see an inviting place' (IHLC 1991a: tape 2). In his 1985 address to the Alaska Eskimo Whaling Commission, Patrick Attungana (whose words also feature in Edwardson's chapter in this volume), another Point Hoper and ordained minister of the Episcopal Church, related an *unipkaaq* (story passed down through the generations) that expresses this even more explicitly:

> When the whales come, ... one of them stops, like it was camping, being caught by the people. ... That one that is like camping... it knows when its relatives are coming back. ... Those that are returning want to listen to what that one that is like camping has to say. That one tells them the stories, that he had a good host with those two, the married ones [the whaling captain couple] ... That one that talks about having good hosts, starts looking forward to going back to those hosts when they return the following year. And the other one that said it did not have good hosts said that it will not camp again but will go to another host. (1986: 5–6)[5]

Thus, assumptions about whale/whale sociality also have consequences for the moral weight Iñupiat place on human social behaviour. This does not simply concern the way in which the whale hunt is conducted but extends to the generosity with which humans treat each other throughout the year. The moral universe is full of social beings acting with intent. To use the language of the risk literature just reviewed, the hazard of impolite human behaviour carries with it the very considerable risk that whales will withhold themselves from the gift relationship. They may simply not show up; they may be struck but slip under the ice; or a wounded whale may be escorted away by two or more of its pod. In my experience, the latter two sorts of instances may be read as evidence that particular individuals had not acted properly. But equally – as in the case of a severe accident several years ago that resulted in the death of someone helping to pull a whale to shore – the responsibility is collective. In this latter case people did not seek to assign individual blame, but rather assumed there had been too much conflict in town and talked about the entire community having to mend its ways and unify itself. At the end of the speech cited above, Attungana concluded that the whale gives itself to all; to receive the gift Iñupiat need to be able to 'hunt in harmony; that is what holds our hunting together' (1986: 6).

From these general statements about the moral aspects of whaling, let us turn to some of the quite specific aspects of human behaviour that North Slope elders consider hazardous to the human/whale relationship. The comments refer to ways that these elders learned to behave in preparation for whaling, during the whale hunt itself, in the immediate aftermath of a successful hunt and during the year overall. Although we begin with references to cleaning ice cellars because this was mentioned so many times as crucial preparatory activity, we should bear in mind that, as Maggie Ahmaogak emphasized when we were talking about the responsibilities of whaling captain wives, the cycle has no clear beginning and no absolute end. The whaling celebration is at once an opportunity to give thanks for a successful season and an opportunity to provide the hospitality that, as we have heard, will encourage whales to give of themselves again in the future.

Ida Koonuk of Point Hope explained why it was so important to clean out ice cellars in March:[6]

> We are told the one we are so expectant about does not like to be laid to rest in a messy cellar. That was one of the foremost teachings we have always heard! My mother-in-law would tell me, 'When you are done with cleaning up of the cellar, before you climb up, say verbally, "you can now expect to be filled".' It has gotten to be a habit with me now, saying it inside the cellar before I climb out of it. (IHLC 1991a: 12)

Carol Omnik, also of Point Hope, concurred:

> It is exactly like one of the former speakers, Ida, said. That the first thing that has to be done is the ice cellar. I, too, grew up when I would see people work to clean out cellars. It has always been a practice from time immemorial, a piece of whale meat from last year cannot be saved until a later time. It has to be taken out. Because the anticipated whale always sees and hears all that goes on. (IHLC 1991a: 13)

Mary Aveoganna, of Barrow, expanded this somewhat:

> We, the Aveoganna crew, my children and their spouses started on an ice cellar, for the proper storage of the mighty bowhead. For it is common knowledge, as we are told from time immemorial, that the bowhead would discern what/how they are to be handled, distributed and stored as they give themselves up to this particular captain and crew. Every one of the crew members gave of their time and labour to get the cellar done in time for whaling. I kept encouraging them, telling them that it will anticipate to be filled with what we all are hoping, praying for. It is so clean and prepared for what we all have awaited for. (IHLC 1991a: 15)

The ice cellar, then, must be prepared as an inviting resting place for the whale. The meat that has been removed in the process cannot be hoarded, as Berna Brower of Barrow related:

> When my daughter-in-law asked what are we going to do with all the meat and fish that were put out from the ice cellar? Shall we put them back into the cellar? [I told her] No!. Just leave enough fish and meat for

the whaling season, for your whalers, then take the extras to the widows and the Elders. So all day she went out and gave away all the meat and fish to different homes that she knew of.

Then one of the Elders spoke and said may she receive something tender and delicious to give away. So that is why we should always give priority to widows and Elders. (IHLC 1991a: 2)

The hope is not that one gives away to get something tasty for oneself, but to receive something worthy of being an appreciated gift again. I want to act properly so that a whale will give itself up to my crew; if that happens, the whale doesn't become 'mine' to have, but the community's to take part in.

The exhortation to share and be generous, especially to those less fortunate, appeared in almost every participant's testimony. Not only Berna Brower, but Ida Koonuk ('take widows and orphans under our wing'), Alice Solomon ('feed the hungry, the orphans, the poor'), Terza Hopson ('What the elders have said about "taking under your wing, so to speak, the poor, the orphans" fits right in with the commandments of our Lord'), Dorcas Tagarook ('we were taught not to omit anyone'), Jennie Ahkivgak ('feed the poor'), Carl Omnik ('take responsibility for the orphans and the elders'), and Mary Aveoganna ('don't hoard') reflected the consistency of this message from across the North Slope region (IHLC 1991a: 2–15).[7]

The need for cleanliness was echoed in the men's session.[8] Eli Solomon drew an explicit parallel with the women's responsibilities on shore: 'Just as the women keep the qanitchat (entry ways) clean, so everything around the tent should be clean – especially the left side of the boat' (IHLC 1991b: 9) [for this way, the whale will 'see' its way to its resting place and be more likely to give itself up].[9] Wyborn Nungasak was also clear that one of the whaling captain's responsibilities was to ensure that 'the environment needs to be clean and acceptable by all' (IHLC 1991d, tape 2: 3).

Words as well as deeds must be treated carefully. 'Watch your words!' Arthur Neakok, originally from Nuvuk (Point Barrow) said to the men; 'refrain your tongue from backbiting', exhorted Carol Omnik while fellow Point Hoper Ida Koonuk emphasized: 'Harsh words do no good; the whale listens in [and reports back to other whales]. Because the whale we are all so eager for listens in, whoever we are dealing with' (IHLC 1991a: 12).

Once the whale has given itself up, it is important to handle the meat with care: treat it 'tenderly' in the process of butchering, storing and preparing the meat for the various feasts during which it will be consumed throughout the year.

> 'It has always been said', according to Carol Omnik, 'that as the whales gather together, they would communicate one to the other, that this particular does not work on me with tender, loving hands. Some would report that this one is the best person to be with. There are some others who would like to go to someone else, all because they want to be worked on tenderly. So the conversation goes on'. (IHLC 1991a: 14)

Above all, women and men reiterated, it is important to 'be in harmony'. Levi Greist remembered a story: 'Long ago, just before going out on a whaling venture, man and wife had a dispute. It was not long after they got to the open lead where they set up camp, that a whale came up and started chopping the ice off with his flukes. Therefore, unity is continually stressed' (IHLC 1991c: 14).

Patrick Attungana underscored the same message on a wider level in his 1985 address to the Alaska Eskimo Whaling Commission: 'When you hunt in harmony, you don't have problems catching the animals. This is what needs to be thought about. If the hunters from Barter to St. Lawrence Island hunt in harmony, the animals will keep going. They will acquire, they will catch the animal' (1986: 16ff). The whaling captain couple, the whaling crew and the whaling crews together are enjoined over and over to 'work together' and to 'be grateful' to the whales for their gift of themselves.

In many important ways, the annual cycle is a marked celebration of whaling. Nalukataq (the spring whaling feast), Thanksgiving and Christmas all incorporate the distribution of shares, the communal consumption of a feast centred on whale meat and maktak, and the clear expression of thanks that whales made this possible.[10] These feasts are intensely social, celebrated in commensality, singing, dancing and prayer, but the exhortations presented above are about the rules of sociality to be followed throughout the year.

The exhortation for humans to be social in particular ways quite explicitly underpins the sociality of the whale/human gift relationship. Messy cellars, messy camps, harsh words and social tensions are all presented as hazards that have the potential to discourage whales from offering themselves. Once a whale has offered itself, thoughtless treatment of the whale's body – either by treating the meat roughly during butchering and storage or by not sharing it fully – is experienced as inhospitable. Those who are not 'good hosts' create the danger that whales will not want to return. Very specific things need to be done, but generally the decisions about how to do them are left open.

To return to the theoretical literature, this set of conversations does not reflect a model that suggests the dangers are 'out there' which must be dealt with socially. The dangers and their potential consequences are both expressed in social terms with social actors – human and non-human – at the centre.[11] These events are very clearly explained as a function of an explicit cause and effect relationship just as the rules guiding proper behaviour are explained as means to a specified end. They are a function of individual actions and individual responsibilities – primarily personified through the whaling captain couple – with consequences for the entire social group. Thus, while we have both rational explanation and institutionalized individual autonomy, the reasoning, self-interested, maximizing economic individual of rational choice theory does not provide us with satisfying explanatory power. Although individuals are left to decide for themselves how to act, for the most part, negative consequences are spoken of in terms of collective responsibility. And as we shall see, the decisions that are made cannot always be predicted in terms of rational self-interest – whether that interest is framed, to borrow from Bourdieu, in terms of material, cultural or intellectual capital.

I do not want to give the impression that either Iñupiaq beliefs or practices are uniform, coherent and somehow hermetically sealed. They are not. How people talk about the social relationships between whales/humans/God varies from person to person, between denominations and between villages. As Isaac Akootchook pointed out, customs at times 'have to be altered to fit our way of life. … What will be effective in your village will not be good for our part of the country' (IHLC 1991c: 1). Nor, clearly, am I trying to reproduce a picture of 'pure' Iñupiaq ideas that can be viewed through intervening layers of Christian doctrines. The participants in both the men's and women's sessions who were quoted above are for the most part practising Christians of several denominations. For many, an active reliance on Christian prayer formed the backbone of proper behaviour. Indeed, Mary Lou Leavitt was firm that 'above all, the woman of the house should be a praying woman' (IHLC 1991b: 3) Just as Terza Hopson drew a parallel between pre-Christian and Christian Iñupiaq practices above, so Jennie Ahkivgak also pointed out that many aspects of the ways in which Iñupiat talk about whaling – whether or not from an explicitly 'Christian' viewpoint – are remarkably consistent.

Especially when I read the Iñupiat Bible, she mused. All that is written thereon is no different from the Iñupiaq customs and way of life. What we knew to be a fact, that our forefathers did not read, but by their verbal expressions it would sound like they were reading the Iñupiat Bible as they gave instructions to live good moral lives. (IHLC 1991a: 12)

Whether from the spirit of God or of the Whale or a combination of both, these moral codes thus provide a backdrop with reference to which a broad range of decisions is generated.

The Institutional Organization of Whaling

We have examined whaling beliefs in terms of what seems to me to be an explicitly moral language of 'risky relationships'; we turn now to contexts in which decisions are made and not just talked about. What emerges clearly is that the Elders' statements we have heard are by no means simply ideal statements; they continue to inform the reasons for fundamental decisions concerning whaling. However, it is clear that improper human behaviour is by no means the only hazard confronting Iñupiaq whalers. Taking a single case example in which 'waste' was defined as a serious problem, we see how discussions include not only moral, but physical and political dimensions. This chapter begins with cultural statements of beliefs in part, as Douglas and Wildavsky affirm, because it is important to get a sense of how people envision a 'good life' before trying to understand how they define threats to it. In this case as well, some of these formal decision-making pathways may look so familiar in non-Iñupiaq settings that it is easy to lose sight of the very specifically Iñupiaq ideas and beliefs that inform particular strategies undertaken on the North Slope. Before turning to the case example, then, let us take a look at the institutions through which whaling strategies are created.

The Alaska Eskimo Whaling Commission (AEWC) is the largest – and the newest – of these formal institutions. Created in 1978 in response to the International Whaling Commission's proposed moratorium on indigenous whaling, it is made up of locally elected Commissioners from each of the ten Alaska whaling villages.[12] In important ways, the AEWC is a bridging organization, representing regional interests to national and international bodies and ensuring that local whaling captains' associations are kept 'in the loop' of information and decision-making. Iñupiaq whalers are keenly aware that without that information, decisions are likely to be taken for them rather than with them. The task of the AEWC is to negotiate with non-Iñupiaq organizations, primarily the US Federal Government and indirectly the International Whaling Commission (IWC), about management plans in general and the quota system in particular.[13] It is also their responsibility to monitor local implementation of the plans once they have been set. As part of this, they mediate the division of the quota among the member villages and keep track of inter-village quota transfers.

The Barrow Whaling Captain's Association (BWCA) is, as it sounds, a community-based organization and has counterparts in all other AEWC member villages. Although not a formally incorporated organization like the AEWC, its status is one of a locally recognized institution and in fact comes out of a long-standing association of whaling captains.[14] According to several Barrow people who talked to me during the 1980s, the umialingat (literally, the whaling captains) used to meet regularly to discuss many issues affecting the community as a whole. Since, as we have already heard, the gift of whales to the community was dependent on their perceptions of proper human behaviour, it was important for the captains to keep track of what was going on in the village. They were a collective decision-making body that played a major role in social life.[15] Today, the BWCA decides on local best practice on matters affecting Barrow crews collectively, a process we shall examine in our case example.

The Barrow Whaling Women's Auxiliary (Utqiagvik Agvigsiuqtit Agnangiich, or UAA) also meets regularly to consider matters that are pertinent to the efficient meeting of responsibilities of the wife's side of the whaling captain couple. In the past few years UAA members have created a Documenting Committee to ensure, for instance, that needed skills in the preparation of the skin boat were not being lost; they have considered how best to prepare feasts for hundreds of people in the safest possible conditions; and they raise funds throughout the year to support the very considerable expenses whaling captains must incur as part of the whaling process.

Each crew is also an organized group unto itself. The whaling captain husband/wife couple, often aided by a co-captain, must make decisions on the intra-crew division of labour, whether to go out on a particular day, and the like. Many of these decisions are discussed as overall responsibilities in the 1991 Elders' Conference. Martha Aiken (2000) asserted that the whaling captain's wife's major responsibility was the safety of the crew. In many ways, as we have already seen, this theme was reiterated by the elders with respect to both halves of the whaling captain couple. Whaling captains are responsible for deciding when and where to cut the ice trails out to the spring camp (most important to be able to return to shore quickly if the ice begins to break); they need to monitor ice conditions constantly, checking for cracks and for flooding. They need to recruit the crew, organize the equipment, prepare the boat and make sure that it is in good repair. Above all, they need to make sure that the crew knows how to do things properly – as emphasized by Isaac Akootchook: 'When we start getting ready for autumn whaling we [captains] teach/talk to everyone involved in whaling, especially to crew members and what is expected of them, also what gear to work on and to bring along during whaling. We also let our crew members know what to do within the boat, etc.' (IHLC 1991c: 2).

'The wife's job is more broad and varied', Wyborn Nungasak suggested (IHLC 1991c: 3) and indeed, it often seems that whaling captains' wives need to be in all places at all times. As we have already heard, they are responsible for the cleanliness of the house, the ice cellars and the entryways. They make sure the crew has adequate clothing, arrange for the sewers to prepare the skin boat cover, prepare the food for the crew as well as the community feasts, help with the butchering, the storing and the preservation of the meat. Like the whaling captains, Jennie Ahkivgak suggested, their job is also to instruct the younger wives and, as Mary Aveoganna pointed out, both husband and wife are responsible for being hospitable – 'good hosts' in an echo of Patrick Attungana. It is their job to make sure help is provided if people are in need. This is carried out by individual wives as well as through the regular meetings of the UAA which take place throughout the year.

Individuals control their own labour and may offer it in a multiplicity of contexts: moving from crew to crew; working with more than one crew; or deciding how much to work in any one season.

Barrow whaling, then, is affected by local decision-making on at least four related but recognisably separate levels: individual, crew, community and regional. At all levels, decisions are constantly being made in response to all sorts of changing conditions. To take a closer look at this process, let us turn to a case example from the 1996/97 autumn whaling seasons.

Case Example: So Many Whales; So Little Time!

Nineteen whales were taken between 10 and 26 September during the relatively short 1996 autumn whaling season in Barrow. On five of those days, between two and five whales were landed on the same day, causing a labour crisis. A mature bowhead produces about a ton of useable food per foot in length. Even 'small' whales (fifteen to thirty feet) thus require a lot of hands to butcher the animal, transport and store the meat, prepare the feast for the entire community and clean up the butchering site. In 1996, the whales landed in Barrow ranged in size from twenty-five to forty-four feet; their mean size was thirty-eight and a half feet. Significantly, only three of the nineteen fell into the twenty-five-to-thirty-foot range that reflects Barrow preferences and eleven of the nineteen (58 per cent) were forty-two feet long or more. Thus, not only were there many more whales than was customary, but they were about fifteen feet longer than usual as well. Fifteen feet means fifteen more tons of meat to butcher for each whale. It was daunting.

In fact, on 12 September, the four landed whales were, respectively, forty-two, forty-two, forty-four, and forty feet long. Just two days later, before people had been able to recuperate, three more whales – forty-four, thirty-seven and forty-seven feet long – were landed within hours of each other. The serious strain on manpower, tempting – even forcing – people to cut corners, and the sudden glut of meat combined to generate the threat of waste. This had the potential to generate unwanted consequences that were explicitly recognized and discussed on multiple fronts:

- It is disrespectful to whales, potentially discouraging their return: a moral hazard;
- It can attract polar bears who pose a physical threat to humans;
- It discourages potential helpers from showing up, thus creating further pressure for the people who do show up: a social hazard;
- It may attract the negative attention of outsiders, potentially weakening the negotiating position of the AEWC with the IWC: clearly framed in political terms.

We have already heard about the general importance of cleanliness. The specific issue of waste is often discussed in formal institutions. Sam Taalak, Edward Hopson and Walter Akpik all spoke at the 1991 Elders' Conference about what they perceived as the larger implications of incomplete storage of whale meat and maktak, with implications for both customary practice and political action on national and international levels. According to Taalak:

> Since I came back to Barrow [from Nuiqsut] this last spring, I have gone out to the dump and have found some maktak in plastic bags, real thick slices of flukes, and meat … I say the captain is to blame for such

wastes – I know the uati meat has a lot of tendon on it ... We should be more careful how we do things ... because one picture like that, when it is shown, they will see to it that our quota is taken all away. Like one speaker said, during Christmas all the uati should be cut up and taken to the feast. (IHLC 1991c: 8)

Edward Hopson, from Barrow, made a similar point:

These meetings I understand are to improve anything about our whaling system ... About the whale, we the Iñupiat ... make our own rules about the whale ... Therefore, we are our own Public Safety about whaling. ... Therefore I feel we should be more careful what we do to the whale. This is not only for Barrow; it involves Nuiqsut too, where one does not take the top layer off only and leaves the rest of it because it froze. Those that oppose whaling will do something drastic when they hear about this. In this meeting we should request AEWC to tell the captains not to throw away any meat or maktak, because when one puts maktak with blubber in the ice cellar, it keeps, no matter how long it stays there. When the top portion from the maktak is cut off, it tastes even better. (Ibid.:13)

Walter Akpik, of Atqusauk, said succinctly: 'Think of what the oil companies can do if they find out ... we do not store the whale meat like we're supposed to. And another thing I do not need to remind you, we all love to eat the whale. Therefore we ought to take into consideration what we do with our share' (ibid.:15).

In each of these statements, the political stakes are posed somewhat differently; all three point to 'external' dangers posed by non-Iñupiaq institutions as well as values defined as Iñupiat; each invokes the notion of responsibility in different ways: political 'bads' and moral 'goods'. Taalak suggests that captains are responsible for wasted meat; the risk is the potential loss of the quota, but then he alludes to the moral rule that uati should be distributed during Christmas feasts, thus defining his concern as thoroughly grounded in Iñupiaq values. Hopson points to the value – and the tenuous nature – of Iñupiaq sovereignty: 'We are our own Public Safety about whaling' and urges more collective care. He identifies the AEWC as the proper institution to encourage captains not to waste meat – but then suggests that much of this meat will taste 'even better' if the top layer is cut off. Walter Akpik specifically identified oil companies as powerfully threatening external entities, couched his fears in terms of collective responsibilities but also reminded listeners 'we all love to eat the whale'. All three are quite clear that Iñupiaq behaviour can generate the risk of adverse actions on the parts of external institutions with whom they are in political relationships, whether they like it or not.

Formal, Collective Decisions: 1997 Responses to 1996 Events

The risks outlined above were the subject of serious discussion as Barrow whaling captains prepared for the 1997 autumn hunt and several strategies were formally adopted by the Barrow Whaling Captains' Association as a whole.

1. Whales migrate in 'waves', grouped roughly by size. The population of the first wave is for the most part significantly larger than that of the second wave, a fact long-known by experienced whalers and corroborated by harvest data generated by the NSB Wildlife Management Department.[16] The Association decided that Barrow whalers should wait for the second migration wave to begin the autumn hunt. The whales would be the smaller, preferred size and the meat would be more tender. Butchering would thus demand less labour power and elders as well as youngers would enjoy the meat more.[17]

2. Again in an effort to limit the demands on available labour power, the BWCA instituted a daily take limit of two whales.

3. Furthermore, the Association instituted a moratorium on crews taking off to whale again until the previous catch had been completely butchered and the site had been cleaned up.

With all of these strategies, the need for coherence was plainly expressed to me by a number of captains. If one crew went out before time, the pressure on others would be intolerable.[18] As with so many aspects of whaling, the view that 'there has to be agreement' was keenly felt.

Quantitative data gathered by the AEWC and the North Slope Borough Wildlife Management Department provides comparative information which illustrates the degree to which decisions taken in the autumn of 1997 resulted in a strikingly different harvest. The total harvest in the 1997 autumn hunt was twenty-one bowhead, slightly higher than the nineteen taken in 1996. Although the size range was also slightly larger, the mean size dropped by seven feet. The mode is even more revealing. In 1997, only three whales were longer than forty feet whereas in 1996 more than half were longer than forty-one feet.

It is also worth comparing the daily take in both seasons. Even though the two seasons began on virtually the same day with the catch of a forty-two foot whale, the 'tempo' of each hunt was strikingly different. In 1996 whalers landed sixteen whales, the vast majority of the season's take, before 20 September; ten of these were forty-two feet or longer. By contrast, Barrow whalers only took three whales in the comparable 1997 period. In 1997, the most intense whaling took place during the last week of September and only two whales exceeded thirty-four feet. Although the two-per-day limit was not strictly followed, no more than three whales were ever landed on one day, a radical cutting back from the previous year. The 1997 season extended almost to the end of October, increasing the likelihood of landing smaller whales and the number of landed whales was much more evenly and reasonably distributed throughout the season, as suggested by the Association. The lessened strain on labour power was evident.[19]

Weighing Up the Risks: What's at Stake in Such a Decision?

As we have said, to reduce the risk of waste (and its accompanying knock-on hazards detailed above), the Barrow Whalers Association made several decisions: to delay the opening of the autumn hunt in order to increase the likelihood of catching smaller whales; to limit the daily catch; to require that whalers not return to their boats until each butchering session was completed and cleaned up. Each of these decisions had some obvious benefits, but also carried their own hazards.

The decision to delay the start of autumn whaling was a conscious calculation based on the knowledge that the 'second wave' of migrating whales are the smaller ones. There are many advantages to this: smaller whales, according to Barrow people, are tastier and more tender; they require less work to butcher and thus do not put the same intolerable strain on available labour. That makes it much easier to clean up, reducing the likelihood of waste.

But of course, neither the BWCA nor individual whaling captains can simply decide when they want to undertake autumn whaling. Weather conditions in the autumn as in the spring are critical factors. Not surprisingly, these are very different. In the spring, for ice-based whaling, as we saw in the opening vignette, the relationship between wind direction and current is a crucial factor in ice movement; in the autumn, when whaling is conducted in ice-free water, wind direction is much less important than wind speed (C. George, personal communication). In the autumn, days may go by during which the wind is too high for whalers to go out at all and differences in weather conditions from year to year will be reflected in different annual harvest patterns. Of most importance to the BWCA discussions, the later one goes out whaling in the autumn, the greater the risk of severe storms, rarely a factor in the spring. Thus, a decision to wait until 16, 20 or 24 September is a decision in which whaling captains calculate quite explicitly how much difference one or two days might make in terms of their knowledge of variability in whale migration patterns, autumn weather patterns and their decision to opt for smaller whales.[20] In these discussions, it should be emphasized that 'the weather' is talked about as a hazard that is 'out there'. It is not talked about in terms of social relations, it cannot be propitiated; it is not a function of improper human behaviour; survival (and for whaling captains, the survival of their crew) depends on taking observant care. Here it seems to me we can think about conscious balancing of 'goods' and 'bads', although what emerges is the extent to which the proposed solution to the threat of waste – a threat that drove the decisions modifying subsequent hunts – must be concerned in terms of further risks.

Not only was the problem of waste discussed in terms of threats that originated in moral, physical and political environments, the solution generated a close examination of further threats that were strategized on (other) moral, physical and political grounds. We are definitely talking about rational choices here – choices that are discussed at length by whaling captains every year. It is, to echo Weber, a moral rationality that begins with the given that whaling is a positively moral goal that underpins all decisions. But even within that moral universe, whaling captains have opted to cut back on the time of the whaling season, and have opted for the most dangerous portion of it. This is in order to land smaller whales which require less labour to butcher. But in a world in which spring whaling is becoming increasingly precarious, the decision to limit the number of whales taken in the autumn means that the captains have opted to restrict the amount of whale meat they can provide to the community and beyond. As we said earlier, a whale provides approximately a tonne of meat per foot in length, so to opt for a thirty-six-foot whale instead of a forty-four-foot one means a reduction of around eight tonnes of meat per whale. Economistic and individually self-interested it is not.

The harvest patterns of 1997 suggest strongly that the strategies put forward by the BWCA were consistently followed by Barrow whalers throughout the season. In 1998 the BWCA decided to wait until 20 September to begin their autumn season in order to maximize their chances of landing primarily small whales and that decision was honoured in full.

Discussion

Various languages of risk have been heard throughout this chapter. That they are neither necessarily mutually coherent, nor inevitably contradictory should be evident from the material we have just examined. In this final section, I want to consider them together more systematically. Accepting for the moment the distinction between 'hazard' and 'risk' as analytically useful, I want to consider the hazards identified in people's statements, the particular risks these hazards were said to pose, the bases of the risks, and the strategies put forward to ameliorate them. In part, this endeavour points out some of the difficulties in such a bi-partite presentation; what looks like a hazard from one perspective becomes a risk from another. Still, trying for such a separation does reveal the extent to which single factors such as 'waste' may be thought to create different orders of unwanted consequences.

The comments reflect three broad types of risk:

* moral: the consequences of improper human behaviour that can result in the whale's withdrawal of the gift itself.
* physical: the threats to a successful hunt, or even survival itself, if environmental conditions are not attended to or if thoughtless decisions are made that put the crew into danger (knowledge of the wind, currents, ice conditions, proper care of equipment, creating ice roads, choosing the place to set up camp, etc.). This clearly engages with both mental and material technology and addresses most particularly the responsibilities of whaling captains and their wives.
* political: the threats to autonomous Iñupiaq conduct of the hunt posed by powerful external institutions such as the International Whaling Commission, the US Government or British Petroleum which very clearly can be influenced by outsiders' perceptions of local actions. 'We are the endangered species', exclaimed Arnold Brower, Jr. at a public hearing some years ago.

In the first and last cases, Iñupiat talk about the dangers that may be created by certain kinds of human behaviour. Both the moral environment within which whales and humans interact and the political environment in which Iñupiat must deal with powerful external institutions are ones in which the hazards and the risks they generate are defined by Iñupiat themselves as social. Both are internal to the social system. The ways in which Iñupiat talked about the physical environment reflect a different sort of classification. Thinning polar ice, shore-fast ice that is not fixed securely to the ocean bottom, high winds, low visibility or the likelihood of severe autumn storms are defined as potentially dangerous, but not as a function of human action. The hazard is thus 'out there'; inasmuch as the risks are defined in human terms – and demand human action – they are social.

I want to return briefly to the issue of political action. Because the focus of this discussion has been on BWCA decisions and not the Alaska Eskimo Whaling Commission (AEWC), we have not examined actions that engage with these external institutions directly. It is worth spending a few moments shifting our institutional focus. Iñupiat are quite clear that others' perceptions of them may be of different orders. Quantifiable 'risk management' policies such as those developed by the International Whaling Commission (IWC) thrive on numbers in which Iñupiaq whaling is defined largely in terms of 'efficiency': whether or not the overall population of bowhead remains healthy enough to reproduce; what the 'struck and lost' numbers are; the length of time it takes a whale to die if hunted with one kind of bomb or another. But these policies also have a moral dimension. If Iñupiaq whaling practices are not seen as being traditional 'enough', Iñupiat risk being defined as 'trophy' or 'sports' hunters who then lose the moral authority underlying their right to continue subsistence whaling. If state or national news media characterize them as 'oil-rich Arabs of the north', then the claim that they need to whale becomes suspect.

Over the years the AEWC has constructed multiple strategies that build on their awareness of these potentially hazardous perceptions. They have invited IWC and Greenpeace officials to Barrow during spring whaling so that they have a chance to experience the depth of feeling whaling generates (and both IWC and Greenpeace accepted the cultural importance of whaling for Iñupiat during the 1990s); they have made trips to non-whaling member nations of the IWC so that AEWC Commissioners can talk to them personally about whaling; they make regular interventions in public hearings of all kinds pertaining to Arctic environmental issues; and they are committed to the kind of science that can both inform their own decisions and be heard at national and international levels.

This brings us to a final, brief, discussion of 'lay' and 'expert' knowledge and, as we discussed in the Introduction, a consideration of the possibility of not only communicating but collaborating across knowledge boundaries. When the Barrow Whaling Captains began to discuss the possibility of postponing the start of autumn whaling, they called in Craig George, a whale biologist working for the North Slope Borough Department of Wildlife Management. He was not called in because he was the expert, but because he was an expert, as were the whalers; he is recognized as knowledgeable and accessible and they wanted to add his knowledge to their own; it is a process that, with local scientists, often works in reverse as well. The very existence of the Department is a direct outcome of struggles over whose knowledge 'counts'. When the IWC first claimed that the bowhead were on the verge of extinction, Iñupiat whalers disagreed. The IWC reaction was that Iñupiat knowledge was not 'scientific' and therefore could be discounted. The local reaction was to form the Alaska Eskimo Whaling Commission, a collective of whaling communities that encompasses the North Slope and beyond. Through the AEWC, the whaling captains lobbied successfully for the right to have the responsibility of conducting scientifically acceptable whale counts and to do this, they established a local body of scientific researchers whose work would be available for peer group assessment and therefore would be accepted within 'the scientific community' but whose work would also grow in conjunction with local interests and would be accessible to them. As Harry Brower, Sr. pointed out in his conversations with Karen Brewster (2004), the history of Iñupiaq/scientist collaborative interactions has roots extending at least back to the establishing of the Naval Arctic Research Lab (NARL) at the height of the Cold War. By the time Bodenhorn was facilitating interchanges between Iñupiaq and Zapotec youth during the first decade of this century, the Department had Iñupiaq as well as non Iñupiaq members and UIC, the village corporation, sponsored an Arctic Research Center (see Bodenhorn 2012).

The extent to which local participants are helping to define research directions is also growing. When a group of National Science Foundation researchers visited Wainwright and Kaktovik to discuss research results and future directions, Wainwright whaling captains had specific suggestions of specific biological research they thought should be conducted in the Wainwright area; what Kaktovik whaling captains wanted was archaeological research done on some whale bones close to the airport. These bones are 'old' – older than the first commercial whaling ventures to take place in the area at the end of the last century. Isaac Akootchook, the senior member of the Kaktovik Whaling Captains Association, was explicit that they wanted any information they could get from archaeologists about the conduct of whaling in the area before Euro-americans showed up. The Wainwright suggestions were primarily about issues the whaling captains themselves were interested in; the Kaktovik suggestion was almost purely political. In my experience on the North Slope, 'science' is neither privileged nor rejected as a way of knowing things. It is precisely a particular sort of knowledge about certain kinds of environments and as such, people are curious about 'it'. Scientists – who are in social relationships – are seen as potential sources of specific sorts of useful information, of valuable support and of irritation, particularly if they are dismissive of Iñupiaq expertise. The divide is in the political definition of authoritative accounts as such, not in the knowledge itself.

Conclusions

We return now to Douglas and Wildavksy's exhortation to understand risk in cultural terms. I have suggested that an underlying ideology asserting the right to life, liberty and the pursuit of happiness might generate different perceptions of risk than one enjoining people to maintain proper relations in a social universe.[21] In many ways, the language of rights as it has developed in the United States is one that presumes that if one does not enjoy them, someone (else) must be accountable. And if it is 'an inalienable right', it must be possible. As I have discussed elsewhere (Bodenhorn 2000), individual Iñupiat certainly have non-negotiable rights – to shares for instance – but these are explicitly connected to the individual responsibility to contribute to the hunting effort. The discussions we have just been considering also centre on notions of responsibility: what are the consequences of our actions and what should we do if they are negative? It is a very 'agentive' position – and one that has served Iñupiat very well indeed in their history of quasi-colonial relations with the world around them. It is perhaps the difference which leads Barrow whaling captains to agree collectively to shorten their whaling period and catch smaller whales in order to ameliorate a risk, whereas the mandate to wear a mask to ameliorate the risk of spreading COVID has created such controversy across the United States.

Within the United States, Iñupiat are clearly operating from a peripheral position – in some ways showing the characteristics proposed by Douglas and Wildavsky (that core groups tend to be present oriented whereas peripheral ones tend to look to the future or to the past) and in other ways departing quite radically from their model. For instance, in a discussion with then NSB Mayor George Ahmaogak in 2000, I asked what issues he felt were most pressing as far as NSB/British Petroleum relations were concerned. His most immediate concern was to begin planning for the time when North Slope oil was no longer viable. BP has derived tremendous profits from North Slope oil fields and he was upset that they seemed 'just not interested' in taking part in any such planning.[22] When I brought up this issue for discussion among BP executives in March 2001, one of the responses was, 'but that isn't going to happen for twenty-five years!' The Douglas and Wildavsky suggestion that peripheral positions are likely to be past and/or future oriented whereas core positions opt for as little change as possible is thus not surprising.[23] However, they also suggest that the peripheral position tends to generate ideologies that are sectarian, demanding ritual statements of allegiance and reflected in a language which suggests the current course is one of disaster, often the product of conspiracy of sorts (1982: 173/4). Here it seems to me that the model simply does not play out. In the conversations I have had in Barrow, the tenor more often than not is open, exploratory, pragmatic and agentive. It is the US President who must appear in public flanked by the American flag and end virtually all speeches with the phrase, 'God bless America'; it is the national political landscape that seems increasingly sectarian in the twenty-first century.

The languages of risk we've heard in this chapter are those used by Iñupiat today. They are languages that reflect values felt to be profoundly Iñupiaq and they are languages that express an acute understanding of connections across a number of systems. We can neither understand these languages in terms of a 'globalization' model that assumes we belong to the same global village, nor can we adopt a relativist position that assumes a kind of cultural difference that prevents intelligible interaction. Iñupiat live in a world in which oil development, global warming and international regimes of animal protection are factors they must take into consideration on a daily basis. There are nonetheless cultural differences which, as we have just discussed, have implications for the ways in which these factors contribute to the perception of risks and the development of options to deal with them. Those discussions are not easy. As Rachel

Edwardson so eloquently points out in this volume, there continue to be heated arguments about what the 'real' risks are and what should be done about them. Ways of talking about the profound importance of sharing which underwrites the whale/human relationship may not be easily grasped by many people who have been brought up in other systems. But the importance of preserving the reproductive capabilities of the bowhead population is as important to Iñupiat as it is to Greenpeace, albeit for different reasons. That many Iñupiat believe in the possibilities of cultural translation is evidenced in their consistent and effective commitment to doing just that. Thus, pace Douglas and Wildavsky, some of the languages we have heard do indeed reflect a peripheral difference, but others assume the possibility of common connection.

What seems to me to be most relevant – whether we are thinking about Iñupiaq strategies, or the process of strategy construction more generally – is that we have not heard a single language of risk, but different languages, revealing incommensurable goods and bads within a single cultural setting. It is not just that different people worry about different things but that the same things may be worried about by the same people for multiple reasons. Difficulties in making decisions, it seems to me, are less often due to a lack of information, than they are because so many orders of values are involved – values that cannot be easily ranked or balanced out.

That these processes must be understood at least in part as a function of governmentality in the Foucauldian sense is probably self-evident. Iñupiat find themselves under increasingly regulatory regimes (to do with the animals they hunt, the ways their children can learn, or the things they can do with the resources at their disposal, for instance) which demand forms to be filled, meetings to be attended and minutes to be filed. In reaction to the IWC challenge in the 1970s, the AEWC continues in 2022 to produce 'evidence' of all sorts and has thus itself instituted methods of surveillance that demand careful record keeping on the parts of whaling captains and North Slope Borough scientists alike. But we cannot usefully understand either Iñupiat discussions of the dangers of autumn storms or of messy cellars through the same framework. In a similar way, although we should recognize the frequency and the ease with which 'science' can become part of governmentality, we need to be wary of assuming this is in the nature of science itself. It is more important to look explicitly at those contexts where 'science' is a marked category as well as others where it is thought of as one of a number of knowledge forms. If Iñupiat can do it, I assume the rest of us can as well.

Acknowledgements

People on the North Slope have been talking to me about whaling and other things for a very long time and I owe a general debt of gratitude for all the hospitality, opportunities to help and information I have been offered since 1980 when I began working for the Iñupiaq Community of the Arctic Slope. I want to remember with thanks Raymond Neakok, Sr. and Mattie Bodfish, both of whom taught me, with humour and patience, teachings that remain after they themselves passed away. I also want to remember Eben Hobson, another long-time friend and conversation partner, who passed away from COVID in September 2021. And to Marie Neakok, George and Debbie Edwardson and their entire families I thank them for their companionship and lively ideas. For the specific purposes of this chapter, I would like to express special thanks to Maggie Ahmaogak, then Executive Director of the AEWC, for detailed discussions about the workings of the AEWC as well as about decisions local whalers have to make for themselves; Martha Aiken, now deceased, who was head of the Documenting Committee of the Barrow Whaling Women's Association when we did this research and was responsible for general discussions about the social responsibilities of whaling captain couples; Craig George, North Slope Borough Department of Wildlife Management, who was always ready to talk about harvest data, provided me with raw data and took the time to create the sorts of tabular versions I kept asking for. Arlene Glenn, who was Oral Historian at the Iñupiaq History, Language and Culture Commission at the time, provided me with access to both photographs and Elders' Conference transcripted material; Frances and Emma Mongoyak took the time to help me learn, through the Iñupiaq transcriptions of the Elders' Conference material as well as the English translations. Thanks too to the students who participated in the Research Methods Class I had the good fortune to teach at Ilisagvik College – especially Fannie Akpik, Dorothy Edwardsen and Arlene Glenn – whose discussions were always acute, far-reaching, informative and full of laughter. They may have been students but they were already grown-ups and experts in their own right. Maggie Ahmaogak, Craig George and Roger Harritt all read the penultimate draft of the paper from which this chapter then developed, for which I am very grateful.

Barbara Bodenhorn was Newton Trust Lecturer in Social Anthropology until 2013 and is currently Fellow Emerita of Pembroke College, Cambridge. Her most recent research interests focus on children's environmental knowledge as well as communally initiated responses to environmental change.

Notes

The ethnography on which this chapter is based was primarily gathered before Barrow's name reverted to Utqiagvik, its original form. In everyday conversations, people use both Barrow and Utqiagvik interchangeably.

1. The research combines archival work at the Iñupiat History, Language and Culture Commission (IHLC), interviews and group discussions with local experts, informal conversations with individuals and participant observation. Fieldwork was conducted during summer visits in 1995, 1996, an extended stay between January and September 1997, and shorter annual follow-up visits between 1998 and 2001. The present chapter relies particularly on the translated transcripts of the 1991 IHLC Elders' Conference held in Barrow (IHLC 1991a, b, c, d). The overall theme of the conference was whaling; the topics under discussion in the men's and women's session placed heavy emphasis on the obligations and responsibilities of crew members in general and of the whaling captain couple in particular. These transcripts were translated by Mabel Hopson and Mabel Paniegeo.
2. See Bodenhorn 1988 on sharing in general; Bodenhorn 1997 on sharing information in particular.
3. This material is taken primarily from the 1991 Elders' Conference held in Barrow, Alaska. Sponsored by the North Slope Borough Iñupiaq History Language and Culture Commission, Elders' Conferences are annual events that provide opportunities for elders from all of the North Slope member villages to participate in several days' intense discussion of specified issues. The women's session took place on 11 July 1991. The session transcript includes comments from (in order of their appearance in the transcript): Rosemary Oviok (Point Hope), Lora Oyagak (Barrow), Berna Brower (Barrow), Mary Lou Leavitt (Barrow), Alice Solomon (Barrow), Terza Hopson (Barrow), Dorcas Tagarook (Wainwright), Jennie Ahkivgak (Barrow), Ida Koonuk (Point Hope), Carol Omnik (Point Hope), Louise Ahkiviana (Barrow), Mary Aveoganna (Barrow). Jana Hacharak (Barrow) and Emma Bodfish (Barrow) presided.
4. The IHLC, as its name implies, is responsible for all manner of cultural and historical documentation, from organizing Elders' Conferences, to collecting genealogies, and publishing land use surveys.
5. In Barrow, Iñupiaq story genres include two general categories: *quliaqtuat* are stories of personal experience whereas *unipkaat* may provide accounts that extend well beyond the narrator's life. Generally translated into English as 'legends', the latter often provide moral, cosmological messages.
6. An ice cellar, built deep into the permafrost that is ubiquitous on the North Slope – for now – is a technology that allows frozen meat storage for up to a year. Because this is where the whale meat will be stored, it is like the whale's home and needs to be made welcoming each year in anticipation of a successful harvest.

7. This reflects sentiments expressed by North Slope residents; when I spent time in Wales, Alaska, the injunction to be generous after a successful harvest was talked about with enthusiasm, but when I mentioned that North Slope elders insisted that their responsibility extended throughout the year, I was met with some bemusement.
8. IHLC 01499tr1. The men's session also took place on 11 July 1991. Those present included, in order of contributing to this session: Ross Ahngasak (Barrow), Kenneth Toovak (Barrow), Noah Phillips (Barrow, Wainwright), Herman Rexford (Kaktovik), Alfred Leavitt (Barrow), Greg Tagarook (Wainwright, Point Hope), Sam Taalak (Nuiqsut, Barrow), Eli Solomon (Barrow), Roxy Oyagak (Barrow), Perry Akootchook (Kaktovik), Arthur Neakok (Point Barrow), Edward Hopson (Barrow), Levi Greist (Kuukpik River, Barrow), Walter Akpik (Atqasuk). Wyborn Nungasak (Barrow) presided; Mabel Panigeo transcribed and translated the tape.
9. This resonates strongly with Ann Fienup-Riordan's (1994) discussion of how important it is for Yup'ik hunters that the passageways between animal and human worlds are kept clear.
10. Maktak is the edible black skin and layer of fat of the bowhead which is highly prized as part of the Iñupiaq diet.
11. That there are also dangers that are perceived to be 'out there' – which also have to be dealt with socially – should not be forgotten. We will turn to these in the next section.
12. Member villages include both North Slope and non-North Slope communities. See AEWC website: http://www.aewc-alaska.org.
13. The AEWC attends meetings, for instance, but does not have voting rights. It was largely through AEWC efforts that the International Whaling Commission was convinced to change its stance from backing a total ban on aboriginal whaling to the present, ever-changing, negotiated quota system.
14. Maggie Ahmaogak alludes to this long-standing association: 'the whalers at the time – way back – had meetings of their own trying to decide what kind of policies and rules they had ... the way they would share with the community – the way they were to give to the poor...' (interview, September 1997).
15. To quote Raymond Neakok, Sr (in Bodenhorn 1988, vol.1: 26), 'Those people will determine exactly how we should treat a person that is breaking the structure of society's running ... how you behave – these were the elders, the *umialigiich*' (see also Marie Adams and Raymond Neakok in Bodenhorn 1988, vol.2: 254).
16. Craig George presented his data to the Barrow Whaling Captains' Association at their pre-autumn season meeting. The figures reproduced here are from the memo prepared for them (George 1997).
17. This would solve more than one problem simultaneously. 'I'm tired of getting big whales no one can eat!' one whaling captain said to Craig George.
18. Although the spring hunt continues to hold a central position, autumn whaling has in fact produced more meat than the spring hunt for the past several years. With spring conditions becoming increasingly perilous, this trend has continued through the first decades of the twenty-first century.

19. Statistics and cross tabulations were provided by Craig George, of the NSB Department of Wildlife. For more comprehensive tabular analysis, see Bodenhorn 2000.
20. George examines a number of environmental factors that are taken into consideration by captains since they influence the likelihood of whales being taken (see also George et al. 1998).
21. I am not suggesting that Iñupiat do not engage in languages of rights. They do – vociferously and effectively. I am suggesting this is not the moral cornerstone that it is in the mainstream US.
22. Interview, September 2000. I approached him before accepting an invitation to talk with BP executives in Cambridge concerning 'ethics and cultural diversity' early in 2001.
23. Of course, from another angle, the common stereotype of 'Eskimos' is that they are present oriented (as I have been told with great certainty by school principals several times over the years) and thus do not adapt easily to 'Western' time constraints. In this light, the respective NSB/BP positions 'ought' to be reversed.

References

Ahmaogak, Maggie. 1997. Interview, AEWC office, Barrow, Alaska, 7 July.
———. 2000. AEWC overview, presentation at 'Whaling in the Western Arctic' NSF workshop, Anchorage, Alaska, April.
Aiken, Martha. 2000. 'Presentation to Research Methods Course at Ilisagvik College, Barrow', in Fannie Akpik and Barbara Bodenhorn (eds), *Learning to Braid 'Real' Thread*, joint publication produced by the Barrow Women's Whaling Auxiliary, Ilisagvik College and the Iñupiat History, Language and Culture Commission, Barrow, Alaska.
Alaska Eskimo Whaling Commission (AEWC). Official website: http://www.aewc-alaska.org.
Attungana, Patrick. 1986. 'Address to the Alaska Eskimo Whaling Commission', reprinted in *Uiñiq: The Open Lead* 1(2): 16ff. Translation, James Nageak.
Bodenhorn, Barbara. 1988. *Documenting Iñupiat Family Relations in Changing Times*, report prepared for the North Slope Borough Commission on Iñupiaq History, Language and Culture and the Alaska Humanities Forum, Barrow, Alaska.
———. 1997. '"People Who are Like Our Books": Reading and Teaching on the North Slope of Alaska', *Arctic Anthropology* 34(1): 117–34.
———. 2000. 'It's Good to Know Who Your Relatives Are, but We Were Taught to Share with Everybody: Shares and Sharing among Iñupiaq Households', in G. Wenzel, G. Hovelsrud-Bruda and N. Kishigami (eds), *The Social Economy of Sharing: Resource Allocation and Modern Hunter-Gatherers*. Osaka: SENRI Ethnological Studies 53, pp. 27–60.
———. 2001, '"It's Traditional to Change": A Case Study of Strategic Decision-making', *The Cambridge Journal of Anthropology* 22(1): 24–51.
———. 2012. 'Meeting Minds, Encountering Worlds: Science and Other Expertises on the North Slope of Alaska', in M. Konrad (ed.), *Collaborators*

Collaborating: Counterparts in Anthropological Knowledge and International Research Relations. Oxford: Berghahn Books.

Brewster, Karen (ed.). 2004. *The Whales They Give Themselves: Conversations with Harry Brower, Sr*. Fairbanks, AK: University of Alaska Press.

Douglas, Mary and Aaron Wildavsky. 1982. *Risk and Culture: An Essay on the Selection of Technological and Environmental Dangers*. Berkeley: University of California Press.

Fienup-Riordan, Ann. 1994. *Boundaries and Passages: Rule and Ritual in Yup'ik Eskimo Oral Tradition*. London: University of Oklahoma Press.

George, Craig. 1997. 'Body Length in Relation to Date of Harvest during the Fall Bowhead Whale Hunt, Memo to Van Edwardsen', Vice President Barrow Whaling Captains' Association, Barrow, Alaska.

George, Craig, Robert Suydam, L. Philo, Tom Albert, Judith Zeh and George M. Carroll. 1995. 'Report of the Spring 1993 Census of Bowhead Whales, *Balaena mysticetus*, off Point Barrow, Alaska, with Observations on the 1993 Subsistence Hunt of the Bowhead Whales by Alaska Eskimos', *Report of the International Whaling Commission* 45: 371–84.

George, Craig, Michael Todd, Harry Brower, Jr. and Robert Suydam. 1998. 'Results of the 1997 Subsistence Harvest of Bowhead Whales by Alaskan Eskimos with Observations of the Influence of Environmental Conditions on the Success of Hunting Bowhead Whales off Barrow, Alaska', report presented to the International Whaling Commission, July 1998, prepared by the Department of Wildfife Management, North Slope Borough, Barrow, Alaska.

Iñupiat History, Language and Culture Commission (IHLC). 1991a. Women's Session, Elders' Conference, Barrow, Alaska, 11 July, Day 2, tape 1; Iñupiaq transcription and English translation, Mabel Hopson.

———. 1991b. Men's Session, Elders' Conference, Barrow, Alaska, 11 July, Day 2, tape 1; Iñupiaq transcription and English translation by Mabel Panigeo, IHLC ref: 01498tr1.

———. 1991c. Men's Session, Elders' Conference, Barrow, Alaska, 11 July, Day 2, tape 2; Iñupiaq transcription and English translation by Mabel Panigeo, IHLC ref: 01499tr1.

———. 1991d. General Session, Elders' Conference, Barrow Alaska, 10 July; Iñupiaq transcription and English translation by Mabel Panigeo.

Latour, Bruno. 1993. *We Have Never Been Modern*. London: Harvester Books.

McCartney, Allen P. (ed.). 2003. *Indigenous Ways to the Present, CCI Studies on Whaling*.

Edmonton: Canadian Circumpolar Institute.

Oquilluk, William A. 1981. *People of Kauwerak: Legends of the Northern Eskimo*. Anchorage: Alaska Pacific University Press, with the assistance of Laurel L. Bland.

Wynne, Brian. 1996. 'May the Sheep Safely Graze? a Reflexive View of the Expert-Lay Knowledge Divide', in Scott Lash, Bronislaw Szerszynski and Brian Wynne (eds), *Risk, Environment and Modernity: Towards a New Ecology*. London: Sage Publications, pp. 44–83.

Afterword
Risk Constellations and the Politics of Polarity

Michael Bravo

Ask almost anyone who lives in the Arctic, young and old, and they will tell you it is a tricky business to navigate life's risks, whether that's looking after one's mental health or caring for cherished places on the land, camps where generations of families lived and subsisted. Nothing stands still. Even where there is continuity in the named features of the land, perhaps an inuksuk (stone monument, or cairn) marking a famous battle between shamans, the floe edge that disappears and reappears in the same place each year, the scent of the air, the taste of melted glacial water, a place whose memory is marred by misfortune, there is movement and change. Everything is in motion, like a dance linking the earthly and celestial realms.

Surveying the sky and the horizon for clues is an important way of knowing in northern societies, a form of gestural knowledge, taking stock, and identifying familiar landmarks. More than that, it is also a way of positioning oneself within what Inuit term *sila*, which is difficult to translate, but approximates to 'the living realm of the air, atmosphere, and sky'. A deeper understanding of *sila* is that it is a cosmological life-force that animates the world. Karla Williamson, Kallalliit scholar, envisages *sila* as a 'force that gives all the living beings air to breathe, and intelligence. With every breath people and animals take, air becomes transformed into energy to be used for intelligence, because as much as there is no life without air, without it there is no intelligence either' (Jessen Williamson 1992: 24).

With climate change, the onset of winter ice comes later in the year and its departure in the spring is earlier; this leaves less time for firm shore ice to form, which complicates the lives of humans and sea mammals alike in the spring – and contributes to coastal erosion during several autumnal storms. Well-formed ice provides health and security to feeding seal pups as well as safety for spring whaling. This interplay between *sila*, *nuna* (the land), *siku* (the ice) and the sea, each of them in flux, the balance altered by a changing climate, can be disorienting as though 'the earth is spinning faster' (Krupnik and Jolly 2002). It is as though the constellations that give order to the universe are shifting. Revising seasonal knowledge and making adjustments to the timing of human-environmental activities like hunting on the ice is therefore not only essential, but sometimes a matter of life and death.

The ecosystems of the Arctic are experiencing unprecedented upheavals, many of these disturbing changes observed in everyday life, some like the tundra and taiga fires of northeast Siberia dramatically so. The chapters in this volume attest to the very tangible experience of living environmental change as it is playing out in different ecosystems of the global cryosphere, notably Arctic Alaska, Canada and Russian Far North, as well as the Alps and Himalayas. Painting an accurate regional picture for the Arctic is deceptively difficult, especially as the beaches, permafrost, ice edges and salinity profiles of the ocean are eroding, dissolving, shifting or giving way. This blurring of boundaries is accentuated by the ebb and flow of geopolitical interests, particularly the competing interests of the three most powerful states in the world, the United States, Russia and China.

The historical incursions of Victorian whaling fleets and naval expeditions into the Arctic archipelagos, reading their twists and turns, dodging icebergs, or devising encounter strategies to avoid provoking violent encounters with northern inhabitants, these all illustrate the constant calculus of risk taking and avoidance inherent in navigation. Managing risk was integral to the construction and description of the Arctic as a geographical imaginary for navigators and their distant readers in ways that still matter today. Commerce, navigation and military power were intertwined in such a way that the language of risk was a way of conceiving and identifying imperial opportunities, to the extent that risk often acquired the status of an organizing principle of these imperial and nationalist ideologies. How best to locate and traverse the Arctic's 'ocean highways', to borrow a phrase from imperial geography, was debated by armchair admirals and hydrographers in Greenwich, Paris and New York. As a mode of analysis integral to the expansion of capital, risk was never just about describing the Arctic. Far more ambitiously, it contained within it organizational logics that imposed an extractivist account of the living Arctic, reforming the contours of the region in ways that colonized and transformed those familiar to its inhabitants.

Newcomers and outsiders generally understood that the best way to control risk in navigating these potentially dangerous archipelagos was to mine the deep knowledge reservoirs of the peoples who had studied its intricacies for hundreds of years. Navigators with experience recognized in the cosmologies of First Nations peoples fine-grained relationships to describe the motives, actions and responses of the living world of humans and non-humans. A spirited landscape offers far more sights, names, stories and other kinds of hooks for orienting oneself. Let's give the name 'constellation' to the shifting patterns governing these relationships observed over countless days, seasons and lifetimes. When a person gathers knowledge of these constellations, instilled through a great deal of practice and repetition, and it becomes second nature, one might describe this navigation as dead reckoning. A newcomer may attribute this knowledge to an inexplicable intuition or mere habit, rather than to skilled attunement to complex patterns of movement. Stillness, particularly in the Arctic, to those with experience and patience, is often seen as an active state, a kind of movement held in suspension, that can announce itself or conceal its presence.

Grasping how the Arctic has acquired its exceptional geopolitical symbolic power is made easier by understanding that 'polar talk', the vocabulary of poles and polarity, is rooted in a very different kind of cosmology, one whose concealments lay elsewhere in the Ptolemaic model of the world which places the polar axis of the earth at the centre of the universe. The imperial desire to rule over the earth's dominions viewing the globe from above, looking down over the North Pole, has close associations with the power of emperors, from Alexander the Great through the Holy Roman Emperors. In this vision of the Arctic, the people or spirits on the edge of the world play a significant role as witnesses paying homage to imperial rulers, a theme replayed over and over in European narratives of exploration (Romm 1992). Early modern cosmography identified the polar Arctic as a crucial site as a source of universal power because it was a unique point on the globe from which worldly time and space (longitude) emanated. This framework of symbolic power, reworked in the creation of northern nation states, is what gave the search for northern sea passages their mythological allure. Indigenous cosmologies must come to grips with the burden of being the liminal linchpins of this imperial legacy, simultaneously being irredeemably 'other' and thereby validating imperial power. Herein lies the key to understanding the competing philosophies of risk, namely that the polar vocabulary of terror, discovery, victory and triumph (popular names for naval ships) invokes a mastery that is only fulfilled by being validated from the periphery.

International relations scholars have for some time speculated that the world order of the twenty-first century is returning towards a multipolar world and carrying with that the risks of global instability, following a long period of relative bipolar stability during the Cold War. Note here how in this political language of risk calculation, the idea of stability is indebted to the advent of systems theory that also emerged alongside military planning during the Second World War and the decades that followed. Something important is being lost when geographical imaginaries privilege scalar visions that situate political power as though it were operating like a magnetic field between two poles of attraction and repulsion. Magnetic fields can be subject to aberrations and distortions, but the language of polarity in international relations constantly struggles to keep up with, or do justice to, the complexity and sheer diversity of the living world.

Generations of international relations students have been taught about the politics of 'poles and polarity'. The realist school in particular, and through no accident, embraced the language of poles in articulating questions about the balance of power and global stability. Famously, Kenneth Waltz, champion of neo-realism, asserted that polarity of the world system was central to determining its stability. 'Almost everyone agrees that at some time since the [First World] [W]ar, the world was bipolar', he wrote, such that 'the emergence of the Russian and American superpowers created a situation that permitted wider-ranging and more effective cooperation amongst the states of Western Europe' (1979: 70). One can recognize in Waltz's bipolar account the role of the Arctic Region during the Cold War as a critical borderland in the American–Russian détente. It is true that his diagnosis of a unipolar world after the fall of the Soviet Union in 1989 may be less useful than constructivist approaches in explaining the framework of international cooperation that enabled the creation of the intergovernmental Arctic Council. However, Waltz left us with an enduring question that matters to anyone who wants to understand how power and risk work in the Arctic, when he asked, 'how should we count poles, and how can we measure power' (ibid.: 129)? The more urgent question today, I would contend, is what we mean by 'pole' and 'polarity', and if they are not up to the job of aligning political and environmental stability, then we need a different framework.

It is against this backdrop of neorealism's Arctic roots, that these chapters offer an alternative relational framework for understanding risk ecologies, and a much better place to begin an analysis of the climate emergency. The cosmic harmony of life is defined by humans and animals recognizing their reciprocal obligations to care for one another (rather than Waltz's account that has its roots in theories of universal political power that emerged in sixteenth-century cosmography). These relational ethics extend beyond animals to the whole living world of plant life that bursts forth each summer, the air from which all living mammals draw breath, and the land whose forms subtly shift with the sunlight across durations near and far. The peoples of the North have for centuries acquired highly detailed knowledge (so much so as often to be baffling to outsiders), very specific linguistic tools, and narrative traditions at their disposal to navigate these relationships with the living world, knowing that they can be prone to sudden and profound change, often with little warning.

When asked today how the Arctic matters to the wider world, northern peoples will often reply that the fundamental importance of the Arctic, and specific places, routes and trails within, is that they are 'home', a place of belonging (Watt-Cloutier 2015). The practical traditional knowledge of receiving clothes, shelter and tools from animals is of course part of the interiority of social life. The decision on a given day to examine the sky to decide whether it is safe or too risky to hunt whales is a means of successfully managing uncertainty. When on a winter's night in March, a hunter may navigate using the three stars high above the horizon to the south called *Ullaktut* (Orion's belt), this constellation is described as sledge runners, but also as hunters who had each become stars because of a transgression of a taboo. This encodes movement and transformation from the profane world of the terrestrial to the celestial realms. Thus, Orion's belt is quite literally a risk constellation in that its stars explain fundamental cosmographical relationships between the affairs of living beings on earth and the celestial or planetary realm. However, I chose the term 'risk constellation' to characterize the work of this volume because the movement of this patterned group of stars across the sky through the night is a source of both moral and spatial navigation, a system of orientation that encompasses knowing one's place in the world.

What then of geopolitics? Where in the geopolitical space that Waltz defined in terms of 'counting poles' is there space for the risk constellations and cosmographical visions of northern peoples? It is a striking fact that in Inuit star lore, the pole star, *Nuutuittuq*, is of comparatively little interest and still of less use because of its stillness. Crucially Inuit do not make the mistake of confusing stillness with stability. Fixed poles of the kind that Waltz envisaged as giving the world stability are less preferred than dynamic relationships between living beings (which includes stars). This is also the case further afield in other cultures such as Bedouin society, where the pole star forms part of the constellation Benetnash, a funeral procession. For Bedouin, the pole star's stillness was traditionally regarded as being suspicious, as though the truth behind it was being concealed or restrained. Thus, readers may choose to be pole counters, which I understand to mean subscribing to a vision of the world based on a fixed or static frame of reference, in which polar claims to authority insist on validation by smaller polities over which power and dominion are exerted. Or they may choose the more ecological, contingent and culturally rich traditions of navigating the world's precariousness through relational strategies. This points to a theory of political power predicated on reciprocity of mutual recognition between centres of power and peripheries. Pole counting on the other hand has the appeal of a clarity born of simplicity and assigns the sovereign power over political ontology to those who hold the reins of power and value their own agency above all others. Risk constellations offer those in power no such satisfaction, reminding them that their well-being is perpetually in the hands of others and subject to complex ethical mediations.

A resolution to the century's defining challenges of the climate emergency and the likelihood of the onset of a sixth major species extinction will very likely require making space for competing kinds of cosmography. The neo-realists show no sign of retreating any time soon while the relational ontologies so beautifully explored in this volume, though lacking political and military power, appear to be ethically indispensable to navigating the twenty-first century. A signal achievement of this collection of chapters is to give readers a very authoritative and reliable picture of the Arctic zodiac, a set of risk constellations that speak to the world's need to find a way forward that comes to terms with the transition that experts agree is now required to keep the earth on any kind of a sustainable trajectory.

Michael Bravo is the Hugh Brammer Fellow in Geography at Downing College, University of Cambridge. He has recently served as Acting Director of the Scott Polar Research Institute, University of Cambridge. He has held visiting professorships at a number of international institutions including the Arctic University of Norway in Tromsø. His books include *Narrating the Arctic* (2002), *Arctic*

Geopolitics and Autonomy (2011), *the Pan-Inuit Trails Atlas* (2014) and *North Pole: Nature and Culture* (2019). The latter was received with acclaim by *New Scientist*, the *Literary Review of Canada* and *Arctic Today*, and featured at the Stoke Newington Literary Festival and the Cambridge Festival of Ideas. Michael's media appearances include BBC Radio 3's 'Free Thinking', Radio 4's 'Daughters of the Snow' and the World Service's 'The Forum'. He currently co-hosts with Adriana Craciun the Arctic Environmental Humanities Workshop.

References

Akpik, F. and B. Bodenhorn. 2001. *Learning to Braid 'Real Thread'*. Barrow, AK: Whaling Women's Auxiliary/ Alaska Eskimo Whaling Commission.

Bodenhorn, B. and O. Ulturgasheva. 2017. 'Climate Strategies: Thinking through Arctic Examples', *Philosophical Transactions of the Royal Society* A. 375:20160363.

Hastrup, K. 2012. 'The Icy Breath: Modalities of Climate Knowledge in the Arctic', *Current Anthropology* 53 (2): 227–30.

Jessen Williamson, K. 1992. 'The Cultural Ecological Perspectives of Canadian Inuit: Implications for Child Rearing and Education', MA dissertation. Saskatoon: University of Saskatchewan.

Krupnik I. and D. Jolly. 2002. *The Earth is Faster Now: Indigenous Observations of Arctic Environmental Change*. Fairbanks, AK: Arctic Research Consortium of the United States.

Martin, K. 2012. *Stories in a New Skin: Approaches to Inuit Literature*. Winnipeg: University of Manitoba Press.

Qitsualik, Rachel. 1998. 'Word and Will – Part Two: Words and the Substance of Life', *Nunatsiaq News*, 12 November, B3.

Romm, J. 1992. *The Edges of the Earth in Ancient Thought: Geography, Exploration, and Fiction.* Princeton, NJ: Princeton University Press.

Waltz, K. 1979. *Theory of International Politics.* London: Addison-Wesley.

Watt-Cloutier, S. 2015. *The Right to Be Cold: One Woman's Fight to Protect the Arctic and Save the Planet from Climate Change*. Minneapolis: University of Minnesota Press.

Williamson, K. 2011. *Inherit My Heaven: Kalaallit Gender Relations.* Nuuk: Government of Greenland.

Index

A

Achi Chokyi Dronma/Drolma, historical figure and deity, 163
adaptation, 18, 20, 32–33, 38, 45, 47, 67, 79, 81, 103, 108–9, 111, 126, 131, 141, 153
adaptability, 31–32, 33, 42, 47, 67, 74, 81
agency, 9, 25, 36, 41, 45, 48, 70, 103, 108, 124, 126–27, 211
agentive, 198–99
agents, 40, 67, 147
Alaska, ix–xii, 10, 18–20, 28, 31, 34, 36, 38–42, 45–47, 90–93, 101–5, 109–10, 116–17, 135, 176, 181–87
Alaska Eskimo Whaling Commission (AEWC), 187–88, 190–92, 196–7, 200–4
Alaska Native (as term of reference), 103–5, 116–21, 145, 176. *See also* Native Alaskans
Alaska Native Claims Settlement Act (ANCSA), ix, 103
Alps, 39, 149, 152–53, 166, 169, 171, 207
Andes x, 152–53, 173
animacy, 2, 5, 8–9, 16, 65, 68
animals, 18, 36, 38, 40, 42–44, 47–48, 90–91, 93 95, 98–99, 107–12, 140, 154, 165, 179, 181, 185, 200, 206, 210
bears, 9, 17, 29, 49, 73, 74, 81, 126, 188, 190
geese, 11, 51
moose, 109, 110
reindeer, 43, 48, 49, 62–66, 70–84
whales, 5, 10, 18, 37–38, 46–48, 96, 98, 113, 179–98, 203, 210
wolves, 49, 74
animation, 7, 65, 70
animated, 4–10, 19, 125
animating, 7–8
animism, 3, 5–10, 20, 50, 62, 64–67, 70, 81–88
Anthropocene, xii, 1–5, 17, 26–27, 34–37, 40, 49, 61, 63, 150, 152
anthropogenic, 44, 59, 62, 72, 161
Arctic, vii, ix–xv, 1–5, 11–50, 58–59, 67–69, 77–80, 89–97, 104–41, 148, 151–52, 161, 168–69, 176, 180, 196–97, 206–11
Arctic Ocean, xii, 21, 46, 59, 95–96, 113, 122, 196, 207
Athapaskan, 30, 40–41, 149, 154
Attungana, Patrick, 10, 38, 98–99, 181–82, 185, 189
autonomy, 64, 179, 186

B
Barrow, Alaska, 22, 31, 38, 46, 48, 176–77
Basso, Keith, 152
Bering Sea, 109, 112, 115
Bodenhorn, Barbara, x, 1, 4–5, 10, 12, 20–21, 26, 28, 32, 36, 38
Bogoraz, Vladimir, 84
Bravo, Michael, 4, 18, 20, 28, 123, 125–26, 130, 151, 206

C
Callison, Candis, 15, 19, 28–29, 31, 35–36, 47, 122–29
Canada, ix, xii, 16, 26, 30–31, 40–42, 51, 122–24, 126–29, 131–41, 207
Canadian Broadcasting Corporation (CBC), 127, 130, 132–38
Chakrabarty, Dipesh, 2, 5, 35
Chang Targo, 156, 158
Chersky, 42
Chukchee, 84
Circumpolar North, viii, x, xii, xiii, 3–4, 11–12, 22, 26–28, 40, 90, 110–11, 132, 150, 167
climate change, x, xi, xii, 3–5, 11–20, 23–28, 31–33, 38–49, 58, 60–63, 75–82, 89–94, 101–16, 122–41, 150–72, 206–10
collaboration, 12, 15, 28–31, 47, 60, 80–81, 96–97, 101, 141
Cold War, viii, 29, 126, 197, 209
colonialism, 35, 40, 63, 115, 126, 128–29, 141
co-constitution, 8, 9, 65–66, 69–70
contamination, 58–59
COP21, 15, 19, 23, 143–44
cosmo-politics, 34, 53, 85, 160
cosmovision, 61, 67, 80–82
Cruikshank, Julie, 30, 37, 40–43, 68, 125
cryosphere, x, xi, xiii, 27, 39, 40–46, 59, 77, 81, 148–53, 155–75
cryocide, 2, 4, 17, 20, 26, 27, 39, 47

D
Dalai Lama XIV, 165, 173
decolonization, ix, 115
degradation, 72–73, 87
environmental degradation, 16, 35, 59, 61–63
deity, deities, 157–60, 163–72
de La Cadena, Marisol, 40, 49, 61, 85, 160
development, viii, xi, 13–15, 36, 40–43, 48, 54–59, 61–62, 67, 72, 96, 104, 111, 125, 131, 141, 151, 199
discrimination, xi, 116
disruption
colonial disruption, 104
environmental, 17, 32, 73
divination, 66, 76, 78, 157, 159–63
djuluchen, 79–80
Douglas, Mary, 13, 23, 53, 205
Drikung Kyabgon Chetsang Rinpoche, 165, 172
drilling, oil, 44

E
earth, x, xiii, 11, 29, 34, 36–37, 49, 58–87, 89–101, 160–66, 207–8, 210–11
ecozone, 4, 26–27
elders, 15, 38, 40, 72–75, 91, 95, 99, 100, 104–7, 109, 113, 138, 180, 181–92, 201–5
endangered species, 180
environment, viii, x, xi–xiii, 1, 2, 7, 12–48, 59–81, 90–101, 105–15, 124–41, 151–68, 177–204
environmental conditions, 1, 80, 90, 167, 195, 207–9
environmental change, 28, 31, 39
process, 26, 32, 35, 42, 46
shifts, 15, 19, 47–48, 113, 177
environmental politics, x, xii, 16, 32, 47, 164, 209
epistemology, 40, 67, 99, 106, 154
epistemic, 63, 150, 167, 169
Eveny, 15, 17–18, 20, 37, 43, 48–49, 58–82
expertise, 12, 15, 18, 29, 30, 48, 62, 64, 77–79, 82, 117, 141, 163, 198
experts, 15, 28–31, 61, 74, 77, 122, 127, 130, 201, 211

Escobar, Arthuro, 39, 61, 64
exploitation, 80, 93–101, 153
extreme events, 17, 21, 31, 33, 38, 49, 160–61, 168

F
Facebook, 123–24, 130, 134, 136–41
Fennoscandia, ix, 42
fires, 17
    fire-fighting, 71
    wildfires, 32–34, 58–60
flexibility, 38, 48, 76, 79
flooding, 38, 45, 72, 154, 189
    floods, 32–33, 58–59, 68, 72, 75, 150, 161–64
food, 78, 98, 135, 139, 190
    food security, 116
    and souls, 5, 181–89
Foucault, Michel, 14, 23, 178
Fourth World, 64

G
generosity
    of animals, 10–11, 51
    between humans, 182
    between humans and animals, 181
    geopolitics, 58, 167, 210–11
cosmo-geo-politics, 4, 37, 49
cosmo-geo-social, 47–48
geoscience, 77
    geoscientists, 76–81
Ghosh, Amitav, 1–2
glacial, 40–42, 149–54, 161–62, 164–67, 206
glaciers, xi, xiii, 20, 30, 40–41, 46, 148–54, 163, 166–72
Greenland, ix, 28, 33, 41–42, 50–51, 122, 131, 149, 153, 169, 174
Gurlha Mandata, 161

H
Hastrup, Kirsten, 28, 35, 41–42, 50, 68, 149, 153, 168
Hawaii, 30
    Native Hawaiian, 30
hazard, 12–14, 44–46, 150–51, 161–4, 179, 180–87, 190, 193–96

Himalaya, x, xii, 39, 149–56, 165–73, 207
Hindukush, 151
human-animal relations, as moral, 73, 83, 106–11, 200
human-environment relations, xii, xiii, 7, 40–41, 44, 62, 67, 81, 194
human-non-human relations, of care, 73, 84, 166, 172, 191, 195, 210
hunting, 95, 98, 100, 151, 178, 182, 198, 207
humanism, 65–66
    humano-centric, 3, 7, 11, 17, 39, 61, 63, 81
hydrocarbon, 59
hydrology, 59, 61, 171

I
ice, x, xii, 34
    glacial ice, xii, 12, 20
    permafrost, x, xii, 15, 18, 34, 39–46, 48–49, 58–82
    shore-fast ice, 189, 196
    sea ice, 17, 27, 33
ice calving event, 176–77
ice melt, x, xiii, 12, 33–34, 40–48, 69–72, 89, 107, 165, 206
Iceland, ix, 166, 172
incommensurability, 157, 168
Indigenous
    knowledge, 3, 16, 22, 30–31, 58, 63–64, 106
    mental health, 19, 103
    publics, 43, 50, 106, 113, 116
    representation, 122–33, 140–41
    voices, 17, 28–29
Ingold, Tim, 152, 154
Inter-species interaction, 26. *See also* human–animal relations
interconnectedness, 63, 80, 111, 153, 157, 165–66
    mercifulness, 48, 73, 80
intimacy, 2–9, 16
Inuit, ix, xiii, 5, 28, 30, 92, 94, 127, 131–43
Inuit Circumpolar Council (ICC), 128, 130–31
Iñupiaq; Iñupiat, 17–18, 36, 51, 181

Iñupiaq History Language and Culture Commission (IHLC), 181–202

J
Jamail, Dahr, 27, 44, 59
Jigten Gonpo, 163
journalism, 122–47

K
Kailash, Mount, 154–59, 160–61
Karakorum, 151
Karmapa Urgyen Trinley Dorje, 153, 165
Kennel, Charles, 167, 172
Keymetinov-Bargachan, Vasily, 72
Kimmerer, Robin Wall, 11, 40, 51
kinship, ix, xiii, 109, 160, 166
knowledge
  contested, 159
  environmental, 3, 4, 11
  expert, 19
  cosmo-geo-ecological, 48–49, 74–80

L
Latour, Bruno, 22, 153, 168, 180
laws, 72, 84, 90, 94
learning,
  through observation, 74
  through practice, 92, 95, 100, 104, 108, 112–14
  through stories, listening, 8, 9, 36
listening, 6, 19, 37, 79, 95, 100, 106, 110, 112
Lhasa, 156, 172
Limi, 161–62

M
Mapham Yuntsho (alias Manasarovar), Lake, 160
marine mammals, 207
Marino, Elizabeth, 44–46, 110, 126
maritime shipping, viii, 44, 126, 161
mining, xi, 6, 42, 58
mobility, 48, 70, 75–76
modelling, 15
  climate modelling, 27, 32

moose, 109–10
morality, 7
  as a condition of animal–human relations, 10, 36, 178
more than climate change, xi
more than human, xiii, 8–11, 61–62, 68, 160
Mt. Rosa, Mountain (Italy), 166
Mt. St Elias, Mountain (British Columbia), 40, 167
myth, 129, 208
  creation myth, 62–63
  aetiological myth, 70

N
Namtsho, Lake/deity, 157, 160
Native Alaskan, 103–5, 116–21, 145, 176
Nepal, 150, 161, 163, 165
New Arctic, x, 123
Norway, ix, 149
non-anthropocentric anthropology, 3, 17, 28, 66, 81
North Slope Borough, ix, 10, 18, 96, 180, 182–203
Northwest Territories, 134, 143
Nuna, 91–92, 207
Nunavut, ix, 28, 30, 134–39
Nyanchen Thanglha Mountain/deity, 156–57, 160

O
One Health, as paradigm, 19, 106, 111–12, 115
ontology, 61–67, 99, 211
Oquilluk, William, 36,

P
Padmasambhava, 156
Papua New Guinea, 168
paternalism, xi
permafrost. *See* ice
persons
  animals as, 18, 40, 47, 95, 98–99, 185–200
  non-human, x, 3, 5, 8, 17, 42, 63, 90–91

personhood, 64–65, 79, 106, 171
Petryna, Adriana, 32, 71
Pleistocene, 42–43
Pope Francis, 166, 172
Porong, 158
post-human
　post-humanism, 63
　post-humanist, 2, 63–66, 81
post-Soviet, 80
Povinelli, Elizabeth, 3–11, 16, 21, 65

Q

qanruyulet, Yup'ik oral traditions, 38, 105, 108
Qayaq, Iñupiaq and Yup'ik; skin boat, 104, 114
Qiu, Jane, 151

R

reciprocity, 36, 37, 80, 84, 211
reincarnation
　and iñua, 10, 179
　multi-species interconnection, 40, 44
　of persons, 109
　of whales, 5, 38, 179, 181–83
reindeer, 43, 48–49, 74
　cosmology, 49
　reindeer herders, 1, 8, 17–18, 38, 58–84
　reindeer-morphic, 62–63, 80
resources, viii, 17, 26, 30, 32–38, 44, 71, 92–94, 117, 126, 153, 174, 200
resource extraction, xi, 35, 94, 99, 134
responsibility, 18, 37, 117, 126, 139, 165, 179, 182–88, 197–98
resilience, xii, 4, 18, 20, 31, 33–34, 38–39, 47, 74, 104–17, 132–41
'right to know', 179, 198
risk, 2, 4, 9–49, 60–78, 114–16, 123–41, 150–64, 177–200
　assessment, 13, 15, 18, 46
　immediate and long term consequences of, 45, 182, 210
　'techno traps', 12–13, 195

Russia, viii, 26, 29, 78, 122, 126, 131, 207, 209
Russian Arctic, ix, xii, 67

S

Saami (Sami), ix, 131
Saami Council, ix
San Francis of Assisi, 166
Sarris, Greg, 5, 8
science, 13, 15, 16, 29, 30, 31–35, 40–41, 66, 77, 82, 101, 115, 129–30, 152–70, 180, 197, 200
　Science-lay divide, 14, 16, 18, 178–93
scientists, 14, 15, 18–34, 40–46, 61–62, 68, 76–81, 96, 111, 122, 130, 151, 197–200
shamanism
　shamanic 5, 18, 65, 67, 81, 83
　shamans, 72, 206
self-determination, vii, ix, 131–32
settler colonialism, ix, 40, 93, 123
sharing, as cultural value, 4, 15, 100, 149, 169, 178, 185, 200
Siberia, xii, 9, 31, 33–34, 42–43, 48, 59–81, 207
Sila, 10, 49, 91–92, 149, 206–7
Silo, 31
　siloed-thinking, 18, 35, 48–49
　silo-effect, 29, 97–99
Sky woman, 11, 51, 62
social media, 19, 29, 89, 122–41
sociality, 9–10, 47, 48, 70, 81, 186
social relations
　inter-species, 26, 36, 40, 182
solutions, 36, 64, 90, 92, 101, 105, 115, 124, 131, 168
sovereignty, ix, 191
Soviet Union, viii, xiii, 18, 209
spirit, 8, 10, 36, 47, 76–79. *See also* iñua
spirituality, 17, 20, 26, 30, 37, 67, 91, 98, 163–9
Stories, importance of, xii, 6, 9, 27, 36–38, 112, 122–41, 149, 154, 182, 208
Strathern, Marilyn, 157, 167, 168
Sweden, ix

T
Takyong, Mountain/deity, 158
technology, xii, 71, 77, 137, 178, 195, 202
TEK
  Traditional Environmental Knowledge, 29–30, 37, 57
'Third pole', x, 151, 173
Tibet, 19, 150, 153–71
Tirakuna, 160, 172
Todd, Zoe, 35, 83
tourism, 143, 161
  'last chance' tourism, xi
Tsing, Anna, 63, 153, 169
Twitter, 123–46

U
uncertainty, 12, 18, 26, 32–33, 39, 44–47, 66, 73–76, 153, 169, 210
United States of America, ix, 13, 40, 92, 96, 97–102, 131, 198–99, 207
Ulturgasheva, Olga, x, xi, 9, 18, 28, 32, 37–38, 58–83

V
Virkkala, Ann-Maria, 77
vitalism, 2, 5–6
voice, x, 26, 28, 31, 165
  eclipsing of, 2, 5, 43

politics of, 3, 15, 17, 36
registers of, 11, 12, 123–41

W
Wenzel, George, 30
'West', the, viii, ix
Weston, Kath, 2–16
whales
  cosmological, 10, 18, 37, 49, 182
  economic, 46–47, 98, 113
  political, 96, 188
  social importance of, 48, 179, 181
whale biology, 192–95
whalers, 179–97
whaling, 10, 20, 28, 97–99, 176–97, 207
Wildavsky, Aaron, 13, 18, 37, 177–78, 187–99, 200
Wynne, Brian, 14–15, 178

Y
youth, 100
  resilience, 103–16
  well-being, 38, 43, 104–12, 114–16
Yukon, 109, 134–35, 138
Yup'ik, Yupiit, 17, 38, 51, 105, 109

www.ingramcontent.com/pod-product-compliance
Lightning Source LLC
Chambersburg PA
CBHW051539020426
42333CB00016B/2006